U0165822

目錄 CONTENTS

★★ 第 5 章　體例　39

★★ 第 6 章　遣詞用字　55

★★
第 10 章　**修辭**　183

「內容豐富，例句實用，條理分明，適合想將英文作文得高分的學習者。」

·康寧大學　邱靖雅

「跳脫傳統上以模仿為主的學習模式，從理論核心切入，更能把基礎紮穩，英文作文實力倍增。」　·北港農工　林明憲

「書中內容詳細、清楚，可以是學生寫作的最好指引。」　　·康寧大學　王盈文

「這是一本對英文寫作真正有幫助的好書！」　　·北港農工　盧美伶

「文字論述恰到好處，舉例適當，簡單易懂。」　　·高雄女中　吳玟欣

"Professor Chiang's book fills a vital need in Taiwan's English composition instruction. Teachers and students will appreciate its clear, logical, step by step introduction to this difficult skill."　·嘉南藥大　Damien Trezise

「本書內容豐富、詳細，適合想在英文寫作上更上層樓的讀者！」·翰陞英文　林達陽

「解說詳盡，例子豐富，敘述易懂、生動。」　　·成功大學　孫鈺媚

「內容深入淺出，創新易懂，非常實用！」　　·北港農工　雷偉斌

「深入淺出、逐條分析、一目瞭然。」　　·高雄中學　陳信堯

「一本不同於坊間寫作書的好書，讓你知道：原來英文作文要這樣寫！」

·嘉義高中　林楨崚

「本書從無到有，一步步引導學習者完成一篇好的作文。作者概念清楚，語言結構強，處處可見其用心著墨，是一本相當好的學測指考英文作文自學書。」

·台南女中　王咏華

「非常推薦這本書。相信這本書將會是學習英文寫作上一塊很棒的墊腳石。」

·家齊女中　王舜薇

「由引導思考清晰作文架構，成為茫茫書海中的一盞明燈！」

・新化高中　鄭予姵

「淺顯易懂，分析的很詳細。」　　　・德光高中　蘇筱雯

「本書循序漸進，深入淺出，措辭幽默，例句豐富，又附解答，必能指點迷津，增進讀者英文寫作能力，並帶來高分。」　　　・台灣聖經公會　梁望惠

「淺顯易懂，循序漸進，是很實用的作文指南！」　　　・崑山大學　洪綺吟

「用字遣詞皆簡單易懂，中英舉例都清晰易懂。本書對要建立作文，甚至英文基礎的人很有幫助。」　　　・道明中學　鄭翰霖

「內容豐富，舉例詳盡，學到很多英文寫作的技巧，真的讓我受益良多。」

・台中高農　林盈宜

"The document is excellently written. The essays are constructed in a logical and easy to follow system. I particularly like the fact that the essays are all concerned with real-life situations which are relevant to students."　　　・康寧大學　白隆堂

「這本書太棒了！Awesome！簡單、完整、實用。向作者敬禮！」

・補教名師　劉力

「編排詳盡，想法獨樹一幟，值得研讀！」　　　・長榮高中　劉哲源

「非常適合短期內需要大幅度進步的考生。」　　　・家齊女中　謝玖吟

「唯一推薦！應考必讀！　　　・嘉南藥大　陳建智

「遣詞用字適中，中、英文舉例清晰易懂。」　　　・家齊女中　鄭曉徽

「這本書的編寫方式異於坊間已出版的寫作參考書籍，可以提供讀者另一種認識寫作方法的觀點。」　　　・師大附中　林秀娟

　　我是蔣炳榮老師的學生，在老師的指導下獲得敦煌書局舉辦的 2012 年大專生英文書評一般組第一名。我曾經修過老師一學年的英文作文課，在修課的期間，著實學到了很多：從標點符號的運用到語句的修辭與變化，為我的英文作文打下了良好的基礎。老師總是很認真的批改每份學生的作文，他說批改學生的作文是在和學生「神交」，透過學生的文章，可以瞭解學生對其周遭事物的看法和處事態度，因此他從學生的作文能對學生有進一步的認識，老師甚至在批改過我在英作課寫的第一篇作文過後一年仍記得我所寫的內容，這點深深地感動了我，證明老師非常的認真教學，相信老師對於撰寫參考書籍也不會馬虎。

　　蔣老師曾經受過多種語言的訓練，包括：法語、西班牙語、日語、美國原著民的語言……等等，再加上老師的語言學專業，使老師對語言本身有深刻的認識，因此對英語有一番獨到的見解，例如：在一般的參考書上，都指出英語有五大基本句型，然而，老師根據英語語法學者所提出的理論指出英語實有七大基本句型。另外，一般我們咸認為英語僅分為單數與複數，但老師曾在課堂上提出英語中的「雙數」，即英語除了單數與複數之外應再多一個雙數的類別，像平常我們使用的英語字彙中有許多是專門處理二項物件，如：both, couple, pair，這個理論就是老師得自美國原著民語言的啓發，可見老師對語言的知識有助於他對英語語法有不同的詮釋與內化，除此之外，老師非常注重原創性，即獨立思考與創新的能力，因此老師不論對學生或對自己都要求必須要有別於他人的想法，故我想老師所寫的書不會落於俗套。

　　一般的教英文寫作的書，可能從書的一開始洋洋灑灑的敘述文章的分類，然後給一大堆的範文，讓讀者無所適從，但老師的書從最基本的「認識英語」開始說起，讓學生從不一樣的角度認識英語，接下來談寫作的技巧與步驟，後來則是聊句法，除了說明句子的文法與結構之外，還列出一般寫作常犯的錯誤，讓讀者認識這些寫作的陷阱才能寫出一篇文情並茂的好作文。除了上述所提的內容外，還包括了遣詞用字、修辭技巧、中翻英……等等，可謂無所不包，循序漸進的介紹英語中「寫」的學問。其實書中有不少內容跳脫了高中英文寫作的程度，直接把大學英文寫作課程之所學放在裏頭，相信準備學測指考的同學讀來必能獲益良多。

當了蔣老師二年的學生，初次被老師教到是在英文作文課上，當初在那門課中受了老師相當嚴格的訓練，我們寫了包含敘述、描寫、定義……等各種不同類型的文章，還設計了英語標語、寫英語履歷，課程內容相當充實，雖然過得很忙碌，卻也值得。現在回想起來，老師的教學方法似乎也反映在他寫書的風格上—想要把一切都教給學生／讀者，老師的書中寫了許多其他參考書所沒有的資訊，讀者讀來或許會覺得煩、覺得累，但若肯咬牙認真地跟隨老師的腳步學習，相信一定會有不同凡響的結果！

黃于綺

國立成功大學心理系

　　回憶大一時，要寫一篇英文作文總會讓我焦慮好一陣子，最後總在時間掐著脖子時，才萬般無奈下筆。這個時候常常只能想到什麼就寫什麼，最終寫出一篇語無倫次僅靠文字堆疊的「文章」。有時過了幾天後，自己再看自己所寫的東西，竟然看不懂或甚至懷疑那是誰寫的。這種窘境直到上了大二英文作文課後才逐漸改變。

　　在大二時修蔣炳榮老師的英文作文課，我們從描寫人物畫像開始，進行圖書館的導覽，描述象棋棋盤，一封請假信（要寄出），定義網球 "deuce"，……最後實際去咖啡廳坐一晚，寫出現場發生的事情。這門課的教學內容和方式深烙在我的記憶中，也從此陪伴我人生中的每一個階段。像進修入學考試有英文作文，繳交的報告要用英文寫作，甚至現職工作也在教這門課。然而卻發現要把這門課教得像自己的老師一樣出神入化，很難。而老師就是能把這門課上得生動有趣，並引導學生一步一步從寫中學，讓學生從完成每一次單元的作業中逐步領悟到作文的結構。經過一年訓練，每個學生終於逐漸能夠呈現出自己的寫作特色，雖然不是個個都成為英文寫作高手，但起碼不至於一遇英文寫作就手足無措，毫無章法地亂寫一通。

　　幾年來，反覆思索老師是如何引領學生進入英文寫作，又如何讓學生體驗英文寫作的樂趣，總難窺其奧堂之妙。如今拜讀老師所寫的這本英文作文書，終於讓我稍能瞭解老師是如何帶領我們一步一步寫出一篇可讓人理解的文章。這本書的基本精神，是以學生的角度來考量面對「學測」與「指考」的英文作文所遭遇的問題，並提出解決之道。讀本書就像老師親自在你身邊一般，一步一步帶你完成一篇大學學測或指考所要求的文章。因此作者一開始就對「學測」與「指考」兩種英文作文考試的特質與差異，做了精闢分析。

　　這本書強調六個技巧與八個步驟。這六個技巧是讀者要時時注意的六個重點，因為除了第六點「掌控時間」外，其餘五點就是閱卷委員的評分指標。這六個技巧是幫助考生拿高分的利器。八個步驟就像寫作歷程，從起點到終點的一段路程。八個步驟包含從平時準備做起，歷經初期的作文題目分析，經過瞭解題目後確立文章大方向，也就是組織「主結構」，然後決定主結構下，小分枝的細節思考，一直到完成一篇英文作文檢查，才算抵達終點。八個步驟就是提

供英文寫作初學者一套「標準作業程式」，只要遵循此一基本動作就不會無所適從，不知如何下筆。

句構變化是附著在六個技巧與八個步驟骨架上的肌肉，句構變化也像身體不同部位有不同的肌肉結構。這本書教導平時最常見到的句型，經過不斷反覆練習，達到得心應手的靈活運用，就是能讓適當的句子出現在適當的位置。轉折詞與連接詞就像筋腱連結不同部位的肌肉，不僅讓不同部位的肌肉能夠強勁的連結，更能讓不同部位肌肉靈活運轉。詞彙就像血液一樣充滿每個句子，氣血順暢與否就要依賴詞彙的運用靈活度。本書重點，句型與詞彙不在多而在於精。

文章組織如開頭、發展和結尾就像人體結構有頭、身體和四肢，開頭寫得好，就像臉孔長得美，能引起讀者繼續讀下去。文章的發展像是身體的曲線，廢話多就會臃腫，內容不足就顯得清瘦體弱，如果能讓文章緊實有緻就像有健壯或曼妙的身材。本書作者提出修練「內容」的要訣，像一位健身教練藉由不同方式訓練不同部位，訓練出您身體上的四塊腹肌，而寫作訓練是從主題、解釋說明、經驗故事、情節發展……影響啟示，訓練出英文作文的「邏輯、具體、細膩、幽默」。

本書概略介紹英語修辭格與音韻節律的基礎知識，目的是好的文章內容還要經過修辭的美化，就像擁有美好身材加上高尚的穿著品味，就更能襯托出整體作品的風采。文章的音律有如個人的儀態，可以讓讀者體會作者在字裡行間的律動，文章的音律就像演講者的手勢與肢體語言，不但呈現作者的情緒也牽動讀者的呼吸。最後，寫作需要平時有充實而規律地閱讀，因為寫作人的思維想法就是文章的靈魂，靈魂是要借由長期的廣讀與精讀來灌溉。

本書把寫一篇英文作文所應具備的要件，都面面兼顧的說明，是一本能引導初學者進入英文寫作培訓的好書。願所有讀者與我一樣在閱讀此書時，有如享受一餐豐盛佳餚，享受到它提供的美味並吸收到它的營養。

預祝所有準備「學測」與「指考」英文作文的考生們都能獲得高分。

鍾瑞明

康寧大學應英系

前　言

很高興也很榮幸能夠將《「學測指考」英文作文的第一本書》呈獻給大家。

　　《「學測指考」英文作文的第一本書》是特地為準備參加學測與／或指考英文作文的同學以及希望從根本學習基礎英文作文的讀者撰寫的考試用專書。全書依據大學入學考試中心所公佈的「英文考科非選擇題閱卷評分原則說明」、「中譯英試題評分說明」、「英文作文分項式評分指標」三個主軸撰寫。全書共十一章，第一至第十章討論基礎英文作文與修辭，第十一章介紹中譯英導論；以英文作文評分指標的「內容，組織，文法句構，字彙拼字，體例」五個項目為經，以中譯英評分標準的「正確、通順、達意」為緯，配合英語構詞、遣詞用字與文法句構的整理與複習，加上基本修辭格式的簡介與練習，透過寫英文作文的技巧與步驟，讓同學、讀者能夠拿起筆從容自在地寫一篇至少 120 個單詞的文章。這樣的培訓，希望能完成作者撰寫這本書的心願─幫嚮往念大學的莘莘學子圓夢，成功地送他們進入心中理想的大學殿堂。接受培訓的同學、讀者就好比駕訓班的學員，從呆板又反覆的機械式操作，久之進而內化成堅定的信心與實力，待考試當下自然能遊刃有餘，達成心中想望。而我必須坦誠地說，撰寫本書的主要目的是要讓同學、讀者可以寫出一篇閱卷委員認可的英文作文，其後的發展因人而異，每個人都有自己的期許與造化，不是嗎？

　　這些年來，教書從作者的興趣發展成為專業，幾乎每一堂課都可以享受到教學相長的快樂。寫書是一種挑戰，挑戰作者的論述，因為它是一種無法依賴肢體語言，卻又必須具有說服力，同時讓讀者如沐春風的紙上教書。我勇於接受這種挑戰。挑戰的結果是我一個人的責任，一切我欣然接受。

　　在這次挑戰的過程中，有眾多戰友的支持與鼓勵。在此，我要好好送上我最誠摯的謝忱。首先，我要謝謝幫我校對英文部分的 Paul Butler 教授、Andrew Stoddart 教授、Vickie Chiang 老師、Elisabeth Keller 老師、Sophie Keller 同學，謝謝他們提供我很多寶貴的建議；也要謝謝台灣聖經公會翻譯顧問梁望惠博士、成大外文所柯孟汝同學，謝謝她們校對了中文部分。我要對

康寧大學的鍾瑞明教授致上無限謝意，謝謝他陪我接受這一次的挑戰，他的「當仁不讓」確實讓我學到很多。此外，我也要感恩這一路走來，始終如一直接或間接提攜關愛我的貴人們，謝謝他們的支持與鼓勵。當然，我更感謝五南圖書公司編輯部的朱曉蘋經理及其高效率的團隊，謝謝他們的學養和經驗。有了他們的指導和投入，本書才能順利出版。

　　個人學識所囿，撰寫本書過程中的錯誤、闕漏，在所難免。竭誠歡迎專家學者、先進同好批評指教，讓我們一起把分享知識的美好事情做得更美好。

蔣炳榮

成大成功湖畔 26602 研究室

2013 年 7 月

敬愛的讀者朋友，您好。本書是一本考試用書，撰寫的原始動機與最終目的是為了幫助大家在參加考試的時候或是在用英文寫作的時候，能夠成績優異、得心應手。如果您正在閱讀這一頁，我猜您應該是下列的讀者朋友其中之一：

1. 高中、高職學生；

2. 要參加「全民英檢」、「托福」、「雅思」等這類型標準測驗的考生；

3. 要打好英文寫作基礎的人士；

4. 英語教師；

5. 對英語有興趣的人士。

本書主要由四個領域組成：文法、修辭、音韻、寫作。讀者朋友各有不同的專業背景，因此身為「作者朋友」，我有義務提供如何使用本書的一些建議：

1. 文法句構基礎訓練不錯的朋友，只要快速翻閱「複習」一下有關句子的合併，特別是形容詞子句和名詞子句的形成。您可以把重心放在第 8~10 章。

2. 時間有限的朋友，只要閱讀第 8~9 章，特別是第 9 章第 7 節有關常用的句型的討論。但是，一定要想辦法自我培訓，能夠依樣畫葫蘆，寫出每句平均長達 10 個單詞的句子。講直接一點，就是「先臨摹，再創作」。

3. 對英語有充分認識，有自我見解的朋友，可以將重點集中在「典型錯誤」（第 7 章第 6 節）、修辭（第 10 章）。

4. 決心要打好基礎，從基本動作開始練功的朋友，最紮實有效的捷徑，似乎必須從開始到最後，一頁一頁地細嚼，而且可能的話，還要附帶將當代英語的文法句構，完整地精讀至少一遍。這種有如「少林寺十八銅人陣」的千錘百煉，如果能持之以恆，一招一式不斷地追根究底，來日必然有成。

「誠意呷水甜」，以上是我誠摯的建議，希望對您使用本書的功效有所幫助。除了以上的建議之外，別忘了全力以赴做好每個章節的練習。

現在，讓我們開始「神交」吧！

縮略與符號

符號	說明	符號	說明
*	後面的結構不合語法	A	（地方）副詞修飾語
（誤）	前面的結構不合語法	C	補語
⇨	句子變形為	O	受詞
=	等於；同義	Od	直接受詞
+	詞序；粘上；後接	Oi	間接受詞
-	詞綴；音節；後接；連字號	S	句子；主詞；主語
[ ]	句子結構；讀音標注	to V	不定詞
【 】	名詞子句	V	（主要）動詞
( )	片語結構；可選的	V-en	過去分詞
/	或	V-ing	現在分詞
___	殘缺結構	vs.	與……相對
---	欠缺	x	乘以
→	擴增為	XYZ	某某單位
←	原來的句構	WH	關係代名詞；關係副詞
…	（英文）省略		
……	（中文）省略		
>	改用為；響度高於		
's/s'	所有格表示		

[請參考7.3.2-4]　[請參考第7章第3節二～四]

第 1 章

認識英文作文

如果有人告訴你「你的中文講得很好」，你會覺得奇怪，會說母語就像是天生的，你認為本來就要說得好。講母語是一種自然習得，也就是說，只要有足夠並且良好的語言刺激，一個正常發育的小孩，就會自然而然地習得身邊同一語言社區的言語。譬如一個從小生長在美國加州洛杉磯 (Los Angeles, California) 的人，天生自然就會講流利的美式英語，而且講的是美國西部地區的美語。但是如果有人說「你的英文好」、「你的日文好」，你會認為是一種讚美。可見學習外國語言是有相當的困難與挑戰，因此會二或三種外國語言是值得高興驕傲的事。

小孩子不用到學校學習就會說非常流利的母語，但是一個沒有人教過閱讀與書寫的小孩，一般情況會是一個文盲。以母語而言，說話可以不用人教就可以表達得很好，但是沒有受過寫作訓練的人，即使是自己的母語說得再好也無法輕易寫出一篇詞達意順的文章，因此寫作是要經過訓練的。所謂的「英文好」必須是「講好英語」與「寫好英文」，但是「講好英語」不等於是「寫好英文」。縱然有人說我書我所說，那只能表達想要說的話，但是無法讓所寫文章成就一格。況且，非以英語為母語的人士，由於生活環境與社交活動不同於英美人士，他們的「英文好」除了「講好英語」與「寫好英文」之外，有時候還要能夠處理流暢通順的中英對譯，當然，也可能是法英、俄英對譯。這裡所說的對譯，嚴謹而言包括口譯和筆譯。

「寫好英文」，不論是對母語或非母語人士而言，都必須要有正規的教和學的過程。就好比騎腳踏車一樣，每個小朋友都需要透過學習才會騎腳踏車，但有些小朋友摔倒很多次才會，有些小朋友摔倒幾次就會了，每個人的學習速度不同，有快有慢，這是「學習上的個別差異」。英文寫作的培訓也是一樣會隨著個別學習差異而有長短難易的區別，英文寫作的學習差異性主要跟學習者獲得英語文刺激的多寡優劣有相當程度上的關係。

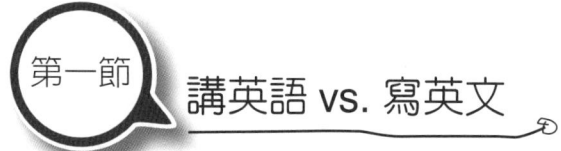

第一節　講英語 vs. 寫英文

講英語和寫英文皆是循序漸進的長期培訓。用英語對談時，說、聽者雙方不會去查詞典，因為在對談的時候，思緒往往是天馬行空，言談之間的話語稍縱即逝，聲音的速度是每秒鐘360 公尺左右，我們看不到聲音也留不住聲音（除非是錄音），於是我們常常要對方將重要的訊息重述一次。但是寫作不同，落筆後，字裡行間用詞選字可不斷重複回溯，而且寫作時必須鋪陳結構琢磨遣詞用字，因此作者會參考值得信賴的詞典以及經常需要查一本以上的詞典以確定所選用的單詞、片語以及文法句構和修辭格式的正確運用。

研究英語的專家學者相信英文寫作優劣與英文閱讀的廣泛度是息息相關並且相輔相成。

俗話說：「熟讀唐詩三百首，不會作詩也會吟。」，就是在說明耳濡目染下的習得。除了廣泛閱讀外，遣詞用字的訓練，也是英文寫作中長期耕耘的培訓之一。當有好幾個單詞可表達同樣或類似的意思時，作者應該力求貼切，選擇精確得宜的單詞或片語。比方說，作者想寫「那位女主人長得很美。」他／她會「美」的相關英文單詞或片語包含 beautiful, pretty, good-looking, gorgeous, lovely, attractive 等。假如時間許可，為了押韻，作者可以有意地「創作出」的片語可能包括 bright and beautiful（聰明又美麗）〔頭韻〕、good-looking and peace-loving（美麗又熱愛和平）〔尾韻〕、gorgeous and generous（美麗又大方）〔頭韻與尾韻〕等。經過對上下文的理解和深思熟慮，作者決定分別選用 beautiful, good-looking 或 gorgeous 作為「美」的對應詞。

第二節 學測指考英文非選擇題高分要點

大學入學考試中心所主辦的「學科能力測驗」（簡稱學測）與「指定科目考試」（簡稱指考）的英文考科均有兩部分：選擇題（占 72 分）與非選擇題（占 28 分），其中非選擇題又分為中譯英（占 8 分）與英文作文（占 20 分），如下圖所示。

學測指考簡易配分示意圖

選擇題 (72%)	非選擇題 (28%)
詞彙、綜合測驗、文意選填、篇章結構、閱讀測驗	中譯英 (8%)、英文作文 (20%)

呼應前文說過「英文好」包含流暢通順的中英對譯，中譯英這項測驗目的即為檢視此能力，只不過「學測」與「指考」僅要求單向的中譯英。中譯英是對華語為母語的考生所提供的「特別待遇」，而托福、多益、雅思等標準測驗則沒有翻譯試題。參加學測、指考英文作文的考生，必須能夠將二個分別長達 20 至 30 個單詞的中文句子翻譯成「正確、通順、達意」的英文。基本上，中譯英試題「評量的重點在於考生能否運用熟悉的詞彙與基本句型」[1]來翻譯。跟英文作文相比，中譯英的限制多，考生只能在被限定的中文句子與語義，去尋找對應的英文。

---

[1] 引號資料來源為大學入學考試中心學科能力測驗與指定科目考試英文考科閱卷參考手冊。

　　相對於翻譯，英文作文可以避開不懂的文法句構或不會的單詞片語，算是一種操之在我的語言創作活動。以 101 學測為例，考生被要求寫一封信勸告他迷上電玩的最好朋友；101 指考作文題目為「請以運動為主題，寫一篇至少 120 個單詞的文章，說明你最常從事的運動是什麼。文分兩段，第一段描述這項運動如何進行（如地點、活動方式、及可能需要的相關用品等），第二段說明你從事這項運動的原因及這項運動對你生活的影響。」勸告電玩迷的文章包羅萬象，諸如勸告對方要以學業為重、注意身體，提醒對方電玩世界充滿暴力與色情等此類的論述。描述、說明「最常從事的運動」的作文，稱得上是海闊天空的發揮題，不會保齡球、足球這些單詞或片語就改成籃球、棒球；不會泳褲、蛙鏡這些單詞或片語就不要寫游泳的運動；不會肌肉、心血管、六塊肌，就轉方向寫健康、團隊精神、大自然等自己可以掌控的詞彙，進一步再談自己有經驗、有把握可以揮灑自如的敘述與舉例。反之，翻譯比英文作文的限制多，考生只能依據限定的中文句子與語義，尋找對應的英文。因此，回答中譯英的題目，必須全方面應對，但也因為受到試題要求所困囿，不但中文要真的看懂，而且必須在有限的英文詞庫裡搜尋正確達意的對應語，往往使考生無法自由發揮大展身手。101 學測中譯英試題是「1. 近年來，許多臺灣製作的影片已經受到國際的重視。2. 拍攝這些電影的地點也成為熱門的觀光景點。」101 指考中譯英試題是「1. 有些我們認為安全的包裝食品可能含有對人體有害的成分。2. 為了我們自身的健康，在購買食物前我們應仔細閱讀包裝上的說明。」試題中的「國際的重視」、「拍攝」、「熱門的」、「觀光景點」；「對人體有害的成分」、「包裝上的說明」的可能的英語對應語，根據「評分說明」，分別是 "international attention," "shoot," "popular," "tourist attractions/spots"; "ingredients (that are) harmful to human bodies," "instructions on the package"。指考的「評分原則」說明中特別強調英文表達之詞序與中文有差異。英文用的是後位修飾，中文用的是前位修飾〔請參考11.1〕，語言對譯所需下的苦功與訓練由此可見一斑。

　　從上述分析結論，學測、指考英文作文和中譯英要考高分必須朝二個目標邁進。第一，「英文作文」要達到內容切題、組織連貫、句子結構與遣詞用字必須正確且能適當表達文意，拼字與標點符號必須使用正確。第二，「中譯英」要達到運用熟悉的詞彙與句構滿足「正確、通順、達意」的要求。

練習1

1. 請舉三個實例說明「講英語」和「寫英文」的不同。

2. 請舉三個實例說明英文作文培訓的過程中，為什麼常需要查閱詞典？

3. 請簡介學測指考的英文作文與中譯英的配分比例和試題的模式。

4. 學測指考的英文作文與中譯英這二項試題，對你而言，哪一個比較簡單？為什麼？

第 2 章

認識英語

　　英語是 21 世紀的世界通用語，也是全球化時代與世界接軌的 USB。講英語的人口最多，使用英語的國家分佈最廣，英語是 21 世紀科技界發表研究成果的主導性語言。身為現代地球村的一員，我們要發展進步、關心國際事務、參加國際活動、擠身世界公民，這一切都需要利用英語這個 USB 做連接，而認識英語是持有與運用這個 USB 的第一步。

　　英語是一種使用拼寫系統的語言，跟很多發展完善的其他語言一樣，具有音、形、義三個元素，就好像一個三角形的三個邊。要能夠靈活運用英語，我們首先必須瞭解它的音、形、義，同時再加上熟悉英語文化，如此使其組成一個對稱的稜錐體，英語語言習得也得以完美建構。

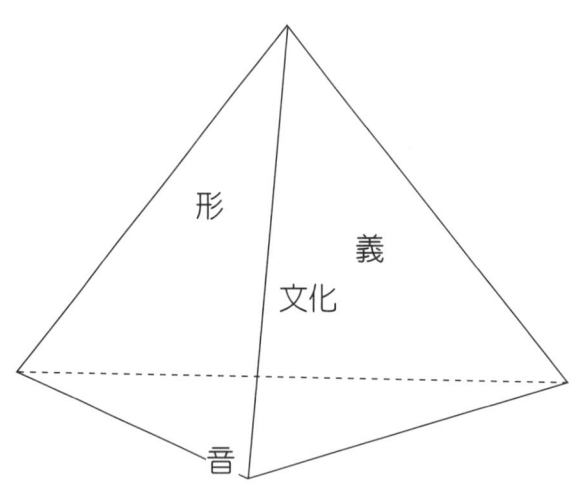

第一節　英語語音

　　我們先來談談英語的語音。瞭解英語語音系統對押韻和在遣詞用字上追求節奏和諧以及平行結構中的詞序排列有很大的助益。一般而言，英語有 24 個子音（輔音），有 17 個母音（元音）。〔請參考附錄 6〕。母音與子音會結合成為音節，例如 me, hi, meet, hike 等。音節的長短 (fur-for)、開閉 (see-seat)、強弱 (can[kæn]-can[kən]) 等，常常會影響句子的節奏，這一點和中文的「抑揚頓挫」非常類似。

　　在寫作及朗誦時，有時候我們還要考慮到重音。在清楚地發出重讀音節的時候，我們會「比較」用力發出該音節，將「比較」多的空氣推出肺部。一般人常含糊地將重音等同於強調，但重音其實可分為兩種：重讀音節與非重讀音節。發音時比較突顯的音節稱為重讀音節，

比較不突顯的音節稱為非重讀音節，例如美式英語 research 當名詞用時，第一個音節為重讀音節，第二個音節為非重讀音節：REsearch；當動詞用時，第二個音節為重讀音節，第一個音節為非重讀音節：reSEARCH。重讀音節一般會有長度、響度、音高的增加，也就是會念的比較長、比較大聲，比較高。基本上，字母 a, e, i, o, u 以及節尾子音後面的字母 y 會形成音節。例如，tomato 有三個音節：to-ma-to; catastrophe 有四個音節：ca-tas-tro-phe; anthropology 有五個音節：an-thro-pol-o-gy。底下，我們引用聖誕歌《平安夜》的第一段來說明在遣詞用字的過程中，押韻所扮演的重要角色。

Silent night, holy night!

All is calm, all is bright.

Round yon Virgin, Mother and Child.

Holy infant so tender and mild,

Sleep in heavenly peace,

Sleep in heavenly peace.

...

顯而易見地，藉由觀察字尾和利用哼唱方式，我們可以感覺《平安夜》有許多押尾韻的單詞：**ni**ght 和 b**ri**ght 押韻、**Mother** 和 **tender** 押韻，**Child** 和 m**ild** 押韻。另一方面，英語也有押頭韻的情形。我們可以聯想到中文裡的「雙聲疊韻」，就很容易瞭解中英文在這個修辭格的運用，稱得上是異曲同工。舉幾個押頭韻的片語為例：（敵友）**f**riend and **f**oe，（搖滾）**r**ock and **r**oll，（可伶可俐）**cl**ean and **cl**ear，（機不可失）**n**ow or **n**ever，（嘻哈）**h**ip-**h**op。押頭韻是一串單詞以相同字母或聲音開頭。〔請參考 10.2.3〕

第二節　英語構詞

構詞是增加新詞彙的基本功。構詞包含分析一個單詞的內部結構與建構新單詞的步驟與方式。我們舉三個例字來討論：breakfasts, unlawful 與 autobiography。breakfasts 由三個成分組合而成：break-fast-s; unlawful 由三個成分組合而成：un-law-ful; autobiography 由四個成分組合而成：auto-bio-graph-y。這裡談到的成分，在構詞學這門專業領域，稱之為詞素，也就是一個語言具有意義的最小單位。break 意指「打破」，fast 意指「齋戒；絕食」，二者形成一個複合詞 breakfast，意義延伸，被詮釋成「停止進食後的第一頓飯」，然後翻譯成「早餐」，-s 是表示複數的字尾。結果，breakfasts 被我們解讀為二頓（含）以上的早餐。運用同樣的分析

原則，law 意指「法令；法律」，-ful 是表示形容詞的字尾，二者形成一個複合詞 lawful，再加上表示「否定」的字首 un-，最後形成 unlawful，意思是「不合法的；違法的」；同樣地，bio 意指「生物的；人生的」，graph 意指「圖表；圖解」，-y 是表示名詞的字尾，三者形成一個複合詞 biography，再加上表示「自己；本身」的字首 auto-，最後形成 autobiography，意思是「描繪自己人生的圖表」，然後翻譯成「自傳」。我們一旦弄懂這些被解構的詞素，按照建構新單詞的步驟與方式的規範，再加上我們的創意，就可以源源不絕地湧出 autobiographies, autobiographer, autobiographical, autobiographically 的衍生詞或詞類變化。

另一種是把詞素當成積木，作合乎構詞規則的組合，例如 automobile（汽車），autoboat（汽船），autobike（摩托車），autofocus（自動聚焦）等，有了信心以後繼續進階建構新單詞，例如 autonomy（自治），autonomous（自治的），autonomously（自治地）等，這種創造力很活躍，就像小時候玩積木一樣過癮。本書附錄 4 按字母排序，有系統地整理出可以快速繁殖你的詞彙量的積木，正等你來大顯身手！

如果你碰巧又知道很多英語的「長」字，一般都指四個音節以上的單詞，例如 de**moc**racy（民主），pho**tog**raphy（攝影），ex**trav**agant（奢侈的）in**dig**enous（本地的），psy**chol**ogy（心理學），phi**los**ophy（哲學）等，還有我們前面提過的 ca**tas**trophe（災難），anthro**pol**ogy（人類學）等，這些「長」字的重讀音節經常落在倒數第三個音節，你就可以輕輕鬆鬆地將這些長相有點「嚇人」的「長」字收服，將它們放進你的詞彙收納箱。這種快樂還真快樂咧！

練習 2

1. 請圈選以「子音（輔音）」為首的單詞。

(1) UFO　　(2) NBA　　(3) undo　　(4) university　　(5) FBI

2. 下列單詞各由幾個「音節」組成？

例：tomato

答：3

(1) apple　　(2) Himalayas　　(3) psychology　　(4) paparazzi　　(5) decaffeinated

3. 下列單詞各由幾個「詞素」組成？

例：reviewed

答：3

(1) breakfasts　　(2) butterflies　　(3) multifunctional　　(4) unfortunately

(5) globalization　　(6) discoveries　　(7) exports　　(8) miscarriages

(9) international　　(10) forewords

4. 請將各組的「詞素」組成一個「合法的」單詞。有些字根需要做一些變化。

例：er　inter　view

答：interviewer

(1) load	up	ing	
(2) ceive	s	er	re
(3) ment	dis	establish	s
(4) er	bean	s	count
(5) law	un	ly	ful
(6) society	al	anti	

(7) ordinary　　　extra　　　　ly

(8) tion　　　　　globe　　　　ize　　　　al

(9) economics　　ly　　　　　　micro　　　al

(10) honest　　　　dis　　　　　y

第 3 章

從詞素到句子；
從擴增到縮減

　　我們在寫英文作文的時候，常埋怨自己的詞彙銀行存款有限，有時候更恨自己的詞彙銀行幾近破產。這種對詞彙量沒有自信的怨尤，常常是因為不知道如何繁殖詞彙、不知道如何建構新詞。前面討論過，詞素是一個語言具有意義的最小單位。books 有二個詞素：book 與 s；interviewed 有三個詞素：inter-、view 與 -ed。有些詞素可以獨立存在，稱之為自由詞素，例如 book 與 view。有些詞素不能夠獨立存在，例如 -s、inter- 與 -ed，必須附著在其他詞素上面，稱之為附著詞素。以英語來說，黏在其他詞素前面的附著詞素，稱之為字首，例如 **re-**(view)，**dis-**(honest)，**im-**(possible)，**de-**(frost) 等。黏在其他詞素後面的附著詞素，稱之為字尾，例如 (review)-**er**，(honest)-**ly**，(balance)-**ing**，(frost)-**y**，(frost)-**ed**。

　　有的單詞由二個（含）以上的自由詞素建構形成複合詞，例如 ice cream (ice+cream)，textbook (text+book)，do-it-yourself (do+it+yourself)。複合詞可以分開寫 (bean counter)，可以用連字號連接 (bean-counter)，也可以連著拼寫 (beancounter)。

　　含有附著詞素的單詞，稱之為複雜詞，例如 careless (care+less)，untrue (un+true)，deceive (de+ceive)，reviewers (re+view+er+s) 等。

　　大家都學過 friend（朋友）和 enemy（敵人），但是很多人就是「不知其所以然」，不會運用「截搭 (blend (ing))」的方法來建構新詞，例如，frenemy（亦敵亦友），brunch (breakfast+lunch)（早午餐），motel (motor+hotel)（汽車旅館）等。「截搭」，又稱混合，是一種構詞方法，常將一個單詞的「頭」截下，然後與另一個單詞的「尾」搭上，混合而成。

　　同樣的道理，我們可以由上下文去解構進而學會 jorts (jeans+shorts)（牛仔短褲、熱褲），turducken (turkey+duck+chicken)（三禽肉，火鴨雞，火雞+鴨+雞），bittersweet (bitter+sweet)（甜中有苦的），birdflu (bird+flu)（禽流感）等。

　　當然，如果有人無意中將 hamburger 錯誤或創意分析為 ham+burger，那麼我們當年拆組積木的頑童赤子之心，就很容易接受與／或創造出 chickenburger (chicken+burger)，cheeseburger (cheese+burger)，fishburger (fish+burger)，vegeburger (vegetable+burger)，riceburger(rice+burger) 這些廣為大家接受、使用的單詞。而且下一次看到 butterfly (butter+fly)，dragonfly (dragon+fly)，firefly (fire+fly) 你會覺得好親近。

　　我們利用詞素來造單詞，利用單詞來組成片語，利用片語透過語法句構來形成句子，利用組合句子來寫一個段落，將主題相關的段落連貫成一篇短文，這種有系統的英文單詞的逐步擴增組合就是英文作文。現在，讓我們來實地操作一番。

文章的大意：我生長在鄉下的一個小村莊。鄉下的空氣很清新。我的父母、爺爺奶奶都很寵愛我，視我為掌上明珠。雖然我們家不富有，但是我們生活很快樂。我愛我的家人。我決心要和我的家人永遠生活在一起。

單詞

我 I	生 be born
長 grow up	鄉下 country
小的 small	村莊 village
空氣 air	清潔 clean
新鮮 fresh	爸爸 father
媽媽 mother	爺爺 grandfather
奶奶 grandmother	視 consider/see
為 as/to be	掌上明珠 the apple of someone's eye/love me very much（很愛我）
雖然 although	有錢的 rich
但是 but	過 live
快樂的 happy	生活 life
愛 love	家人 family
決心 determine	要 want
永遠 forever	和 and/with
他們 them	住 live
一起 together	

造片語

was born, grew up, in the country, small village; clean and fresh; father, mother, (parents); grandfather, grandmother, (grandparents); not rich; lead a happy life; love my family, want to live; with them。

文法句構與修辭

was born and grew up（平行結構）；a small village in the country（後位修飾）；clean and fresh（平行結構，詞序）；my parents and my grandparents（平行結構）；see me as the apple of their eyes（成語）；although we are not rich（從屬連接）；live a happy life（搭配；同系受詞）；happy and harmonious（押頭韻）；love my family ... so that... want to live with them forever（因果）。

遣詞用字

視之為 (see ... as)，寵愛我 (love me very much/spoil me/the apple of their eyes)，過生活 (lead/live a ... life)，決心要做某事 (be determined to V ...)，永遠在一起 (with them forever)。

組成段落　（60 字左右）

I was born and grew up in a small village in the country, where the air is clean and fresh. My parents and my grandparents (my parents and their parents) see me as the apple of their eyes. Although we are not rich, we live a happy and harmonious life. I love my family so much that I am determined to/want to live with them forever.

*毋*庸置疑地，這是一個很有意義的實地操作，因為，我們只要再加一個長達 60~70 個單詞的第二段，就可以滿足一篇至少 120 個單詞的文章的要求，同時又可以順利獲得滿意的分數，進而考上理想的學校。這是一個淺顯易懂的道理，更重要的是，這個實地操作絕對不會是一蹴可幾，更不會是遙不可及。

底下，我們來探討二組例句。比方說，我們造了三個句子：我有一位好朋友。(I have a good friend.) 這位朋友住在臺北。(The friend lives in Taipei.) 臺北是臺灣北部的一個大城市。(Taipei is a big city in northern Taiwan.)

因為修辭的考量，我們決定將第二個句子改成形容詞子句。結果，我們有了底下的二個句子：I have a good friend who lives in Taipei. Taipei is a big city in northern Taiwan. 也許，我們決定要將三個句子合併為一。我們決定用二個形容詞子句。

於是，我們造出了後面這個句子：I have a good friend who lives in Taipei, which is a big city in northern Taiwan. 我們想到句型要有變化，我們覺得這裡不想用二個形容詞子句，因為我們等一下還要用到形容詞子句，而且，我們有把握處理「同位語」的句構，於是我們寫出了底下的

句子：I have a good friend who lives in Taipei, a big city in northern Taiwan. 在專有名詞 Taipei 的後面接上一個指涉相同人地物的名詞片語，形成一個並列結構，從修辭的角度來說，這是一種同位關係，也就是「同位語」的處理與表現。

　　同樣地，我們要用英文寫出這個句子：「幾天前，我偶然遇見了一位女孩，那位女孩年輕、時尚、美麗。」我們會的單詞片語整理如下：

幾天前 a few days ago; the other day	偶然 suddenly; unexpectedly; by chance
遇見 meet; come across; bump into	年輕 young
時尚 fashionable; fashionably-dressed	美麗 beautiful; pretty; attractive

　　經過遣詞用字、文法句構與修辭的考量，我們可以造出底下的句子：A few days ago I came across a girl who was young, beautiful, and fashionably-dressed. 我們的遣詞用字功力告訴我們 come across 等於 meet ... by chance，因此不再累贅使用副詞 unexpectedly 或 by chance；同時，考慮到「詞序排列與節奏」，我們將「年輕、時尚、美麗」的英語對應語排成 "young, beautiful, and fashionably-dressed" 的詞序。

　　我們轉個方向，來討論縮減。縮減是擴增的反面。縮減從英文作文的角度來說，基本上，是語法的運用。理論上，我們可以將句子縮減為片語，將片語縮減為單詞，將單詞縮減為詞素。但是，考試的時候，最常用、最實用的是依照文法句構與修辭的規範，將句子縮減為片語。

練習 3

1. 底下有二組單詞，請說明 A 組成員與 B 組成員在構詞上的最大不同之處。

（提示：rainbow = rain+bow　vs.　reviewer= re+view+er）

A 組：(1) rainbow　(2) textbook　(3) girlfriend　(4) brainwash　(5) redneck

B 組：(1) reviewer　(2) washing　(3) foolish　(4) careless　(5) unlawful

2. 造片語：請利用下列各單詞造出由至少三個單詞組成的「合乎語法的」片語。請不要組成一個完整的句子。

例：city

答：a city in Taiwan

　　(1) model　(2) life　(3) bright　(4) reporters　(5) homework

3. 造句：請利用下列的單詞或片語，各造成一個由至少八個單詞組成的「合乎語法的」句子。

例： city

答： Tainan is a beautiful city in southern Taiwan.

    (1) models   (2) a happy life   (3) bright   (4) fashion   (5) packaged food

第4章

寫英文作文的技巧與步驟

本章討論寫英文作文的技巧與步驟。這裡的技巧跟學測指考的分項評分原則是相對應的。

第一節　技巧

一、第一個技巧：一致

一致就是文章要清楚切題、要具有整體性。一篇文章是由 10 到 15 個左右的句子組合而成。以堆積木作比喻的話，這 10 到 15 塊積木，要拼裝成一個有主題的作品。就一致性而言，這些句子必須跟文章的主題相關，切忌離題。基本上，要達到一致就是從頭至尾不要造出與主題不相關的句子，然後，利用句子的合併以及轉承語，將這些相關卻零散的部分成功組合。

以 101 年學測為例。你要寫一封信勸告你最好的朋友不要常常熬夜打電玩，要以學業為重，免得被父母責備。你設計要寫三段。第一段開頭鋪陳。先說最近注意到你的好朋友上課不是遲到、缺課就是打瞌睡，放學後匆忙離校去打工，作業不是忘了交就是到了學校才找同學的作業抄襲，成績退步，被父母責備，後來你知道他迷上了電玩。第二段支撐發展。你以好朋友的身份規勸他不要迷上電玩，要節制，每個星期以玩 4 個小時為限，星期六與星期天上午各二個小時，而且萬萬不可熬夜打通宵而造成第二天上課打瞌睡。接著，你勸他不要為了買遊戲卡而去打工賺錢。你們現在是學生，應該以學業為重，爭取好成績，讓父母感到驕傲。第三段收場結尾。你鼓勵你的好朋友，每天晚上跟你到公園慢跑 30 分鐘，既減肥又強身。你提議你們再加上同學大偉，每個星期一三五的晚上在圖書館一起讀書、討論功課。你們約定要念同一所大學而且要從同一所大學畢業。最後，你依照書信的格式，加上開頭的稱呼 (Dear Ken/Barbie)，信尾致辭 (Best regards, Best wishes, Take care,)，簽名，成功完成由三個段落組合，清楚切題具有一致性的文章。

其實，根據歷屆學測指考英文作文的提示，我們寫二段即可。也就是說，我們可以將第二段與第三段合併成為一段。

我們在第三章討論從遣詞用字，到造片語造句子，到利用文法句構與修辭變化句型，到善用轉承語組成段落。我們來演練一下遣詞用字，造片語，造句子。

詞彙 （第一段）

注意	notice that ...
打瞌睡	doze off
倉促地	hastily; in a hurry
兼職工作	part-time job; work part-time
忘了交作業	forget the homework
抄襲	copy
同學的作業	your classmate's homework
成績	academic performance; grade
退步	not as good as it used to be
被父母責備	your parents blame you; be blamed by your parents

詞彙 （第二段）

沉迷於	be addicted to
打電玩	play video games
節制	set a limit
四個小時為限	a maximum of four hours
熬夜	stay up
遊戲卡	game cards
以學業為重	school work is our (top) priority
努力學習爭取好成績	work/study hard to get good grades
讓父母感到驕傲	make our parents be proud of us
慢跑三十分鐘	jog thirty minutes
減肥	lose weight
強身	get in shape
在圖書館一起念書	study together in the library
討論功課	discuss homework
承諾	promise; make a promise
念同一所大學	go to the same university
畢業	graduate from

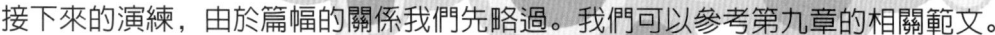

接下來的演練，由於篇幅的關係我們先略過。我們可以參考第九章的相關範文。

二、第二個技巧：連貫

連貫就是將所寫的零散句子，整理成一個段落，然後將主題一致的二個或三個段落，組合成「有開頭、有發展、有結尾」的一篇完整文章。中文作文常提到的「起承轉合」就是這裡所指的連貫。有一點要說明的是，除非是撰寫對比題材的文章，例如比較中學生打工的優缺點，或比較中學生住校舍的優缺點等，否則很少要用到「起承轉合」的「轉」。學測指考的英文作文要求文長至少 120 個單詞，如果我們決定寫二段，那麼第一段用 50 個字左右寫開頭，介紹我們的想法、主張、論點等，第二段就用 70 個字左右充分解釋、說明、舉例與／或提出有效的建議與解決方案等，最後加上一個簡短的結論。

提供一個口訣供參考如下：一段 50 提論點；二段 70 舉例說明建議作結論。

三、第三個技巧：支撐

支撐，又叫支持，是文章整個發展的主幹。作者有義務提供足夠的證據來說服讀者。這些所謂的證據包括事實、定義、解釋、舉例、資料等。這些證據必須具體、明確、完整，也就是要有說服力，讓讀者點頭認同。以 100 年指考為例：「提示：你認為畢業典禮應該是個溫馨感人、活潑熱鬧、或是嚴肅傷感的場景？請寫一篇英文作文說明你對畢業典禮的看法，第一段寫出畢業典禮對你而言意義是什麼，第二段說明要如何安排或進行活動才能呈現出這個意義。」作答時，你在第一段，依主觀看法用 50 個字左右寫出畢業典禮對你個人的意義；例如，我不喜歡畢業典禮，因為像大拜拜；例如，我很期待畢業典禮，因為它代表了結束也意味著開始。你如何敘述畢業典禮的意義，閱卷委員不會有太大的意見。但是，你的第二段必須用 70 個字左右來支持發展第一段，根據試題的指示，寫出你要如何安排進行活動，以呈現出這個意義。

你大約有 70 個字的篇幅可以說明你的做法，試題的提示規定你要說明如何安排或進行活動。你可以提出具體的做法，例如 (1) 舉辦一場師生都沒有拘束的派對或座談會；(2) 邀請成功的校友返校演講；(3) 將舉辦畢業典禮預算金額的一半捐給慈善機關做公益；(4) 請畢業生承諾，畢業後每年必須向母校進言建議，如何讓母校茁壯成長永續經營。別忘了，你只有 70 個單詞左右可以寫。平均用 20 個單詞寫一項活動。如果你有良好的訓練跟演練，這實際上是一點問題也沒有。

四、第四個技巧：遣詞用字和體例

　　高中 7000 個單詞足夠應付遣詞用字的挑戰。中等程度的學生不需要擔心自己可用的單詞太少。一般的詞典用來下定義解釋的詞彙約在 2500 個單詞左右，你的詞彙銀行如有 5000 個單詞，就綽綽有餘。就像有 5000 塊積木，在有創意又懂得靈活應用的幼童的手中，可以無限地創造出令人讚賞的組合。

　　同樣地，只要遣詞用字精確得宜沒有錯誤，只要你遵守大小寫、縮寫、標點符號的規定，你選擇用 prevent 或 prohibit 或 stop 或 ban 或 curb 來表示「禁止」，所得到的分數都一樣。例如，禁止酒駕，我們可以用 prevent drunk drivers from driving 或 prohibit drunk drivers from driving 或精簡為 stop drunk driving。因此，不要有一定要用藻麗詞彙的迷思，就用自己最有把握的 stop drunk driving 吧！

五、第五個技巧：有效變化

　　有效變化的目的是同中求異，必要時異中求同。有效變化有四種應用方式：遣詞用字、句子長短、句型結構、標點符號。我們可以利用不同詞彙、長中短句、句型變化以及應用標點符號，使句子結構變化萬千。例如，表示因果關係的果，我們可以用 lead to 或 result in 或 as a result 或 thus resulting in 或 so that ... 等；我們可以利用平行結構、倒裝句、同位語，從屬連接，虛主詞／虛受詞、主動／被動、加強語氣的重複等不同的句型，讓閱卷教授肯定考生有變化句構的能力；我們可以善加利用逗號 (,) 句號 (.) 以外的標點符號，例如分號 (;)，破折號（--），引號（" "），底線（＿＿＿），脫字號 (∧) 等，突顯我們對標點符號的掌握。總之，有效變化就是避免單調、千篇一律的句子結構。

六、第六個技巧：掌控時間

　　學測指考英文考科的考試時間分別限定為 100 分鐘與 80 分鐘，考生必須在規定的時間內做完第壹部分選擇題的 50 多個單選題與第貳部分的非選擇題。如果第壹部分 50 多個選擇題，每題平均要 45~60 秒作答，那麼就要用掉 40~50 分鐘，剩下的 40~50 分鐘時間，要完成二題翻譯與一篇至少 120 個單詞的英文作文。假如我們用 10 分鐘完成二題中譯英，那麼我們就剩下約 30~40 分鐘寫作文。30 分鐘寫 120~150 字，等於一分鐘寫 4 到 5 個單詞。冷靜一想，也不是那麼困難。

結論是，用 40 分鐘完成選擇題，包括檢查答案與劃卡，用 10 分鐘作翻譯題，用 30~50 分鐘寫作文。平常多模擬演練幾次，考試就會胸有成竹，鎮靜淡定。

第二節　步驟

接著，介紹撰寫學測指考英文作文的八個步驟。前三個步驟屬於考試前的預備作業，後五個步驟屬於考試當下搶高分的方法。

一、第一個步驟：猜題

猜題就是預期會出什麼主題的作文。我們彙整最近十年的主題，發現學測指考的英文作文與/或翻譯題目常跟當年的社會熱門議題；一般民眾的道德標準；休閒養生；高中生的家庭生活、學校活動；社群網路等有關。

英文作文有 (1) 不要佔用博愛座（公德心）。(2) 沒有電的世界（節約能源）。(3) 拾物不昧（道德）。(4) 不要沉迷電玩（休閒）。(5) 捐出樂透彩金（公益）。(6) 其他，例如廣告、音樂、旅遊、考試、被人冤枉、最難忘的氣味等。

中譯英有 (1) 高房價。(2) 國產影片。(3) 臺灣的夜市。(4) 太空科技。(5) 殘而不廢。(6) 飲食健康。(7) 核能安全與綠色能源。(8) 少子化。(9) 網路票選讓玉山成為世界奇觀。(10) 全球糧食危機。(11) 大眾運輸與高鐵。(12) 無煙的用餐環境。(13) 地球村與參與國際活動。(14) 科技犯罪與網際網路詐財。凡此等等。

根據以上的整理，在參加考試之前，我們可以「大膽地」預測 20 個主題，例如，前一陣子的中菲緊張關係，讓我們多花一點心思在「主權國家」(sovereignty)，「外交」(diplomacy)，「國防」(national defense)，「司法獨立」(independent judiciary)，「國際組織」(international organization)，「人權」(human rights)，「自助者人助」(Heaven helps those who help themselves.) 等議題上面。因為猜題，我們會多做一些準備，會多背一些單詞片語與句子，有備無患，「得之我幸，不得我命，如此而已」，沒有壞的副作用，何樂而不為呢？平常多閱讀英文時事報導可以幫助我們猜題與準備相關的詞彙與片語。

二、第二個步驟：準備 150 個單詞，50 個片語，10 種句型

　　單詞，例如「實用的」(practical)，「有機的」(organic)，「文化」(culture)，「特徵」(characteristic)，「協商/談判」(negotiation) 等。片語，例如「組成」(be composed of)，「酒駕」(drunk driving)，「理所當然認為」(take it for granted that)，「稍縱即逝」(now or never)，「色情與暴力」(sex and violence) 等。句型，例如平行、倒裝、分詞構句、從屬連接、對等連接、重複、平衡、設問等等〔請參考第 10 章〕。一開始，我們會覺得像是亂槍打鳥，甚至以為是不切實際。但是，我們看到電影裡的武術學校，練武場二側總是擺著各式各樣兵器；海軍艦艇上面展示的武器與戰鬥機，其目的是要讓自己和別人知道我們已經準備好了。再說，學測沒用到的單詞與片語，也可能在指考用到，而指考沒用到的單詞與片語，以後上大學、念研究所總會用得到。更何況，你在詞彙銀行存的錢越多，你的詞彙金庫就越飽滿充實，當然要高興去做。〔請參考附錄 8〕

三、第三個步驟：精選轉承語〔請參考附錄 2〕

　　前面提過，學測指考的英文作文通常只需要「起承合」加上說明、措施與舉例等，因此，我們儘量讓自己熟悉表達「承合」與「說明、舉例、解釋」的轉承語，辨識這些轉承語，最後的驗收是要能夠靈活運用它們。表達「承合」的轉承語，例如 moreover, furthermore, in addition 等。表達「對照」的轉承語，例如 however, nevertheless, by contrast, on the contrary 等。表達「因果」的轉承語，例如 therefore, consequently, as a result 等。表達「舉例」的轉承語，例如 for example, for instance, to illustrate 等。就應付考試而言，夠用就好了，不要太貪心，必要時，死忠於同一個轉承語，要寫表達「舉例」的轉承語，就用 for example 就是了。其他等考上大學以後再說！

四、第四個步驟：看清楚題目，消化題目

　　考試的規定或提示沒有變化的話，字數是至少 120 單詞，寫二段。一定要確定第二段是舉例或是說明或是解釋原因或是方法措施等。從看題目開始就要隨時注意時間的分配，盡可能留個三分鐘給第八個步驟。

五、第五個步驟：構思二段的組織架構

　　其實，沒有變化的話，學測、指考的提示都會「很體貼地、很清楚地」指導我們如何構

思。底下分別是 100 學年度和 101 學年度的指考英文作文提示。

(100) 提示：你認為畢業典禮應該是個溫馨感人、活潑熱鬧、或是嚴肅傷感的場景？請寫一篇英文作文說明你對畢業典禮的看法，第一段寫出畢業典禮對你而言意義是什麼，第二段說明要如何安排或進行活動才能呈現出這個意義。

(101) 提示：請以運動為主題，寫一篇至少 120 個單詞的文章，說明你最常從事的運動是什麼。文分兩段，第一段描述這項運動如何進行（如地點、活動方式、及可能需要的相關用品等），第二段說明你從事這項運動的原因及這項運動對你生活的影響。

我們就像新兵出操，一切照表操課，So easy, right？

六、第六個步驟：畫圈圈圖或畫樹狀圖

畫圈圈圖是將主題用一個大圈圈框起來，畫在最中間；跟主題有關的論述各用一個中圈圈框起來，畫在大圈圈的四周；支撐論述的舉例、說明、解釋、做法、細節等各用一個小圈圈框起來，畫在中圈圈的四周。一個圈圈等於一個單詞或片語或句子。基本上，我們要在 5 分鐘內迅速地劃出 10~15 圈圈，然後利用擴增的方法，來形成句子、組成段落。

我們來為 100 學年度指考英文作文畫圈圈，如下：（圖 1）

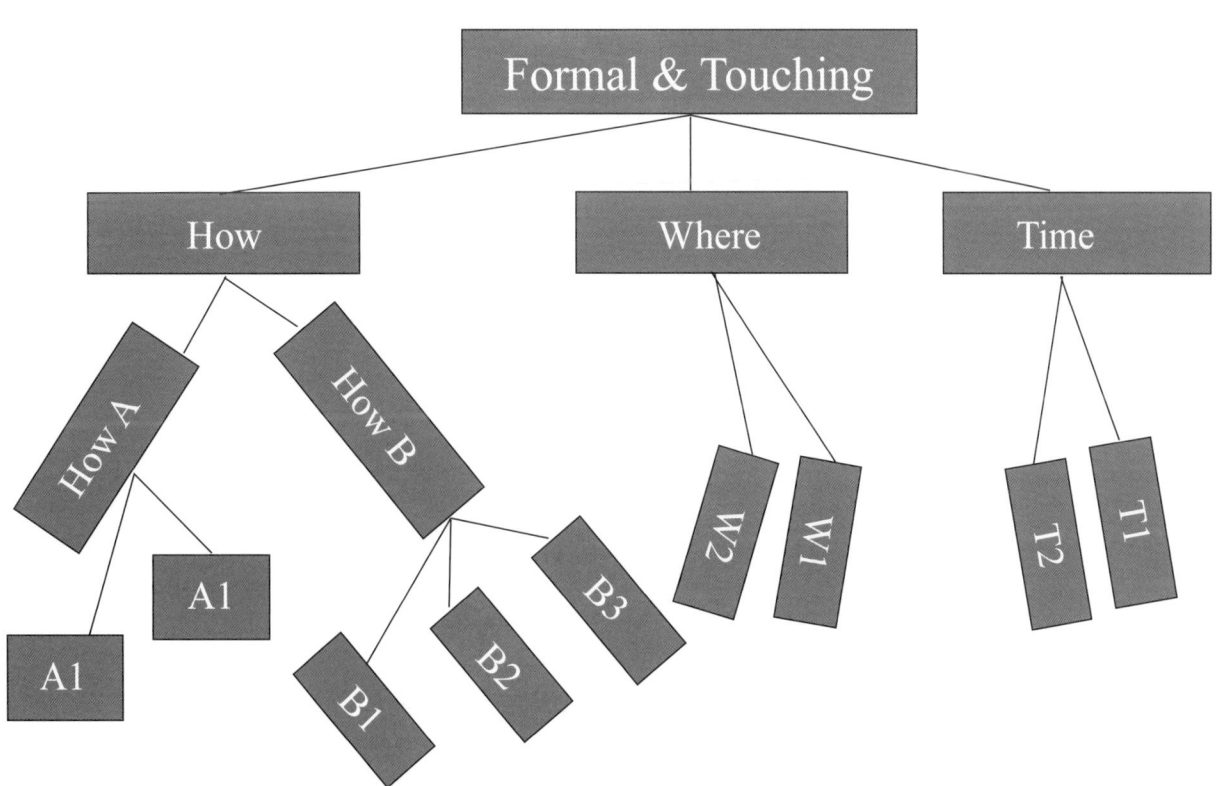

當然也可以用畫樹狀圖代替畫圈圈圖。如下：（圖2）

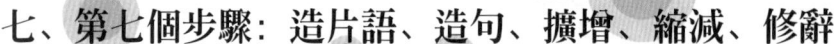

七、第七個步驟：造片語、造句、擴增、縮減、修辭

基本上，將造好的名詞片語附上造好的動詞片語，加上時、空、因、貌 (when, where, why, how) 的描述，就會組成好的句子，因為一個句子等於名詞片語加上動詞片語（或再增加副詞片語或介系詞片語）。接著運用擴增以及縮減的技巧讓句子字數增加或精簡，最後再運用有把握的修辭格，成功寫出 120 個單詞以上的文章。一位訓練有素的考生會放鬆心情來進行這個步驟，因為已經駕輕就熟了。

八、第八個步驟：檢查校對

如果時間快到了，不要更改內容。寫了就寫了。剩下的三分鐘用來檢查校對以下各項：

(1) 文法。(2) 拼寫。(3) 冠詞是否欠缺或多餘。(4) 句子是否出現二個動詞。(5)有無不當地用逗號連接二個句子。〔請參考 7.6〕

常言道：「養兵千日，用在一時。」只要平常按部就班勤加練習，考試時一定可以輕鬆以對，情況好的話，說不定能夠振筆疾書揮灑自如哩！

第三節　模擬練習

> 說明：1. 請依提示寫一篇英文作文。2. 文長至少 120 個單詞 (words)。
> 提示：請以流浪犬為主題，寫一篇英文作文，說明如何減少狗兒在街頭流浪。文分二段，第一段說明狗兒被原先飼主棄養的原因，第二段提出減少流浪犬的有效方法。

考試當下要採取的步驟如下：

1. 看清楚題目，消化題目。
   (1) 主題是「流浪犬」，不是在街頭流浪的寵物。
   (2) 主題是要說明「如何減少」狗兒在街頭流浪，不是要捕殺在街頭流浪的狗兒。

2. 構思二段的組織架構。

(1) 根據平常的訓練，決定採用 2：3 的分配，第一段寫 4~5 句，約 50~60 個單詞，第二段寫 6~7 句，約 70~80 個單詞。

(2) 依照提示，第一段寫 2~3 個「狗兒在街頭流浪的原因」，第二段寫 3~4 個「減少流浪犬的有效方法」。

3. 畫樹狀圖。

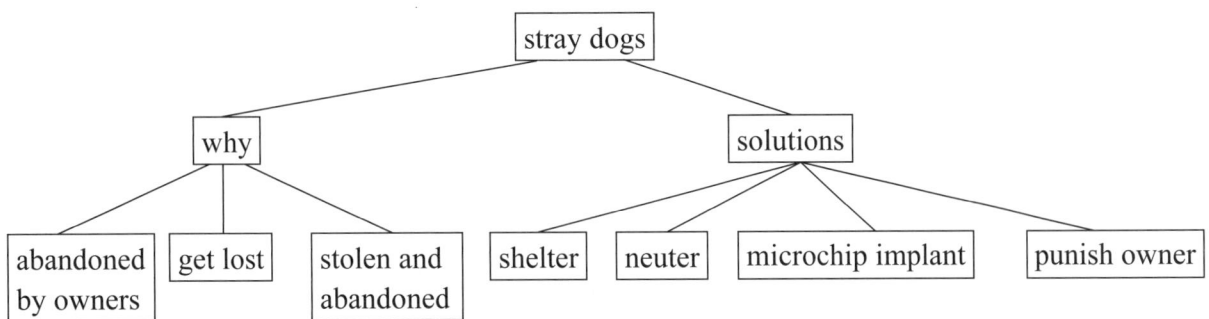

在畫樹狀圖的時候，框框內的關鍵字詞儘量用英文，必要時，當然也可以中英文並用。關鍵字是用來提醒、規範你造詞、造句的步驟。

Stray dogs 流浪犬

Whys 原因

abandoned by owners 飼主棄養

get lost 迷路

stolen and abandoned 被偷然後被拋棄

Solutions 解決方法

shelter 動物收容所

neuter 閹割

microchip implant 植入晶片

punish owner 懲處飼主

humane societies 人道團體

4. 造片語、造句、擴增、縮減、修辭。在進行本步驟的時候，要時時以「一致、連貫、支撐、遣詞用字、變化、修辭」等為念。

單詞與片語

   (1) 普遍 common; not uncommon

   (2) 在街道上 on the streets

   (3) 飼主棄養狗兒 the owners abandon these dogs

   (4) 不道德的行為、不人道的對待 immoral behavior, inhumane treatment

   (5) 由於某種原因 for some reason or other

   (6) 走失而回不了家 get lost and have no home; get lost and end up homeless

   (7) 被偷然後被拋棄 be stolen and then be abandoned

   (8) 有關當局 the authorities concerned

   (9) 採取有效措施 should take effective measures; effective measures should be taken

  (10) 防止飼主棄養 to prevent owners from abandoning their pet dogs

  (11) 我的建議如下 my suggestions are as follows:

  (12) 嚴厲的懲處 severe punishment; to severely punish the owners

  (13) 建立動物收容所 build animal shelters

  (14) 請求人道團體協助 ask for help from humane societies

  (15) 實施閹割或結紮 to have your "companion animals" neutered

  (16) 防止不要的和意外的產仔 to prevent the births of unwanted and accidental litters

  (17) 嚴格執行 should be strictly enforced

  (18) 植入晶片 microchip implant

造句

（因為時間有限，有些單詞不會或沒有把握，而且又不想寫太多，因此決定只寫二個原因，四個解決方法。）

第一段：四句

(1) 近年來在臺灣到處看得到在街頭流浪的狗兒。

   Recently, in Taiwan we can easily see stray dogs everywhere on the streets.

(2) 這些流浪的狗兒的飼主棄養他們。

   The owners abandon these dogs.

(3) 棄養你的「動物夥伴」是不道德的行為，更是不人道的對待。

   It is immoral to abandon your "companion animals." It is an inhumane treatment.

(4) 在街頭流浪的狗兒是因為他們回不了家。

   Some dogs become strays because they have no home.

第二段： 六句

(5) 減少流浪犬的一些有效措施。

There are effective measures to decrease the number of stray dogs.

(6) 立法嚴厲懲處故意棄養狗兒的飼主。

We need to make laws to severely punish the owners who purposely abandon their pet dogs.

(7) 建議對「動物夥伴」進行閹割，防止不要的及意外的產仔。

We suggest that owners should have their "companion animals" neutered to prevent the births of unwanted and accidental litters.

(8) 規定對「動物夥伴」植入晶片，防止狗兒走失。

We have to enforce "microchip implant" regulations to prevent dogs from getting lost.

(9) 建立動物收容所。請求人道團體提供協助。

We need to build enough animal shelters. We can ask for help from humane societies.

(10) （結論）我們要將狗兒視同家人。我們不得棄養他們。

We regard our pet dogs as our family members. We shall never abandon them.

擴增、縮減、修辭

(1) Recently, in Taiwan it is not uncommon for us to see stray dogs here and there. （說明：用了虛主詞句型 it is ... for ... to v 使句構富於變化；利用雙重否定 not uncommon 加強語氣；利用平行結構 here and there「到處」；同時刪掉 on the streets。）

(2) Most of the stray dogs are purposely abandoned by their owners. （說明：用了被動語態，改變詞序；將 stray dogs 移到句首，準備利用形容詞子句合併 (1) 和 (2) 句；加上副詞 "purposely" 以突顯狗兒的可憐。）

(3) Abandoning your companion animals is immoral behavior. In fact, it is an inhumane treatment. （說明：將虛主詞結構 it is ... to abandon 改用動名詞 abandoning 因為要避免用太多 "it"。改用 "companion animals"「動物夥伴」以達到「語言上的政治正確」及用字得宜；加上轉承語 in fact 使語氣更順暢。）

(4) For some reason or other, some dogs get lost on the streets and end up becoming strays. （說明：加上轉承語 for some reason or other 呈現「因果」關係；利用片語動詞 end up 強調意外的結果；利用遣詞用字 strays = stray dogs。）

(5) As far as minimizing the number of stray dogs is concerned, some of the effective measures are discussed as follows: （說明：利用轉承語及「步驟句」句型 as far as ... be concerned，承前接後，準備提出有效的解決方法；利用遣詞用字，選用自己事先準備

33

好的單詞 minimize「減至最小量」。）

(6) To begin with, we need to make laws to severely punish the owners who purposely abandon their pet dogs.（說明：利用轉承語 to begin with 介紹第一個解決方法；利用 v ... to v 的句構表示「目的」。）

(7) Second, we suggest that owners should have their pet dogs neutered to prevent the births of unwanted and accidental litters.（說明：利用轉承語 second 介紹第二個解決方法；利用 that 引導名詞子句。）

(8) Third, we have to strictly enforce "microchip implant" regulations to prevent dogs from getting lost.（說明：利用轉承語 third 介紹第三個解決方法；利用動詞片語 prevent ... from v-ing 表示「防止」；加上副詞 strictly「嚴格地」，藉以要求飼主們遵守相關規定。）

(9) Last, we must build enough animal shelters, and when necessary, we can ask for professional help from humane societies.（說明：利用轉承語 last 介紹最後一個解決方法；利用對等連接詞 and 連接二個相關的獨立單句；加上轉承語 when necessary (when it is necessary) 呈現「時空」關係；加上形容詞 professional「專業的」，藉以加強語氣；選用情態助動詞 must，使其與 need，have to，must 等營造遣詞用字上的變化。）

(10) In conclusion, if we regard our pet dogs as our family members with loving care, we shall never abandon them. We never shall.（說明：利用轉承語 in conclusion 引導結論句；利用從屬連接詞 if 引導「條件」；利用情態助動詞 shall 強調所主張的解決方法「必定」實現。最後加上僅由三個單詞組成的短句，鏗鏘有力地作 ending。）

結合成二段式短文

Recently, in Taiwan it is not uncommon for us to see stray dogs here and there, most of **which** whom are purposely abandoned by their owners. Abandoning your companion animals is immoral behavior. In fact, it is an inhumane treatment. For some reason or other, some dogs get lost in the streets and end up becoming strays. As far as minimizing the number of stray dogs is concerned, some of the effective measures are discussed as follows:

To begin with, we need to make laws to severely punish the owners who purposely abandon their pet dogs. Second, we suggest that owners should have their pet dogs neutered to prevent the births of unwanted and accidental litters. Third, we have to strictly enforce "microchip implant" regulations to prevent dogs from getting lost. Last, we must build enough animal shelters, and when necessary, we can ask for professional help from humane societies. In conclusion, if we regard our pet dogs as our family members with loving care, we shall never abandon them. We never shall.

接著進行「檢查校對」，發現要將第一句的 which 改成 whom，因為用表「人稱」的關係代名詞 whom 可以突顯對狗兒的尊敬。校對後的文章長 172 個單詞。

如果要刪減的話，我們可以刪掉「對『動物夥伴』進行閹割這句話」，那麼文長就是 150個單詞，當然還可以再精簡。要注意的是，如果「閹割」、「結紮」、「晶片」、「人道的」等單詞或片語不屬於你已有的或事先準備好的詞彙時，要用同義字詞或定義性的描述來取代，例如，「閹割」改用 "remove an animal's reproductive organ"；「人道的」改用 "treat animals in a kind way"。果真是「黔驢技窮」時，只好捨棄不用。我們可以轉個彎，另外提供一個造成狗兒流浪的原因：原先的飼主要移民外國或是因為繳不出貸款，房子被銀行收回，因而無處飼養；另外討論一個解決方法：請獸醫代為尋找願意認養的新飼主或是對久病難癒的老寵物實施安樂死。

第四節　102 學年度學測、指考英文作文試題

（102學測；資料來源：大學入學考試中心）

說明：1. 依提示在「答案卷」上寫一篇英文作文。
　　　2. 文長至少 120 個單詞 (words)。
提示：請仔細觀察以下三幅連環圖片的內容，並想像第四幅圖片可能的發展，寫出一個涵蓋連環圖片內容並有完整結局的故事。

（102 指考；資料來源：大學入學考試中心）

> 說明：1. 依提示在「答案卷」上寫一篇英文作文。
> 　　　　2. 文長至少 120 個單詞 (words)。
> 提示：以下有兩項即將上市之新科技產品：

產品一：隱形披風 (invisibility cloak)

穿上後頓時隱形，旁人看不到你的存在；同時，隱形披風會保護你，讓你水火不侵。

產品二：智慧型眼鏡 (smart glasses)

具有掃瞄透視功能，戴上後即能看到障礙物後方的生物；同時能完整紀錄你所經歷過的場景。

　　如果你有機會獲贈其中一項產品，你會選擇哪一項？ 請以此為主題，寫一篇至少 120 個單詞的英文作文。文分兩段，第一段說明你的選擇及理由，並舉例說明你將如何使用這項產品。第二段說明你不選擇另一項產品的理由及該項產品可能衍生的問題。

練習 4

1. 請寫出本章討論的寫英文作文的六個技巧。

_____

_____

_____

_____

_____

2. 英文作文五項評分指標的其中一項是「文句結構富於變化」。請簡單說明何謂「變化」。

_____

_____

_____

_____

_____

3. 請將底下各句以至少二種不同的句型或方式改寫，以達到「有效變化」。

例： The youngest player broke the record.

答： (A) The record was broken by the youngest player.

(B) It was the youngest player that broke the record.

(1) My sister gave me a guitar for my birthday.

_____

_____

_____

_____

(2) That we should use English-English dictionaries is important.

(3) The cheerleaders worked very hard but our team lost the game.

(4) We are devoted to social reforms and we are devoted to judicial reforms.

(5) My parents practiced day and night so that they can participate in the singing contest.

第 5 章

體例

由於篇幅的關係，我們只討論在學測指考英文作文中，比較實用的體例。

依照「評分指標」，體例占 2 分 (10%)，包括有格式、標點與大小寫。格式指的是正確的寫作風格，標點指的是標點符號，大小寫基本上指的是大寫與縮寫的規定。

第一節　格式

格式是指導、規範作者和編輯人士編排、設計書面文件的準則。撰寫正式文章，特別是研究報告時，我們必須遵守一些約定俗成的規定。每個專業領域都有自己的準則與偏好，例如文學領域的 MLA（Modern Language Association 現代語言協會）格式與社會科學領域的 APA（American Psychological Association 美國心理學協會）格式。本書主要依據 MLA 手冊，簡要介紹最基本的格式規範。

1. 紙張：8.5 英寸 × 11 英寸；即 A4 紙張。
2. 空白邊緣：每頁上下左右各留一英寸的頁邊空白邊緣。
3. 題目：在第一行置中。題目必須遵守大寫規定：
    (1) 題目的每一個字的第一個字母一律大寫，(2)-(5) 除外。
    (2) 題目中間的冠詞 the, a, an 的第一個字母不可以大寫。
    (3) 題目中間的介系詞，如 by, for, in, to 等的第一個字母不可以大寫。
        當代英語的編輯格式有將四（含）個字母以上的介系詞，如 between, through, without 等的第一個字母大寫的趨勢，特別是報章雜誌的標題。
    (4) 不定詞 (to v) to 的第一個字母不可以大寫。
    (5) 對等連接詞 and, but, or, nor 等的第一個字母不可以大寫。
4. 注意事項：
    (1) 人稱代名詞所有格 my, your, his, her 等、指示代名詞 this, that 等、關係代名詞 who, which, that 等的第一個字母一律大寫。
    (2) 有些短的單詞如 as, out, up 等可以作介系詞用也可以做副詞用，作副詞用時第一個字母一律大寫；在題目中間作介系詞用時，不可以大寫。
5. 題目不需要劃底線、加框、斜體等。當代英語有將題目用粗題字型與/或加大字型的趨勢。
6. 每一段的第一個字必須內縮 (indentation)，從頁左邊空白邊緣內縮半英寸或是空五格 (space)。

7. 每一句的第一個字的第一個字母必須大寫，句尾必須標以句號（.），問號（?），驚嘆號（!），或冒號（:），或省略號（...）。相關標點符號的討論，請參考第 5 章第 2 節。

8. 二個句子之間要空二格。當代英語常只空一格。

9. 沒有其他規定的話，原則上隔行書寫或打字 (double-space)。

　　長久以來，學測指考英文作文並不要求考生寫題目。以上有關撰寫正式文章的格式的介紹，目的是讓同學有備無患。因此考試的時候，我們只要注意 1 英寸的頁邊空白和插字的規定即可。如果我們不想用立可白修正液/帶，就將要更正的字詞或是要插入的字詞工整地寫在該行的正上方，然後用一個脫字號 (Λ) 標示位置。請比較：

*I come apologize for breaking your daughter's heart.

*   *to*

I come ∧ *apologize for breaking your daughter's heart.*

*"Government of the people, by the people, and for the people, will not perish from the earth."

    shall

"Government of the people, by the people, ~~and~~ for the people, ~~will~~ not perish from the earth."

      ∧

第二節　標點

　　標點就是標點符號。英文的標點符號興起於 14 世紀左右，到了 15 世紀，由於活版印刷術的發明，印刷業基於需要，建立了一套標準化的標點符號，一直到了 19 世紀，英文的標點符號才算是真正地標準化。但是，為了經濟原因，為了節省打字機的色帶，為了節省時間、油墨和紙張，從 20 世紀中葉開始，標點符號的使用被減少到最低程度。

　　使用標點符號的基本原則是避免歧義，也就是避免有兩種語義解讀。我們來看看這個有名的一對例子。"eats shoots and leaves" vs. "eats, shoots, and leaves"。 前面的例子可以解讀為 "someone eats the shoots and then he or she leaves"; 後面的例子可以解讀為 "someone eats, someone shoots, and someone leaves"。這裡是所謂斷句的問題，跟中文的「下雨天留客天留我不留」，「天天天藍」，「歐陽明」是同一回事。語言強調的是約定俗成，遵從主流用法，考生原則上必須遵守「較嚴格」的規範，等哪天麻雀變了鳳凰，我們再來打破傳統，展翅高飛，不理語言的約束。

一、句號（.）(period/full stop/point/dot)

句號前面沒有空格。句號後面要空二格，然後再開始新的句子。

1. 用於直述句之後。

   This is an interesting story.

2. 用於縮略詞之後。

   I will see you on Tues., Feb. 18, 2014, at 3:00 p.m.

   （當代英語有用 pm 取代 p.m. 的趨勢。別忘了約定俗成，目前 p.m.還是王道。）

   pp. 17~25 (pp. = pages)

3. 當小數點用。

   Enclosed please find a check for $75.30.

4. 用於大綱項目的字母和數字之後。

   I.

   A.

   1.

   a.

5. 用於註明幕別與場別。

   Julius Caesar 3.2（《朱利阿斯・凱撒》第 3 幕，第 2 場）

二、逗號（,）(comma)

逗號前面沒有空格，逗號後面要空一格。

1. 分隔平行結構的成分。

   We ordered a hamburger, two large fries, and two Cokes.

   比較：We ordered a hamburger, two large fries and two Cokes.

   （當代英語有 and 前面不用逗號的趨勢。）

2. 分隔從屬子句與主要子句。

   Because I got a cold, I did not go to the meeting.

3. 分隔分詞構句。

   Walking in the park, I met my English teacher.

4. 分隔呼語。

Professor Lin, can I ask you a question?

5. 用於信函的稱呼和信尾致辭之後。

Dear Ken,　　Hello Ken,

Best regards,　Sincerely,

6. 分隔轉述動詞和引語。

The passenger replied, "I don't care."

(= The passenger replied: "I don't care.")

(= "I don't care," replied the passenger.)

(= "I don't care," the passenger replied.)

三、分號（;）(semicolon)

分號前面沒有空格，分號後面要空一格。

1. 分隔二個關係緊密的獨立子句。概略而言，此時的分號，約等於逗號加上 and，or，but。

My major is history; her major is chemistry.

比較：My major is history, and her major is chemistry.

2. 分隔已有逗號的平行結構的成分。

He is going to have concerts in Taipei, Taiwan; Shanghai, China; and Sydney, Australia.

3. 與連接副詞/轉承語使用，分隔從屬子句與主要子句。

I got a cold; therefore, I did not go to the meeting.

四、冒號（:）(colon)

冒號前面沒有空格，冒號後面要空一格。

1. 美式英語信函的稱呼語，演說詞的稱呼語之後。

Dear Professor Johnson:

My fellow citizens:

Ladies and gentlemen:

2. 引導表示舉例、補充、說明、解釋等的單詞或片語或句子。

冒號後面的第一個字母可以大寫。傳統嚴謹的規定，冒號前面的句子，結構必須完整。

There are four seasons in a year: spring, summer, fall, and winter.

I see your point: People change.

3. 分隔主標題與副標題。

English Composition for High School Students: An Introduction

4. 分隔時間的時分秒。

10:25:38 a.m.

5. 分隔聖經的章節。

Genesis 3:1~3

五、連字號（-）(hyphen)

連字號前面後面都沒有空格。

1. 用於複合詞。

up-to-date; ex-husband

2. 用於字根與字首，字根與字尾之間。

mid-60s; anti-lock; move-ment; teach-er

3. 用於對手之間，比分之間。

the San Antonio Spurs-the Miami Heat game

The final score was 6~4, 6~4, 7~6.

4. 用於地名之間。

the Taipei-Seoul flight

六、省略號（...）(ellipsis)

省略號前面後面都要空一格。在句尾時，前面沒有空格，後面加上句號、問號或驚嘆號。當代英語有很多實例並未在句尾加上句號，只用省略號而已。

1. 用於省略單詞、片語或句子。

Government ... shall never perish from the earth.

... that all men are created equal....

2. 用於表示語句中間的停頓。

Tell Laura ... I need her ... may be late ... that cannot wait....

七、破折號（--）(dash)

破折號前面後面都沒有空格。打字時，用連續二個連字號形成一個破折號，因此，破折號是連字號的二倍長度。有些作者不區別連字號與破折號。

1. 用於表示語句中突然轉變的想法或結構。

   Would you--if you have a car--take me to the airport?

   The young singer is eager to meet his fiancee--even right away.

2. 分隔非限制性的同位語或附加說明。

   Are there four seasons--spring, summer, fall, and winter--on your island?

八、問號（?）(question mark)

問號前面沒有空格。

1. 用於問句之後。

   Is Mary your sister?

2. 用於表示存疑。

   Julius Caesar (100~44?BC)

九、驚嘆號（!）(exclamation mark)

驚嘆號前面沒有空格。有人主張正式文章，除了引用之外，不要過度使用驚嘆號。

1. 用於驚嘆句之後。

   What a sexy dancer!

2. 用於加強語氣的命令句之後。

   Listen up!

   Run!

十、引號（" "）(quotation mark)

引號前面空一格，後面接其他標點符號時沒有空格，沒有接其他標點符號時空一格。美式

英語將逗號、句號等置於引號內；英式英語將逗號、句號等置於引號外。

1. 用於直接引述。

The Princess replied, "I'll never kiss a frog."（美式英語）

比較：The Princess replied, "I'll never kiss a frog".（英式英語）

2. 用於表示作者的特殊目的。

The robot has a better "brain"?

She is not a "roommate"; she is a "friend."

3. 用於翻譯。

The next number is C'est la vie, "Such is life."

十一、底線（＿＿＿）(underscore)

底線是在字或字母的正下方劃上橫線。底線，嚴格上來說，是一種字型符號，用來代替斜體字 (italics) 的字體。在用印刷體字體或手寫時，我們以劃底線來代替斜體字，表示下列的辨識功能。

1. 用於書籍、報紙、雜誌、期刊、電影、廣播與電視節目等的名稱。

Harry Potter (*Harry Potter*)

The New York Times (*The New York Times*)

參考：當代英語有不將報紙名稱用斜體字或劃底線的趨勢，例如 The New York Times。

2. 用於英文文本中的外國文字。但是，當代英語常用引號代替底線，或是以一般文字處理。

Veni, vidi, vici vs. "Veni, vidi, vici" (I came, I saw, I conquered.)

El Niño vs. "El Niño"（厄爾尼諾現象；聖嬰現象）

第三節 英文書信格式

英文書信主要有三種格式：靠左對齊式、縮排式、改良靠左對齊式。

靠左對齊式 (block style) 是將書信的分隔部分，1 至 10 全部向頁面左邊的空白邊沿對齊，除了另有規定之外，各個部分，包括正文段落，中間隔開一行。段落的正文不用隔行書寫。

縮排式 (indented style) 是將 1~2 與 6~10 的分隔部分，往右移到信紙中間，靠左對齊，信的正文每一段的第一個字必須內縮，從頁面左邊空白邊沿內縮半英寸或是空五格。改良靠左對齊式 (modified block style) 與縮排式唯一的不同之處是正文每一段的第一個字都不必內縮。

信的分隔部分 1 至 10，說明如下：

1. 信頭 (heading)，又稱回信地址 (return address)。信頭是信紙上所印製的公司或機關名稱和地址，或是個人姓名和地址。例如：

   Department of Foreign Languages and Literature

   National Cheng Kung University

   1 University Road

   Tainan, Taiwan 70101

   ROC

2. 日期 (date) 是撰寫這封信的日期，例如 January 18, 2014。請參考附錄 3，有關日期的寫法。

3. 信內收信人地址 (inside address) 是收信人的名稱和地址。按照慣例，信內收信人地址和日期中間隔開三行。

4. 稱呼 (salutation) 是信函開頭對收信人的稱呼語，即某某先生、女士、經理、校長鈞鑒等。例如 Dear Mr./Ms./Miss White；Hello David；Hey Judy 等。

5. 正文 (body) 是信的內容。

6. 信尾致辭 (closing) 是信函結尾的致意，即敬上、敬啓等。例如 Respectfully,（恭敬地，常用以向尊長致敬）；Sincerely, Sincerely yours, Yours sincerely, 或 Yours truly,（謹上；敬上，常用於正式信函的致意）With best regards, Best regards, 或 Best,（謹致問候，常用以好友之間較為正式的問候）；Love,（愛你的；All my love, 全心愛你的；或 Lots of love, 深深愛你的，常用於給家人、朋友或愛人的信尾致意）等。

7. 簽名 (signature) 是發信人的簽字署名，一般使用手寫草體。不一定和打字簽名一樣，有時候並不容易辨讀。

8. 打字簽名 (typed signature) 是列印發信人的姓名，一般都用印刷體，容易辨讀。按照慣例，信尾致辭與打字簽名中間隔開四行，方便發信人簽字署名。

9. 副本資訊：(copy/cc:) 是註明副本抄送的資料，通常用 cc: (carbon copy to)，例如 cc: Chair of DFLL, William（副本抄送：外文系系主任、威廉）等。

10. 附件資訊：(enclosures:/enc:) 是註明附在信函裡面的文件，例如 Enc: Copy of transcripts（附件：成績單）等。

靠左對齊式

1 信頭／回信地址

2 日期

3 信內收信人地址

4 稱呼

5.1 正文第一段（不內縮）

5.2 正文第二段（不內縮）

5.3 正文第三段（不內縮）

6 信尾致辭

7 簽名

8 打字簽名

9 副本資訊

10 附件資訊

縮排式

1 信頭／回信地址

2 日期

3 收信人地址

4 稱呼

*****5.1 本文第一段（內縮）

*****5.2 本文第二段（內縮）

*****5.3 本文第三段（內縮）

6 信尾致辭

7 簽名

8 打字簽名

9 副本資訊

10 附件資訊

改良靠左對齊式

| 1 信頭／回信地址 |

| 2 日期 |

| 3 收信人地址 |

| 4 稱呼 |

| 5.1 正文第一段（不內縮） |

| 5.2 正文第二段（不內縮） |

| 5.3 正文第三段（不內縮） |

| 6 信尾致辭 |

| 7 簽名 |

| 8 打字簽名 |

| 9 副本資訊 |

| 10 附件資訊 |

範例

David Lin
389 Yuer Street
Taichung, Taiwan 404
ROC

December 18, 2013

Professor P. J. Chiang
1 University Road
Tainan, Taiwan 70101
ROC

Dear Professor Chiang:

I am writing in regard to your ad posted on the bulletin board at the Department of Foreign Languages and Literature concerning your need for a research assistant. I am interested in working with your team. I believe I can offer technical knowledge, backed by my experience in Dr. Tera Chen's language lab between July 2012 and June 2013.

I have enclosed a copy of my resume and a copy of the transcripts issued by National Cheng Kung University. I would welcome any opportunity to talk with you about my training in Phonetics and in Audio Recording. Please feel free to call me at (06) 2757575 or e-mail brjiang@mail.ncku.edu.tw.

Sincerely,

David Lin

cc: Julia Fang
Enc: Resume, Transcripts

練習 5

1. 英文作文分項式評分指標的其中一項是「體例」。請簡單說明「體例」。

---

2. 下列的句子均有不符合標點與／或大小寫規定與／或格式的錯誤，請予以更正。

例：It was pouring, however the fans were energetic and enthusiastic.

答：It was pouring; however, the fans were energetic and enthusiastic.

(1) We completed our project ahead of schedule, we felt very proud.

(2) Hurry up, We are supposed to pick up the manager at p.m. 3.30.

(3) The patient screamed and shouted at the nurse. 'leave me alone'.

(4) The committee promised to give us a answer by 2013 October 18.

(5) The man's restrooms are on the 1th floor, the ladies's restrooms are on the 2th floor, we also have childrens' restrooms on the 3th floor.

(6) "The old man and the sea" is an novel written by Hemingway in 1951.

(7) The picnic basket was filled with: sandwiches, apples, drinks, candy bars.

(8) When did the internet come into being. The early 80S or the mid nineties?

(9) According to my dictionary, who is a abbreviation for World Health Organization.

(10) 「......government of the people......shall never perish......。」

3. 下列的英文作文題目均有不符合標點與／或大小寫規定與／或格式的錯誤，請予以更正。

例： A Dream after my Mother

答： A Dream after My Mother

(1) The Art Of Listening To Classical Music.

(2) Elementary English Composition for Highschool Students:an introduction.

(3) Taiwan Stand up!

(4) Can Money Buy Everything for us?

(5) The Future of Teaching English As a second Language.

第 6 章

遣詞用字

　　遣詞用字就是措詞，也就是挑選使用精確得宜的單詞和片語，特別是挑選所謂的實義詞。英語的「實義詞」有名詞、動詞、形容詞與副詞。寫文章必須言之有物，言指的是動詞，物指的是名詞。我們常用副詞修飾動詞，用形容詞修飾名詞，因此確實掌握、靈活運用實義詞是一個基本訓練。現代英語的詞序是主詞-動詞-受詞 (SVO)，而這個主詞和受詞都是名詞片語。因此選對了名詞和動詞幾乎等於寫好了一個單句。當然，基本條件是沒有文法錯誤。

　　我們在第三章概略談過遣詞用字，這裡我們再舉二個例子來討論。我們想寫的句子是「很多學生迷上電玩。」我們要處理的遣詞用字，因人而異。「很多」讓我們聯想到的單詞及片語有 many, so many, a lot of, a number of, a large number of, a great number of, a huge number of 等；「迷上」有 like ... so much, indulge in, be addicted to, be interested in, take passionate interest in 等；「電玩」有 computer game, video game, PC game 等。我們的文法知識告訴我們，學生和電玩要用複數，用了複數就不要再加定冠詞 the; the, many 和 a number of 都是中間限定詞，不可以重疊使用；這個句子的「迷上」是指常態性的敘述，也就是習慣性的動作，要用現在簡單式態；addicted 常用於 be addicted to 的句型，而且這裡的 to 是介系詞，必須後接名詞或 v-ing，凡此等等。

　　我們要如何挑選精確得宜的單詞和片語呢？答案簡單又清楚。只挑選有把握的。如果有把握的超過二個，那就選最有把握的。這個挑選過程包括拼字、大小寫、文法、句構、語義的差別等。

　　準此，我們可能會寫出類似下列的句子：Many students indulge in computer games. A large number of students are addicted to computer games. A huge number of students take passionate interest in playing video games. 如果沒有把握拼對 video 就捨棄不用，不會 indulge 就捨棄不用，不會被動語態的 be addicted to something 就捨棄不用，就這麼簡單。再說，其他條件相同的情況下，上述三個例句得到的分數都一樣。

　　同樣地，我們想寫的句子是「我小時候常常跟我表哥到他家後面的小溪游泳。」這個句子由二個句子組成：「我小的時候。」與「我常常跟我表哥到他家後面的小溪游泳。」可供我們挑選使用的單詞和片語有 I was little, I was young, in my childhood 等；often went swimming, like going swimming, like to go swimming, used to go swimming 等；behind his house, in the rear of his house 等；a creek, a river, a small river, a stream 等。考試當下沒有必要追求完美，不必計較 little 和 young 有何語義上的差異，like going 和 like to go 是否完全一樣，creek 是不是等於 small river 或 stream 等。只要記得用一個表示時間的從屬連接詞 when 把二個句子成功連接即可。結果，我們造出了一個長達個 18 單詞的複句：When I was little, I used to go swimming with my cousin in the stream behind his house.注意到了沒有？像這樣的句子成功地寫 7 個，再加上適當的轉承語，就會形成一篇 120 個單詞以上的的文章。難嗎？不難！

第一節　屈折變化與衍生變化

當代英語的詞綴分成二種：屈折詞綴、衍生詞綴。屈折詞綴一共有 8 個，都是字尾。衍生詞綴，又稱派生詞綴，俗稱詞類變化。常用字首、字尾、字根，有幾百個。本節介紹八個屈折詞綴，有關常用的衍生詞綴請參考附錄 4。

八個屈折詞綴

1 -s	名詞複數	books, buses
2 's -s'	名詞所有格	women's, Venus's, ladies'
3 -s	第三人稱單數現在式（三單現）	cooks, washes
4 -ed	過去式	cooked, washed
5 -ing	現在分詞（進行時態）	speaking, writing
6 -en	過去分詞（完成時態；被動語態）	spoken, written
7 -er	比較級	faster, better
8 -est	最高級	fastest, best

不規則的屈折變化就不在這裡討論。如果你挑選的名詞和動詞的屈折變化是不規則的，而你又沒有把握拼對的話，建議重新挑選，以免拼錯被扣分。例如，你要寫「放」，可是你沒有把握是 "lay, laid, laid" 或是 "lie, lay, lain" 時，很簡單，捨棄不用，改用 "put, put, put"。同理，沒有把握「起床」是 "rise, rose, risen" 或是 "arise, arose, arisen" 時，改用 "get up"。屈折變化不會改變原來單詞的意義。

衍生變化是在一個單詞的前面與／或後面加上衍生詞綴來形成一個具有新的意義的單詞。許多衍生變化也連帶造成詞類變化。例如，名詞 beauty，加上尾綴-ify 變成動詞 beautify，加上尾綴-ful 變成形容詞 beautiful，再加上尾綴-ly 變成副詞 beautifully。我們會發現衍生變化是倍數增加詞彙的好方法之一。

第二節　常用字首、字根、字尾〔請參考附錄 4〕

第三節　口語英語與書面英文

　　口語英語，又稱英語口語，是講話時候用的一種英語，例如 Why not...? No problem. See you around. Beat it.（滾開！）等，書面英文，又稱英語書語，是寫文章，特別是寫正式文章的時候用的一種英語，例如用 "I apologize for being late." 比 "I'm sorry I am late."；"Go away." 比 "Beat it."；"I am exhausted./I am very tired." 比 "I'm beat." 分別來的正式。考試的時候，除非是要引用故事主人翁的對話，否則我們強烈建議一律用書面英文。要熟悉書面英文可以從閱讀以英語發表的總統就職演說詞一類的文章開始，循序漸進，一方面廣讀，一方面精讀。平常多閱讀正式英文，待實力累積夠了，日後撰寫英文作文勢必如魚得水。

　　我們建議考生讀者先研讀美國總統林肯 (Abraham Lincoln) 1863 年的蓋茨堡演說詞 (The Gettysburg Address)，美國總統甘迺迪 (John F. Kennedy) 1961 年的就職演說詞，美國民權運動領袖馬丁‧路德‧金恩二世 (Martin Luther King, Jr.) 1963 年為終止美國的種族主義的一場公開演說。著名的片語和句子 "of the people, by the people, for the people"；"And so, my fellow Americans: ask not what your country can do for you--ask what you can do for your country...."；"I have a dream." 分別來自他們三位上述的演說詞。〔請參考附錄 1〕

第四節　美式英語與英式英語

　　當代英語有二個主要的方言：美式英語 (American English) 與英式英語 (British English)。概略地說，美式英語指的是在美國 (the US) 所使用的英語；英式英語指的是在聯合王國 (the UK) 所使用的英語。由於歷史、政治、經濟以及其他的因素，美式英語與英式英語在發音、拼寫、語法、語義等方面，各有很明顯的特色。本書將重點鎖定在考試要注意的拼寫和語法二方面。

一、拼寫

拼寫	美式	英式
ze/se	civilize	civilise
	organize	organise
er/re	center	centre
	theater	theatre
or/our	color	colour
	labor	labour
log/logue	catalog	catalogue
	dialog	dialogue
se/ce	defense	defence
	offense	offence
ll/l	fulfill	fulfil
	skillful	skilful
l/ll	canceling	cancelling
	traveiing	travelling
m/mme	aerogram	aerogramme
	program	programme
e/ae	esthetic/aesthetic	aesthetic
	encyclopedia	encyclopaedia
ay/ey	gray	grey

二、語法

美式

1. We ***don't have*** enough cash.

2. What ***did you have/have you got*** in your backpack?

　　3. You **have got to/have to** leave.

　　4. His wife **left** for Japan already.

　　5. The team **is** going to win the game.

英式

　　1. We **haven't** enough cash.

　　2. What **did you have** in your backpack?

　　3. You **have to** leave.

　　4. His wife **has left** for Japan already.

　　5. The team **are** going to win the game.

　　今天的臺灣是一個多元的社會。考生同學和閱卷教授來自不同的地方、不同的社會背景。有人學的、講的是美式英語，有人學的、講的是英式英語，有人二種都學過都會用，有人比較會用其中的一種，有人比較喜歡用其中的一種，不一而足，更沒有對錯。最重要的原則是考試的時候，如果做得到的話，必須堅持一致，儘量不要混合使用，從頭到尾只用美式英語或是英式英語。

第五節　重要的遣詞用字規範

　　學測指考的英文作文分項式評分指標對字彙、拼字的要求是「用字精確、得宜，且幾無拼字錯誤」，做到了這三點要求，本項目就可以拿到滿分。

　　不要有拼字錯誤應該不是問題，不會或沒有把握的，就改用其他的同義字。從現在要開始使用，或繼續使用，而且堅持使用英英詞典。最重要的理由是這樣做會讓你學測指考英文作文拿高分。舉例說明如下：*Longman Dictionary of Contemporary English*, 5th edition 對「入迷，沉迷」(addicted) 這個單詞下的定義是 "liking so much that you do not want to stop doing it or having it"，接著列出一個搭配 addicted to 以及一個例子 "kids addicted to surfing the Net"；《麥可米倫高級英漢雙解詞典》(2008) 對 "addicted" 下的定義是 "enjoying a particular activity very much and spending as much time as you can doing it"，接著列出+to 以及一個例子 "I don't want the kids getting addicted to stupid TV programmes."。

　　如果，我們平常就是使用英英詞典，一旦累積深厚的英文功力，那麼 101 學測英文作文

有關你最好的朋友最近迷上電玩的主題句，不就迎刃而解了嗎？一則，你可以很精確地用詞條 "addicted" 造出正確的片語 be addicted to playing video games 或 got addicted to video games；一則，你可以在文章中靈活應用定義 "spending a lot of time playing video games" 或 "like video games so much that he does not want to stop playing them"。

一、精確

精確就是精準正確，不要模糊。下午三點二十分不要說成三點左右或是下午時分。「化裝舞會」（100 年學測）不要寫成 make-up party 或 cosmetic party。要嘛，就用美式英語的 masquerade，要嘛，就用英式英語的 fancy dress party，不然就利用《朗文詞典》為 masquerade 下的定義 "a formal dance or party where people wear masks and unusual clothes"。使用英英詞典是長期，甚至於是終生累積詞彙實力的不二法門，「持之有恆，久自芬芳」。加油！

二、得宜

得宜就是合適恰當，基本上跟文章的體例密切相關。寫信的稱呼 Dear Mr. President, To Whom It May Concern, Hey Ken 等、信尾致辭 Sincerely, Respectfully, Love, 等，因為與收信人的關係以及寫信的目的，可能會有不同的選用；舉例說明的 first/firstly, second/secondly, next, then, finally 絕不能用 one, two, the last 等代替，以免不得宜。遣詞用字不得宜會使讀者或閱卷者疏遠，會讓他們覺得格格不入，結果就拿不到高分。寫給朋友的信，遣詞用字可以輕鬆隨意、口語化。相對而言，寫正式文章，遣詞用字就必須正經、嚴肅。常見的遣詞用字不得宜的例子如下：

1. 語言上的種族歧視。2008 年 11 月 4 日 Obama 當選美國第 44 任總統，第二天臺灣的主流平面媒體和電視新聞幾乎都用「美國第一位黑人總統」當作頭條，當時很多人都覺得「黑人」這二個字可能會有語言上的種族歧視。果然，當天的晚報以及第二天以後的媒體，都將「黑人」改成「非洲裔美國人」或「非洲裔美人」(African American)。另外一個例子。2012 年 2 月 18 日，美國專門播放體育節目的有線電視聯播網 ESPN 的一位作者在新聞內容提要用 "Chink in the Armor" 諷指 NBA 名將林書豪 (Jeremy Lin)，結果因為使用了具有種族歧視的 Chink（中國佬，影射華人眼睛的上斜窄縫狀），導致全球「林來瘋粉絲 (Linsanity fans)」譁然抗議，最後遭到解雇。不要使用會冒犯特定族群的字詞。不要用 Indian（印第安人），改用 Native American；同理，「臺灣原住民」，不一定要用 aborigines，用 Native Taiwanese；「女人」避免用 females，用 women 或 ladies。

2. 語言上的冒犯與歧視。遣詞用字應該使用「語言上的政治正確 (political correctness)」，避免冒犯常遭歧視的族群。考試可能會碰到的情形討論如下：

(1) 「殘障人士」用 the physically-challenged 或 the differently-abled 代替 the disabled，用 the disabled 代替 the handicapped。

(2) 「老年人」用 (the) senior citizens 代替 the elderly，用 the elderly 代替 the old。但是，有些成語還是要遵守「約定俗成」，例如「老少」(young and old)。

(3) 我們可以運用「委婉」的修辭技巧，將「窮人」(the poor) 寫成 people (who are) not so rich；「老人」(the old) 寫成 people (who are) not so young 等。

3. 語言上的性別歧視。女性主義的興起以及兩性平權的推行已經讓很多作者避開含有 man 或 woman 的複合詞。很多是將 man 或 woman 去掉，有些是將 man 或 woman 改成 person 或 people，有些是改用別的字詞，舉例對照如下：

(1) 主席，主任 chairman > chairperson > chair

(2) 業務員，推銷員 salesman/saleswoman > salesperson > sales

(3) 員警 policeman/policewoman > police officer

(4) 服務員 waiter/waitress > server

(5) 郵差 postman > mail carrier

(6) 主持人 host/hostess > host

(7) 主播 anchorman/anchorwoman > anchor

(8) 空服員 steward/stewardess > flight attendant

(9) 前夫／妻 ex-husband/-wife > ex

(10) 人力資源 manpower > human resources

4. 使用粗魯的言語、禁忌語或冒犯性言語。有些言語，例如 Damn it!（他媽的！）；Fuck!（他媽的！）；Shit!（媽的！）等，對某些閱聽者、在某些場合是不適當的，這也是正式與非正式、粗魯與非粗魯的主要分界線。好朋友在一起喝茶打屁，開開黃腔，開開玩笑，無可厚非，當然過頭也會翻臉的。考試作答是非常嚴肅的事情，絕對不要跟自己的寶貴分數開玩笑。舉例對照如下：

不得宜	得宜	
cock/prick	penis	陰莖
cunt/pussy	vagina	陰道
chick/babe	woman	女生
dude/jack	man	男生
tits/boobs	breasts	乳房
fucking delicious	very delicious	非常好吃
have the shits	have diarrhea	腹瀉

　　「得宜」對臺灣的學生而言不是困擾，因為我們的英語環境太正式了，通常是應付教室活動的作業，所以我們很少會用到方言、俚語、羞辱性言語、冒犯性言語或非正式的言語。總之，為了分數，不要矯情、不要冒險，儘量用正式的表達方式就對了。等考上了，跟朋友慶功宴時再秀兩句「不得宜的」言語也不遲，你說是嗎？

練習6

1. 請寫出下列單詞或片語的美式英語或英式英語的對應語。必要時，請參考詞典。

　　例：tin

　　答：can

　　(1) elevator　　(2) trolley　　(3) candy　　(4) vest　　(5) subway

　　(6) football　　(7) queue　　(8) chips（炸馬鈴薯條）　　(9) cinema

　　(10) elementary school

2. 請依據「語言上的政治正確」原則，將下列單詞或片語做適當的更換，以避免語言上的「種族歧視」、「性別歧視」、「冒犯與歧視」、「粗魯」、「禁忌」等。必要時，請參考詞典。

　　例：chicks（美眉；妞）

　　答：girls; women; ladies

　　(1) nigger　　(2) American Indians　　(3) chairwoman　　(4) fireman

　　(5) the handicapped　　(6) female writers　　(7) old people

　　(8) un-fucking-believable　　(9) Chinks　　(10) pussy (for young women)

第 7 章

文法、句構與分類

第一節　文法

　　文法，比較廣義的用詞是語法，它是使用語言的一套規則。語言專家學者，常把語法分成三類：描述性語法、規範性語法、教學性語法。

　　顧名思義，描述性語法著重描述，主要在於清楚說明語言使用者對自己語言所具備的知識；規範性語法著重規範，主要在於制定一套規定使用者應該如何正確使用語言的文法規則；教學性語法著重教學，主要在於編寫一套規定說明使用者學習外國語言的文法規則。一般而言，規範性語法和教學性語法相對比較嚴謹，也是考試時的最主要依據。簡單地說，考試的時候就是要按照課本的文法來造片語和句子，碰到必須選擇的時候就要以教學性語法為第一優先，其次是規範性語法，最後才是描述性語法。雖然有點無奈，但是這樣處理可以幫你拿高分，幫你圓夢。

　　不要硬碰硬，不要用「老外就是這樣用」的說法來「麻醉」自己或是閱卷教授，考試的作答，一律根據教學性語法與規範性語法就對了。例如，不要用 "I did not do nothing." 要用 "I did not do anything."；不要用 "between you and I" 要用 "between you and me"；不要用 "It's real hot." 要用 "It's really hot."；不要用 "For who are you waiting?" 要用 "For whom are you waiting?"；不要用 "We consider the activities as unnatural." 要用 "We consider the activities unnatural." 等等。

　　限於篇幅，本章只討論在準備學測指考英文作文時，比較容易疏忽的部分。

第二節　基本句型

　　傳統上，我們習慣認為英語有五大基本句型 (1)-(5)，但是許多現代英語語法專家學者主張再加上 (6)-(7) 二個句型，形成有七大基本句型。

1. S-V	The secretary never lies.	
2. S-V-O	The secretary broke the window.	
3. S-V-Oi-Od	The secretary bought us the tickets.	
S-V-Od-P-Oi	The secretary bought the tickets for us.	
4. S-V-C	The secretary is young.	
	The secretary is his sister.	

5. S-V-O-C   We consider the secretary efficient.

                                We consider the secretary our best friend.

6. S-V-A   The secretary is upstairs.

7. S-V-O-A   The secretary put the coffee on the table.

（S=主詞；V=動詞；O=受詞；Oi=間接受詞，通常是人；Od=直接受詞，通常是物；P=介系詞；C=補語；A=副詞修飾語，常表地方）

第三節　句子的結構與分類

一、句構

　　句構就是句子的結構。以七個句型作為基礎，經由擴增、縮減、變形的步驟而達到句構的多樣性，加上修辭的潤飾，可以組合成變化萬千的一篇文章。學好英文是一輩子的事，英文作文的功力應該是今天比昨天好，明天比今天更好。

　　我們將比較重要、比較實用的句子結構，依照不同的功能分析如下：

二、分類

依修辭效果： 平衡句、鬆散句、掉尾句、倒裝句、重複句。

1. 平衡句：二個獨立子句的組成部分，全部或幾乎全部相似的句子。

"Choose what you love and love what you choose."

「選你所愛，愛你所選。」

"You may change your position but you may never change your profession."

「你的職位可能會晉升，但是你無法改變你的專業。」

Today you are proud of your school; tomorrow your school will be proud of you.

今日你以母校為榮，明日母校以你為榮。

2. 鬆散句：主要子句在前，從屬子句在後的句子。

They canceled the game because there was a typhoon.

We will win the contest if we work hard.

3. 掉尾句：從屬子句在前，主要子句在後的句子。

Because there was a typhoon, they canceled the game.

If we work hard, we will win the game.

4. 倒裝句：詞序不是 SVO 的句子。（請參考 10.9）

Rarely has a concert attracted so many people. <=

A concert has rarely attracted so many people.

Inside the package are an invoice and a photo. <=

An invoice and a photo are inside the package.

5. 重複句：句子的組成部分，全部或幾乎全部重複的句子。

There was no food; there was no water; there was no power; there was nothing.

I will be a singer and I will be an actor and I will be a director.

依邏輯關係： 肯定句、否定句。

1. 肯定句： I smoke.

I will fall in love again.

2. 否定句： I do not smoke.

I will not fall in love again.

Never will I fall in love again.（倒裝）

依組合關係： 單句、合句、複句、複合句。

1. 單句： I am a teacher.

I teach English.

I was late.

I had a bad cold.

I did not hand in my homework.

I was absent.

2. 合句： I am a teacher and I teach English.

3. 複句： I was late because I had a bad cold.

Because I had a bad cold, I was late.

4. 複合句： I was absent and I did not hand in my homework because I had a bad cold.

I did not hand in my homework because I was absent and because I had a cold.

依語氣態度：直述句、疑問句、祈使句、驚嘆句。

1. 直述句：Her advisor has a reputation for honesty.

　　　　　All languages change through time.

2. 疑問句：Does her advisor have a reputation for honesty?

　　　　　Do all languages change through time?

3. 祈使句：Be here before five pm.

　　　　　Class, line up please.

4. 驚嘆句：What a wonderful woman your mother is!

　　　　　How beautiful the dancer is!

第四節　句子的合併

　　句子的合併就是將句子擴增變形，使得文章不是千篇一律的簡單句。一般而言，句子的合併有二種：對等連接與從屬連接。對等連接就是利用對等連接詞 and, or, but 等將二個獨立子句，連接形成一個合句。從屬連接就是利用從屬連接詞 if, when, although, so 等（引導副詞子句）；利用 who, which 等（引導形容詞子句）；利用 that, how 等（引導名詞子句）；或是利用連接副詞 therefore, however, moreover 將二個句子連接，形成一個複句。由從屬連接詞引導的句子稱為從屬子句，另一個獨立子句稱為主要子句，也就是說，從屬連接以後的二個句子會有主從之分。主從之分只是邏輯與強調的考量。

一、對等連接

（一）and 表並存。有時候 and 也會呈現先後順序和因果關係。

Peter went back to college and he got an MBA.

Peter 回大學念書，拿到企管碩士學位。

They were married in 2009 and they have three kids.

他們在 2009 年結婚，他們有三個小孩。

（二）or 表選擇、排斥。

You must stop beating my daughter or I will call the police.

你不要再打我女兒了，要不然我要報警。

You can have fun with us or you can wait in the room.

你可以跟我們一起玩，要不然你就在房間等。

（三）but 表對照、反面。

She is rich but she is not happy.

她有錢，但是她不快樂。

He worked very hard but he failed the exam.

他很用功，但是他沒有通過考試。

　　也可以利用片語對等連接詞，也就是相關連接詞，來進行對等連接。常用的片語對等連接詞：both ... and; not only ... but also, not ... but; either ... or, neither ... nor.

"Not that I loved Caesar less, but that I loved Rome more."

「我愛凱撒，我更愛共和。」

Either you return the money to me or I will sue you.

你不還錢，我就告你。

二、平行結構

　　平行結構是一種基本的修辭格，在寫作中扮演一個非常重要的角色。平行結構是利用 and, or, but，其中 and 用的最多，將二個（以上）結構相同的語法單位，例如形容詞、名詞片語、句子連接而成。外觀上，平行結構是 A and B 或是 A, B(,) and C。除了結構相同以外，我們還要考量到語義相關，節奏和諧，詞序排列。〔請參考 10.2.1-4〕

young, sexy, and beautiful（三個形容詞）

年輕性感又美麗

financial independence, social respect, and professional achievement（三個名詞片語）

經濟獨立，社會尊敬與專業成就

I missed my flight, I forgot my cell phone, and I lost my luggage.（三個句子）

我錯過班機，我忘了帶手機，而且我把行李弄丟了。

 第五節 從屬連接

從屬連接是利用從屬連接詞將二個單句合併的一種使句子擴大增長的方式。利用從屬連接，合併後的句子有「主要子句」與「從屬子句」的區別。

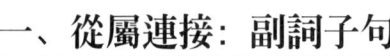

一、從屬連接：副詞子句

（一）利用表示「時間」的從屬連接詞：after, before, when, while 等。

We were playing computer games while she was taking a shower.

我們在打電玩的時候，她在洗澡。

（二）利用表示「地方」的從屬連接詞：where, wherever 等。

"Where there is a will, there is a way."

「有志者，事竟成。」

（三）利用表示「原因」的從屬連接詞：because, for, since 等。

I share my secrets with you because/for/since you are my best friend.

我跟你分享我的秘密，因為你是我最好的朋友。

（四）利用表示「結果」的從屬連接詞：so, so that 等。

The players practiced very hard, so they won the championship.

The players practiced so hard that they won the championship.

球員們很努力練習，所以贏得冠軍。

（五）利用表示「條件」的從屬連接詞：if, provided (that) 等。

If you need my advice and assistance, please feel free to call me.

Please feel free to call me, provided (that) you need my advice and assistance.

如果你需要我的建議和協助，請不要客氣，打電話給我。

（六）利用表示「讓步」的從屬連接詞：although, though 等。

Although the director is rich, he leads a frugal life.

雖然那位導演很有錢，但是他生活節儉。

（七）利用表示「目的」的從屬連接詞：so that, in order that

My sister is on a diet so that she can lose weight.

我姐節食，爲的是減肥。

（八）利用表示「做法」的從屬連接詞：as, as if 等。

"When you are in Rome, do as the Romans do."

「入鄉隨俗。」

（九）利用表示「比較」的從屬連接詞：as, than 等。

I was as you are; you will be as I am.

從前我和你一樣，以後你會和我一樣。

（十）利用表示「對照」的從屬連接詞：whereas, while

A horse is an herbivore whereas a tiger is a carnivore.

馬是草食動物，而老虎是肉食動物。

（十一）利用表示「限制」的從屬連接詞：as long as, so long as 等。

As long as you have a visa, you can stay in our country.

你只要有簽證，你就可以留在我們國家。

（十二）利用表示「類比」的從屬連接詞：just as ... so, as ... so 等。

Just as fish need water, so humans need love.

就如同魚需要水一樣，人類也需要愛情。

二、從屬連接：形容詞子句

（節錄自書林 (2013) 出版，蔣炳榮所著之《簡明當代英文法》第 294~303 頁。）

形容詞子句又名關係子句，因為常由 wh- 字，如 who, which 等關係代名詞引導，所以也常被稱為 WH 子句。形容詞子句是一種名詞後位修飾語，其最常見的句型，圖示如下：

... NP wh-
- ____ V O ...（____ 表示缺主詞）
- S V ____ ...（____ 表示缺（動詞的）受詞）
- S V P ____ ... => P wh- S V ...（____ 表示缺（介系詞的）受詞）
- ____ N V ...（____ 表示缺限定詞）

說明

1. NP (noun phrase) 名詞片語，是 wh- 的先行詞，與 wh- 指涉相同的人事物。

2. wh- 字，通稱為關係代名詞，代替前面提過的 NP。

3. 空格線 ＿＿＿＿ 代表 wh- 字在後面出現的句子（形容詞子句）中所缺漏的名詞片語及其所扮演的語法角色。這個角色會是主詞 (S)，受詞 (O) 或是限定詞 (D)。傳統上，我們分別稱之為 wh- 字的主格，受格或是所有格。

4. 扮演受詞的 wh- 字會出現在及物動詞 (V) 的後面，或是出現在介系詞 (P) 的後面。當代英語必須將當受詞用的 whom, which 前移至先行詞後面，也同時常將在句尾落單的介系詞前移至 wh- 字前面。結果會形成新的結構：先行詞 + 介系詞 + whom/which ...〔請參考附錄 1.2 精讀分析 3〕

例句：

> I know the professor ＿＿＿＿＿＿＿ won the award.（who; 主詞）
> I know the professor ＿＿＿＿＿＿＿ you will marry.（whom; 受詞）
> I know the professor ＿＿＿＿＿＿＿ you are talking about.（whom; 受詞）
> = I know the professor about ＿＿＿＿＿＿＿ you are talking.（whom; 受詞）
> I know the professor ＿＿＿＿＿＿＿ son was killed.（whose; 限定詞）

（一）形容詞子句是一種名詞後位修飾語

　　形容詞子句是由 who-whom-whose 或 which-whose 引導一個結構不完整的關係子句，作形容詞用，修飾 wh- 字所代替的先行詞。所謂不完整的子句，是指句子裡面會缺少一個主詞或受詞或限定詞。而這個所欠缺的語法角色會由 wh- 字來補足。

> I know *the man*. *The man* is a professor of economics.
> 我認識那個人。那個人是經濟學教授。
> 利用形容詞子句合併句子：（the man 是指涉相同人物的名詞片語）
> ⇨ I know the man *who* is a professor of economics.
> 我認識那個人，他是經濟學教授。
> （who 代替先行詞 the man，扮演後面形容詞子句中動詞 is 的主詞。）

73

I know *the man*. The committee has nominated *the man* as the director.

　　我認識那個人。委員會已提名那個人為導演。

⇨ I know the man the committee has nominated *whom* as the director.（誤）

　　（whom 必須前移至先行詞 the man 後面）

⇨ I know the man *whom* the committee has nominated as the director.

　　我認識已被委員會提名為導演的那個人。

　　（whom 代替先行詞 the man，扮演後面形容詞子句中動詞 has nominated 的受詞。）

I know *the man*. Your daughter will be married to *the man*.

　　我認識那個人。你的女兒要嫁給那個人。

⇨ I know the man your daughter will be married to *whom*.（誤）

　　（whom 必須前移至先行詞 the man 後面）

⇨ I know the man *whom your* daughter will be married to.

⇨ I know the man *to whom* your daughter will be married.

　　（在句尾落單的介系詞 to 前移至 whom 前面）

　　我認識你女兒要嫁的那個人。

I know *the man*. *The man's* son is the conductor of a symphony orchestra.

　　　我認識那個人。那個人的兒子是一個交響樂團的指揮。

⇨ I know the man *whose* son is the conductor of a symphony orchestra.

　　（whose 代替先行詞 the man 的所有格，扮演單數可數名詞 son 的限定詞，組成合乎語法的名詞片語）（說明：單數可數名詞必須前接限定詞。）

　　我認識那個人。他的兒子是一個交響樂團的指揮。

（二）判斷選擇正確的 wh- 字

1. 先行詞的語義屬性。

　　這裡所提到的語義屬性指的是「人稱」或「非人稱」，也就是說 wh- 所代替的先行詞是屬於「人稱」的人，如 the man, a professor, your daughter 等，或是屬於「非人稱」的事物，如 the committee, economics, a symphony orchestra 等。

　　表「人稱」的先行詞後面可以選用關係代名詞：who, whom, whose。

　　表「非人稱」的先行詞後面可以選用關係代名詞：which, which, whose。

　　另一種研判的方法如下：

先行詞可用下列代名詞代替時	判斷選用的 wh- 字
I, we, you, he, she, they（主格）	who
me, us, you, him, her, them（受格）	whom
my, our, your, his, her, their（所有格）	whose
it, they（主格）	which
it, them（受格）	which
its, their（所有格）	whose 或 of which

2. wh- 字在所引導的形容詞子句中的語法角色。

　(1) 在動詞前面當主詞時，選用 who 或 which。

　(2) 在動詞或介系詞後面當受詞時，選用 whom 或 which。

　(3) 在名詞前面當限定詞時，選用 whose 或 of which。

3. 簡單圖示如下：

先行詞 ＼ wh-字的語法角色	主詞（主格）	受詞（受格）	限定詞（所有格）
人稱 the man	who	whom	whose
非人稱 the book	which	which	whose/of which

（三）whose 與 of which 的互換

NP whose N = NP of which the N = NP the N of which

　　傳統上，研究英語語法的學者主張將非人稱的名詞，利用 of 片語來表示「歸屬關係」。當代英語則常出現用撇號（'）加上 s 的用法。因此在很多情況下，我們可以用 of which 或 whose 來表示「非人稱」先行詞的「歸屬關係」。例如：

Japan's technology = the technology of Japan （日本的科技）

the school's poor students = the poor students of the school （學校的貧困學生）

準此，非人稱先行詞後面的 whose 可改寫為 of which 的結構。

比較：
- My grandfather gave me a pocketknife whose handle is made of ivory.
- = My grandfather gave me a pocketknife of which the handle is made of ivory.
- = My grandfather gave me a pocketknife the handle of which is made of ivory.

我爺爺送我一把小摺刀，刀柄是象牙做成的。

參考：My grandfather gave me a pocketknife *with* an ivory handle.

比較：
- I live in a run-down apartment whose staircase is shaky and unsteady.
- = I live in a run-down apartment of which the staircase is shaky and unsteady.
- = I live in a run-down apartment the staircase of which is shaky and unsteady.

我住在一間破舊的公寓裡面，公寓的樓梯搖搖欲墜。

參考：I live in a run-down apartment where the staircase is shaky and unsteady.

I live in a run-down apartment with a shaky and unsteady staircase.

（四）關係副詞 (relative adverbs)

關係副詞有：when, where, why, how。關係副詞必須引導一個結構完整的關係子句。

1. 先行詞表「時間」時，用 when 引導關係子句。

先行詞為 "time" 或表「時間」的名詞如 year, (in) 1990 等，用 when 引導關係子句。

She always remembers the day *when* he went down on one knee and proposed to her.

她一直記得他單膝跪下向她求婚的那一天。

In the summer of 1990, *when* she was traveling in Europe, she was robbed of her purse.

1990 年夏天她在歐洲旅行的時候，她的錢包被搶。

2. 先行詞表「地方」時，用 where 引導關係子句。

先行詞為 "place" 或表「地方」的名詞如 city, situation 等，用 where 引導關係子句。

She was born in a place *where* people despised baby girls.

她出生在一個人們鄙視女嬰的地方。

We are facing a difficult situation *where/in which* nobody wants to be a volunteer.

我們正面臨一個沒有人要擔任志工的困境。

3. 先行詞表「理由」時，用 why 引導關係子句。

先行詞為 "reason" 或表「理由」的名詞如 cause, motive 等，用 why 引導關係子句。這個 why 也常可省略。

Give me two reasons (why) women love underwear trimmed with lace.

告訴我二個為什麼女人喜歡鑲有花邊的內衣的理由。

That was the motive (why) she ran away from home.

那就是她離家出走的動機。

4. 先行詞表「方法」時，不要用關係副詞。

先行詞為 "way" 或表「方法」的名詞如 method, procedure 等，可直接引導關係子句，不必加關係副詞。或是省略先行詞，直接以 how 引導關係子句。

I hate the way he humiliates his subordinates.

I hate how he humiliates his subordinates.

我討厭他羞辱部屬的做法。

This is usually the method they solve their financial crisis.

This is usually how they solve their financial crisis.

這就是他們解決財務危機所常用的方法。

（五）when, where, why, how 與介系詞 + which 的互換

因為介系詞片語常作副詞用，因此表「時間」、「地方」、「原因」、「方法」的 when, where, why, how, 可以改寫成介系詞 + which。

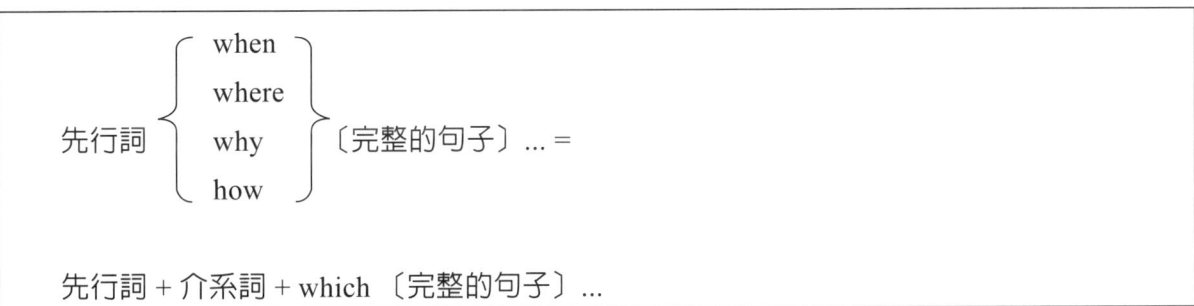

Everyone in the meeting remembers the year *when* the US declared independence.

= Everyone in the meeting remembers the year *in which* the US declared independence.

會議中的每個人都記得美國宣佈獨立的年份。

The date *when* we hold the election will be posted on our website.

= The date *on which* we hold the election will be posted on our website.

我們辦理選舉的日期會在我們的網站公佈。

We are looking for the cathedral *where* the mass will be held.

= We are looking for the cathedral *in which* the mass will be held.

我們在尋找要舉行彌撒的那間大教堂。

They went back to the room *where* the girl was murdered.

= They went back to the room *in which* the girl was murdered.

他們回到女孩遇害的那個房間。

That is the reason *why* we closed down our overseas branches.

= That is the reason *for which* we closed down our overseas branches.

= That is the reason we closed down our overseas branches.（省略 why）

參考：That is why we closed down our overseas branches.

　　　那是我們將海外分公司關閉的理由。

Tell me the cause she refused your proposal.（不用關係副詞）

= Tell me the cause *for which* she refused your proposal.

參考：Tell me what caused her to refuse your proposal.（以 what 取代先行詞及關係副詞）

參考：Tell me why she refused your proposal.

　　　告訴我她拒絕你求婚的理由。

This is the normal procedure the police uses to handle a rape case.（不用關係副詞）

= This is the normal procedure *with which* the police handles a rape case.

參考：This is how the police handles a rape case.（以 how 取代先行詞及關係副詞）

這是警方處理性侵害案件的正常程序。

The specialist is teaching us *the way* we should manage a company.（不用關係副詞，無 the way how 之說法）

= The specialist is teaching us the way *in which* we should manage a company.

參考：The specialist is teaching us *how* we should manage a company.

　　　這名專家在教導我們應該如何管理一家公司。

（六）現代英語有用 that 代替 who, whom, which, why 的趨勢

The man *who* spoke to you on the phone was my parole officer.

= The man *that* spoke to you on the phone was my parole officer.

跟你通電話的人是我的假釋審查官。

The man *whom* we trusted betrayed our party.

= The man *that* we trusted betrayed our party.

我們所相信的人出賣了我們的黨。

We moved into an apartment *which* has four bedrooms and three bathrooms.

= We moved into an apartment *that* has four bedrooms and three bathrooms.

我們搬進一間有四個臥室，三個浴室的公寓。

The reason *why* she sold out all her shares is still a mystery.

= The reason *that* she sold out all her shares is still a mystery.

她將所有的股份賣掉的理由仍然是個謎。

（七）用 that 代替 wh- 字引導形容詞子句

先行詞由 all, any, every, the only, the + 最高級形容詞（如 the most beautiful girl）等表示「強列指示」的限定詞或表示「唯一」的形容詞所限定時，常用 that 代替 wh- 字引導形容詞子句。

All *that* glitters is not gold.

= All is not gold *that* glitters.

外表好未必是真好。

The painter lost the divorce case and his wife took everything (*that*) he had.

那位畫家離婚官司敗訴，因此他老婆拿走他所有的一切。

I no longer believe any promises (*that*) a politician makes.

我不再相信政治人物所做出的任何承諾。

Record every promise (*that*) she makes.

將她許下的每一項承諾都記錄下來。

She is the only woman *that* works for a local law firm.

她是本地一家律師事務所唯一的女職員。

Your daughter is the most talented ballerina (*that*) I have ever seen.

你女兒是我見過的最有才華的芭蕾舞演員。

This is the last cigarette (*that*) I will ever smoke.

這是我抽的最後一根香菸。

（八）省略關係子句中扮演受詞的 whom, which 或 that

在省略後如果不會影響句子語義的清晰時，可以省略扮演受詞的 whom, which 或 that。

Do you know the programmer *whom* we are going to interview?

= Do you know the programmer we are going to interview?

你認識我們打算採訪的那位程式設計師嗎?

This is the tape *which* you have been looking for.

= This is the tape you have been looking for.

這就是你們一直在找的那卷錄影帶。

The wardrobe is the only property *that* we have.

= The wardrobe is the only property we have.

這個衣櫃是我們僅有的財產。

（九）缺先行詞或先行詞是未知或不確定的人事物時，用 wh-ever

也就是說沒有先行詞的時候，分別用 whoever, whatever, whichever 引導形容詞子句。也有語法學者稱這種 WH 子句為名詞性的關係子句。

wh-字的語法角色　　　　 先行詞不確定	主詞（主格）	受詞（受格）	限定詞（所有格）
人稱	whoever	whomever	whosever
非人稱；指涉物	whatever	whatever	---
非人稱；指涉人物	whichever	whichever	---

基本上，whichever 等於 whatever。不同的是 whichever 強調「選擇」。

Whoever cheats in the exam will be suspended from school.

任何人考試作弊都會被勒令停學。

We certainly will respect *whomever* the committee has nominated.

我們一定會尊重委員會所提名的任何人。

Whatever you have said in the interview will be kept secret.

你在受訪時所說的任何話都將被保密。

Whatever happens, keep running and running.

無論發生什麼事，你就一直一直跑。

There is no rush. You can choose *whichever* you prefer.

不要急，你喜歡哪一個就選哪一個。

Change the oil every six months or every 3,000 miles, *whichever* comes first.

每六個月或三千英里換一次機油，哪一個先都一樣。

whatever 與 whichever 也可作限定詞。

比較：
> *Whatever lotion* you use, you have to keep it in a cool place.
> 不管你用什麼樣的乳液，你必須把它放在陰涼的地方。
> E-learning will be the trend, *whichever way* you look at it.
> 不管你用哪一個角度來看，網路學習是未來的趨勢。

（十）限制性關係子句 vs. 非限制性關係子句

限制性關係子句是用來辨識、確認先行詞的一種名詞後位修飾語，其所提供的資訊經常是必要的，而且有助於限定先行詞的意義。非限制性關係子句，提供有關先行詞的額外訊息，不具有限定先行詞意義的作用。在書面英語中，我們常用逗號（,）來分開先行詞與非限制性關係子句，而先行詞與限制性關係子句之間則不用逗號（,）分開。

比較

The woman whom you hired is the judge's wife.

被你們雇用的那個女人是法官的老婆。（限制性）

My mom, who is in her 40s, is the judge's wife.

我媽今年四十幾歲，她是法官的老婆。（非限制性）

The university that won first place is a private one.

獲得第一名的那所大學是一所私立大學。（限制性）

Harvard University, which is a prestigious university in the US, is known for its law school.

哈佛大學是美國享有盛名的一所大學，以法學院著稱。（非限制性）

形容詞子句，又稱關係子句，或稱 WH 子句，是一種常見的後位修飾語，利用 wh- 字引導一個關係子句提供訊息來辨識、確認或限定先行詞。形成關係子句時，主要有三個考量：第一，有沒有先行詞 (who vs. whoever)。第二，先行詞是指涉人稱或非人稱 (who vs. which)。第三，先行詞由 wh- 字取代後，在關係子句中扮演下列哪一個角色：主詞、受詞或限定詞 (who vs. whom vs. whose)。

三、從屬連接：名詞子句

（節錄自書林 (2013) 出版，蔣炳榮所著之《簡明當代英文法》第 307~313 頁。）

名詞子句是從屬子句的一種，基本上是包孕在句子裡面的句子，相當於名詞（片語），扮演句子的主詞、受詞、補語、同位語的角色。名詞子句是由 that 或 WH 詞引導一個直述句所形成。換言之，原先的疑問句型，在形成名詞子句時，都必須還原為 S-V 或 S-助動詞-V 的直述句。

（一）名詞子句是表示一件事情的名詞片語

我們常用一個單句來敘述一件事情。如果我們要擴增我們的句子，使原先這個敘述一件事情的單句降階成為一個名詞（片語），這種變形，就是在形成名詞子句。

We have to be honest.
我們做人要誠實。（單句；獨立子句）

形成名詞子句：
that we have to be honest
我們做人要誠實（從屬子句）

名詞子句作句子中的主詞：
【That we have to be honest】is very important.
我們做人要誠實。這是很重要的事情。

名詞子句作句子中的受詞：
I know【that we have to be honest】.
我知道我們做人要誠實。

（二）名詞子句的形成

在形成名詞子句之前，我們有二個考量。

1. 原先的單句是不是問句？

    (1) 不是問句時，則直接在句首加上 that，形成名詞子句。

    (2) 是問句時，則進入下一個考量。

2. 原先的問句是一般的是否問句，如 Are you OK?或是由 WH 詞引導的 WH 問句，如 Where are you from?。

> (1) 是否問句時，
>
> ①將由 be (am, are, is; was, were) 或助動詞 have (have, has; had) 所引導的問句，還原為直述句，記得將 be, have 歸位。
>
> ②將由情態助動詞 (will, can, may; would, could, might ...) 所引導的問句，還原為直述句，記得將情態助動詞歸位。
>
> ③將由 do (do, does; did) 所引導的問句，還原為直述句，刪掉助動詞 do，記得還原主要動詞的時式。
>
> ④在所還原的直述句前面加上 if 或 whether 或 whether or not 或 whether ... or not。

> (2) WH 問句時，將問句還原為直述句，同時
>
> ①保留 wh- 詞。
>
> ②將 be, 助動詞 have 或情態助動詞歸位。
>
> ③刪掉助動詞 do。記得還原主要動詞的時式。

現在我們逐步實際演練一下，將下列各「原句」形成名詞子句。

> 原句：Noise can hurt our hearing ability.
>
> 　　　噪音會傷害我們的聽力。
>
> 分析：原句不是問句，直接在句首加上 that。
>
> 形成：【that noise can hurt our hearing ability】

> 原句：Are there creatures living on Mars?
>
> 　　　火星上面住有生物嗎？
>
> 分析：原句是動詞 be 引導的是否問句，(1) 將原句還原為直述句：there are creatures living on Mars；(2) 將直述句句首加上 if 或 whether (or not) 或 whether ... or not。

形成：【if there are creatures living on Mars】

　　　【whether (or not) there are creatures living on Mars】

　　　【whether there are creatures living on Mars or not】

原句：Have you ever heard the wolf cry?

　　　你曾經聽過狼哭嚎嗎?

分析：原句是一般助動詞 have/has/had 引導的是否問句，(1) 將原句還原為直述句：you have ever heard the wolf cry；(2) 將直述句句首加上 if 或 whether (or not) 或 whether ... or not。

形成：【if you have ever heard the wolf cry】

　　　【whether (or not) you have ever heard the wolf cry】

　　　【whether you have ever heard the wolf cry or not】

原句：Does your next-door neighbor believe in God?

　　　你的隔壁鄰居相信上帝嗎?

分析：原句是一般助動詞 do/does/did 引導的是否問句，(1) 將原句還原為直述句：your next-door neighbor believes in God（說明：刪掉 does，同時還原主要動詞 believe 的時式）；(2) 將直述句句首加上 if 或 whether (or not) 或 whether ... or not。

形成：【if your next-door neighbor believes in God】

　　　【whether (or not) your next-door neighbor believes in God】

　　　【whether your next-door neighbor believes in God or not】

原句：When is your birthday party?

　　　你什麼時候開生日派對?

分析：原句是有動詞 be 的 WH 問句，將原句還原為直述句：(1) 保留 wh- 詞；(2) 將動詞 be 歸位，即移到主詞 your birthday party 後面。

形成：【when your birthday party is】

原句：What have you done to your coffee maker?

　　　你對你的咖啡機做了什麼?

分析：原句是有助動詞 have/has/had 的 WH 問句，將原句還原為直述句：(1) 保留 wh- 詞；(2) 將助動詞 have 歸位，即移到主詞 you 後面。

形成：【what you have done to your coffee maker】

原句：How can she pay off her debts?

　　　她如何能夠還清她的債務？

分析：原句是有情態助動詞 can 的 WH 問句，將原句還原為直述句：(1) 保留 wh- 詞；(2) 將情態助動詞 can 歸位，即移到主詞 she 後面。

形成：【how she can pay off her debts】

原句：Where does your research assistant come from?

　　　你的研究助理是哪裡人？

分析：原句是有助動詞 do/does/did 的 WH 問句，將原句還原為直述句：(1) 保留 wh- 詞；(2) 刪掉 do，同時還原主動詞 come 的時式。

形成：【where your research assistant comes from】

（三）名詞子句的語法功能

　　名詞子句等於一個名詞片語，可以扮演主詞、受詞、補語或同位語的語法角色。除了名詞子句扮演同位語的用法之外，如果我們將名詞子句從一個句子移除，那麼會造成一個不完整的句子。

1. 名詞子句作句子的主詞。

【That dolphins have complicated communication systems】has surprised scientists.

海豚具有複雜的溝通系統這件事令科學家感到驚奇。

（名詞子句作動詞 has surprised 的主詞）

參考：＿＿＿＿＿＿＿＿＿＿＿ has surprised scientists.（句子缺主詞）

【Whether or not the governor will withdraw from the election】is uncertain.

州長是否會退出選舉是一件不確定的事。

（名詞子句作動詞 is 的主詞）

參考：＿＿＿＿＿＿＿＿＿＿＿ is uncertain.（句子缺主詞）

【What we will do next】has nothing to do with you.

我們下一步會做什麼與你無關。

（名詞子句作動詞 has 的主詞）

參考：＿＿＿＿＿＿＿＿＿＿＿ has nothing to do with you.（句子缺主詞）

【How he will divide his property】affects everyone in his family.

他會如何分財產這件事影響到他家裡的每一位成員。

（名詞子句作動詞 affects 的主詞）

參考：＿＿＿＿＿＿＿＿＿＿＿ affects everyone in his family.（句子缺主詞）

2. 名詞子句作句子主要動詞（單及物動詞）的受詞。

> Experts believe【(that) noise can hurt our hearing ability】.
> 專家們相信噪音會傷害我們的聽力。
> （名詞子句作動詞 believe 的受詞）
> 參考：Experts believe ＿＿＿＿＿＿＿＿＿＿.（句子缺受詞）

> Scientists wonder【if there are creatures living on Mars】.
> 科學家對火星上面是否住有生物一事感到疑惑。
> （名詞子句作動詞 wonder 的受詞）
> 參考：Scientists wonder ＿＿＿＿＿＿＿＿＿＿.（句子缺受詞）

3. 名詞子句作雙及物動詞的直接受詞。

> The tour guide told them【that breakfasts were included】.
> 導遊告訴他們早餐是包含在內的。
> （名詞子句作雙及物動詞 told 的直接受詞）
> 參考：The tour guide told them ＿＿＿＿＿＿＿＿＿＿.（句子缺直接受詞）

> Our teacher informed us【that the speech contest had been canceled】.
> 老師通知我們演講比賽已經取消。
> （名詞子句作雙及物動詞 inform 的直接受詞）
> 參考：Our teacher informed us ＿＿＿＿＿＿＿＿＿＿.（句子缺直接受詞）

4. 名詞子句作介系詞的受詞。

　　基本上，that 所引導的名詞子句不可以直接作介系詞的受詞。如果 that 所引導的名詞子句要直接作介系詞的受詞時，必須先將該介系詞去掉。相對而言，wh- 所引導的名詞性子句可以直接作介系詞的受詞，有時候這個介系詞可以省略。

> *People have complained *about*【that many government officials are corrupt】.（誤）
> People have complained【that many government officials are corrupt】.（正）
> 人們抱怨有很多政府官員腐敗。

> *She is not sure *of* that she will work for her ex-boyfriend.（誤）
> She is not sure【that she will work for her ex-boyfriend】.（正）
> 她不能確定要不要替她的前男友工作。

Your final grade depends *on*【what you have done in the conference】.

你的最終成績取決於你在本次研討會上的表現。

（名詞子句作介系詞 on 的受詞）

參考：Your final grade depends on _____.（句子缺受詞）

We have been wondering (*about*)【when the recession will end】.

我們一直弄不清楚景氣低迷到底什麼時候才會結束。

（名詞子句作介系詞 about 的受詞）

參考：We have been wondering about _____.（句子缺受詞）

5. 名詞子句作主詞補語。

Our decision is【that students must wear sneakers in PE classes】.

我們的決定是，學生們上體育課時必須穿運動鞋。

（名詞子句在連繫動詞 is 後面，作句子的主詞補語）

參考：Our decision is _____.（句子缺主詞補語）

My question is【if we will receive our pay checks by Friday】.

我的問題是我們是否在星期五之前會拿到薪資支票。

（名詞子句在連繫動詞 is 後面，作句子的主詞補語）

參考：My question is _____.（句子缺主詞補語）

6. 名詞子句作同位語。

Her suggestion【that all employees should work on Saturdays】was ridiculous.

她提出所有的員工每個星期六要上班的建議實在荒謬。

（名詞子句作主詞 her suggestion 的同位語）

參考：Her suggestion _____ was ridiculous.（句子沒有同位語）

The police must strictly enforce the rule【that no one should drink and drive】.

警方必須嚴格執行任何人都不應該酒後駕車的這條規定。

（名詞子句作受詞 the rule 的同位語）

參考：The police must strictly enforce the rule _____.（句子沒有同位語）

（四）that 的省略

在不會影響句子語義清晰的原則下，引導名詞子句作受詞或主詞補語的 that 可以省略。

I know *that* you will turn down his invitation.
⇨ I know you will turn down his invitation.
我知道你會拒絕他的邀請。

Their prediction is that the opposition parties will win the election this time.
⇨ Their prediction is the opposition parties will win the election this time.
他們預料反對黨會在本次選舉中獲勝。

（五）名詞子句與先行主詞 it 的互動

句型：It + 連繫動詞 +（形容詞）+【that ...】

有時候因為考量到修辭，英美人士會將「冗長」的主詞，從句首移到連繫動詞或是補語的後面，而由一個先行主詞 it，又稱虛詞，去填補原先「冗長」的主詞移位後所留下來的空缺。語法學者常稱這種變形為外位式變形 (extraposition)，而將這個先行主詞 it 稱為虛主詞。

【That patients should have enough rest】is important.
⇨ _____ is important【that patients should have enough rest】.（後移）
⇨ *It* is important that patients should have enough rest.（補上先行主詞／虛主詞）
病人應該要有足夠的休息，這是一件很重要的事。

【That the bank will not OK her car loan】seems clear.
⇨ _____ seems clear【that the bank will not OK her car loan】.（後移）
⇨ *It* seems clear that the bank will not OK her car loan.（補上先行主詞／虛主詞）
很明顯，銀行不會核准她的汽車貸款案。

> 句子合併是要將句子擴增拉長，就是要將二個（以上）的單句擴增為合句或複句。名詞子句是將句子擴增的一種重要方式，也稱得上是一種修辭格式，目的就是要建構「句中句」。英語學習者只要按部就班，勤加練習，自然駕輕就熟。

文法重點整理與典型錯誤

一、主詞與動詞在數目上一致

　　就文法而言，主詞是決定動詞數目的一個名詞片語，這個名詞片語通常表示人、事、物、觀念。單數的主詞用單數的動詞，複數的主詞用複數的動詞。單複數的屈折變化，由動詞組的第一個元素來標記，通常會是助動詞或主要動詞。中文的動詞沒有單複數的區別，所以考生要特別注意本觀念。

---

1. My friend is coming to my birthday party.
2. My friends are coming to my birthday party.

3. My friend has visited the museum many times.
4. My friends have visited the museum many times.

5. My friend does not lie to me.
6. My friends do not lie to me.

7. My friend plays tennis well.
8. My friends play tennis well.

二、善用現在簡單式態

　　現在時式簡單時態的動詞，常用來表示 (1) 恒常為真的事實，(2) 習慣的動作，(3) 目前的想法，(4) 討論小說、電影等的情節，(5) 表示排定的、非尋常人力所能任意改變的未來動作、情況，(6) 表示「歷史的現在」等。

　　寫敘述文的時候，「歷史的現在」非常適用，用「現在簡單式態」來描述一個過去的事實，可以讓閱聽者身臨其境，感同身受。

---

(1) There are twelve months in a year.

　　The moon moves around the sun.

---

(2) I teach English.
We go to church on Sundays.
(3) I like to have a cup of coffee.
We believe in God.
(4) The movie is a romance. It is in the spring of 1912. It tells the story of the Titanic.
(5) Summer break is only two weeks away.
The graduation ceremony is next Saturday.
(6) The batter takes a big, long swing, and hits the ball. It's a home run.

三、V + V-ing vs. V + to V

　　英語不允許二個限定動詞緊鄰出現，除了極少數幾種結構以外，V+V 是錯誤的結構。考生同學在寫英文作文的時候，很容易蹦出 V+V 的錯誤，這很可能是受到母語的影響，因為中文有類似「我們喜歡去逛街。」這種三個「動詞」連在一起的結構。英語不可以這樣寫。like 是表示目的的「階段動詞」，後面常接 to V, go 是表示動貌的「階段動詞」，後面常接 V-ing，所以要寫成 "We like *to go* shopping." 或 "We like *going* shopping."。

1. V + V-ing：表示情緒、動貌的動詞後面接 V-ing。

> 情緒、動貌動詞：admit, appreciate, avoid, celebrate, consider, continue, delay, deny, detest, dislike, enjoy, finish, forget, go, imagine, keep, lie, like, mind, postpone, regret, remember, resist, risk, sit, stand, stop, suggest ...

　　My boyfriend enjoys listening to classical music.

　　Do you mind leaving us alone?

　　Please stop smoking here.

2. V + to V：表示目的的動詞後面接 to V。

　　表示目的的動詞數目最多，不勝枚舉。就準備考試而言，我們只要記住上述的情緒、動貌動詞後面要接 V-ing，以及少數幾個動詞後面可以接 V，其他的動詞原則上後面接 to V。

　　I've come to help you and your family.

　　She decided to sell her piano.

　　They refuse to apologize for being rude.

3. V + V 的情形：come, go, help 後面接 V。

My parents used to help pick up my kids.

Her mom always helps cook the meals for us.

I want your girlfriend to come visit us.（美式英語）

I want your girlfriend to come and visit us.（英式英語）

> Go ask the tour guide.（美式英語）
>
> Come have a drink with us.（美式英語）
>
> 美式口語英語中，come 和 go 後面的 and 常被省去，造成 V + V 的結構。
>
> Go and ask the tour guide.（英式英語）
>
> Come and have a drink with us.（英式英語）

比較

go + V-ing 表示「前往進行休閒或職業活動」。

We go swimming every Monday.

They have just gone shopping.

四、代名詞的指涉模稜兩可

　　這是作文初學者很容易犯的錯誤。通常是一個句子裡的代名詞或關係代名詞，在語法上可以指涉二個以上的名詞片語。身為作者，我們有責任寫出語義清晰的句子，讓讀者毫無疑惑地知道、追溯代名詞所指涉的名詞片語。假如我們告訴讀者說：「麗華告訴美華說她醉了。」讀者會弄不清楚是誰醉了。麗華？美華？還是另有其人秋華？因為代名詞「她」的指涉模稜兩可。碰到這樣的情形，我們必須改寫句子，讓讀者很清楚地知道代名詞和關係代名詞的指涉。例如，Peter told his cousin that he had failed the exam. 這個句子裡面的 "he" 有可能是 Peter，也有可能是 his cousin，也有可能是第三者，所以必須改寫。可能的改寫方式是 Peter told his cousin that his cousin had failed the exam. 或 Peter told his cousin that Peter had failed the exam. 或 Peter told his cousin that John had failed the exam. 當然，為了避免句子拗口，我們也可以利用轉述結構配合標點符號來處理類似的問題：Peter said to his cousin, "You have failed the exam." 或 Peter said to his cousin, "I have failed the exam." 等等。同理，The TV was put on the second floor which we bought in the new shopping mall. 必須改寫成 The TV which we bought in the new shopping mall was put on the second floor. 其實，要避免模稜兩可的指涉並不困難，考試時，寫到 he, she, it, we, they, which, who, that 等的時候，必須確認該代名詞的指涉為何，這樣就不會犯錯了。

五、懸擺修飾語

懸擺修飾語 (dangling modifier)，又稱垂懸修飾語，是一個句子裡的修飾語沒有特定、明確的修飾對象，或是作者誤以為是的對象在邏輯上講不通。最常見的含有懸擺修飾語的句構，是以非限定動詞 (V-ing, V-en, to V) 引導，而逗號後面的主要子句裡的主詞，卻不是該非限定動詞所修飾的對象。造成懸擺修飾語的原因是在形成非限定動詞片語的時候，特別是分詞構句，作者錯誤地省略二個不相同的主詞的其中一個。要避免懸擺修飾語，最簡單的方法是在省略主詞的時候，必須先確定它和主要子句裡的主詞是同一個人物，或是將句子還原，甚至於是改寫句子。

---

*Jogging in the track, a bullet pierced my girlfriend's left lung.

判斷：在慢跑 (jogging) 的是誰？不會是子彈 (bullet)，不會是左肺 (left lung)，是我的女朋友。

處理 1： Jogging in the track, my girlfriend had her left lung pierced by a bullet.（確定主詞）

處理 2： When my girlfriend was jogging in the track, a bullet pierced her left lung.（改寫）

---

*Made of crystal, the bartender handled the wine glasses very carefully.

判斷：用水晶玻璃做的當然是酒杯，不太可能是調酒師。

處理 1： Made of crystal, the wine glasses were handled very carefully by the bartender.（確定主詞）

處理 2： Because the wine glasses are made of crystal, the bartender handled them very carefully.（改寫）

---

*To produce a good film, a touching story is needed.

判斷：誰要製作一部好電影？是人，不是一個感人的故事。

處理 1： To produce a good film, we need a touching story.（確定主詞）

處理 2： If we want to produce a good film, we need a touching story.（改寫）

六、誤置修飾語

誤置修飾語 (misplaced modifier)，又稱錯位修飾語，是修飾語放錯了位置，通常是介系詞片語、形容詞子句、分詞/形容詞片語放在錯誤的先行詞後面，或是副詞放在錯誤的動詞前面或後面。誤置修飾語常常會造成歧義，除非是要刻意營造幽默，否則應該避免。

*The movie star married the director **with three children**.

問題：是 movie star 還是 director 有三個小孩?

處理 1：The movie star married the director who had three children.

處理 2：The movie star who had three children married the director.

處理 3：With three children, the movie star married the director.

---

*My best friend and I used to enjoy a first-run film **with a large bucket of popcorn**.

問題：是 My best friend and I 還是 film 吃爆米花?

處理：With a large bucket of popcorn, my best friend and I used to enjoy a first-run film.

---

*The sexy and beautiful dancer walking down the stage **gracefully** bowed to the judges.

問題：是優雅地 (gracefully) 走下舞臺，還是優雅地向評審鞠躬?

處理 1：The sexy and beautiful dancer who gracefully walked down the stage bowed to the judges.

處理 2：The sexy and beautiful dancer gracefully walking down the stage bowed to the judges.

處理 3：The sexy and beautiful dancer walking down the stage bowed to the judges gracefully.

處理 4：The sexy and beautiful dancer walking down the stage bowed gracefully to the judges.

語法學者將這種可以同時修飾前後二個動詞片語（walked 與 bowed）的副詞 (gracefully) 稱為「交叉修飾語」(squinting modifier)。

---

*My brother took my scooter to the mechanic **that needed a change of oil**.

問題：是誰需要換機油? scooter? mechanic?

處理：My brother took my scooter that needed a change of oil to the mechanic.

---

*The business of our shop was very good; we **nearly** made NT$5,000 last night.

問題：「範疇副詞」nearly 放錯了位置，是差點就賺到? 還是賺了將近新臺幣五千元?

處理：The business of our shop was very good; we made nearly NT$5,000 last night.

本類型的「範疇副詞」：about, almost, approximately, just, merely, nearly, only, scarcely 等。

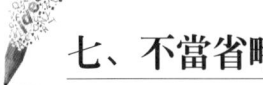

七、不當省略

省略是一個句子裡有一部分因為精簡、強調、修辭的原因而被刪除。不當省略就是省略後的句子結構有瑕疵、有錯誤。最常見的不當省略有二種：被比較的元素是語義屬性不相同的人

事物；結構中必要的單詞或片語被省略。原則上，被省略的部分，根據語法與/或語義的考量，應該是可以追溯、還原的。

1. 被比較的元素是語義屬性不相同的人事物。

> *The house prices of this year are higher than last year.
>
> 問題：（房子的）價格在跟時間（去年）做比較。
>
> 處理： The house prices of this year are higher than **those** of last year.
>
> 　　　（those = the house prices）

> *Today's temperature is lower than yesterday.
>
> 問題：溫度在跟時間做比較。
>
> 處理 1： Today's temperature is lower than **yesterday's** (temperature).
>
> 處理 2： Today's temperature is lower than **that** of yesterday.
>
> 　　　（that = the temperature）

> *My backpack is more expensive than you.
>
> 問題：背包在跟人做比較。
>
> 處理 1： My backpack is more expensive than **your backpack**.
>
> 處理 2： My backpack is more expensive than **yours**.

2. 結構中必要的單詞或片語被省略。

> *Every student in my class was interested and surprised at the story.
>
> 問題：interested 後面的 in 被不當省略了。
>
> 處理： Every student in my class was interested **in** and surprised at the story.

> *We are grateful and proud of your help with the graduation ceremony.
>
> 問題：grateful 後面的 for 被不當省略了。
>
> 處理： We are grateful **for** and proud of your help with the graduation ceremony.

> *My husband always has and always will remember to take our kids to Disneyland once a year.
>
> 問題：has 後面的 remembered 被不當省略了。
>
> 處理： My husband always has **remembered** and always will remember to take our kids to Disneyland once a year.
>
> 參考： I love you. Always have. Always will.
>
> 　　　我愛你，永遠愛你。

*My daughter is as intelligent if not more intelligent than her son.

問題：intelligent 和 if 中間的 as 被不當省略了。

處理 1：My daughter is as intelligent **as**, if not more intelligent than, her son.

處理 2：My daughter is as intelligent **as** her son, if not more intelligent.

處理 3：My daughter is as intelligent **as** her son, if not more intelligent than her son.

考試的時候如果沒有把握，就不要省略。不要犯錯是考高分的最高原則。

八、動詞後面的介系詞或介副詞忘記寫了

有很多不及物動詞接上介詞就成為及物動詞，例如 look(for), listen(to) 等；有些動詞與介副詞組合，成為片語動詞，有雙字動詞，例如 turn on, look up 等，有三字動詞，例如 look forward to, keep up with 等。或許是受到母語的影響，考生同學有時候會把動詞後面的介系詞或介副詞給忘記寫了。

中文：我老婆非常驚愕地盯著醫生。

問題：*My wife stared the doctor in shock.

處理：My wife stared **at** the doctor in shock.

中文：聽說她猝死，我很傷心。

問題：*I was heartbroken to hear her sudden death.

處理：I was heartbroken to hear **of/about** her sudden death.

中文：我不知道要如何清除那些用過的電池。

問題：*I do not know how to dispose the used batteries.

處理：I do not know how to dispose **of** the used batteries.

中文：這些幫派分子在販賣毒品。

問題：*These gangsters are trafficking drugs.

處理：These gangsters are trafficking **in** drugs.

九、把表「存在」的「有」(there be) 用 "there have" 表示

中文：那裡以前有一個公園。

問題：*There used to have a park over there.

處理：There used to **be** a park over there.

中文： 你的文章裡面有很多文法錯誤。

問題： *There have a number of grammatical mistakes in your essay.

處理： There **are** a number of grammatical mistakes in your essay.

比較： Your essay is full of grammatical mistakes.

十、把 "happen" 當成及物動詞

中文： 我們不知道昨天早上發生了一起兇殺案。

問題： *We do not know that yesterday morning happened a murder.

處理： We do not know that **a murder happened** yesterday morning.

中文： 這間俱樂部近來發生了一些怪事。

問題： *The club recently has happened many strange things.

處理： **There have been** many strange things happening in the club.

十一、主動 vs. 被動

把必須用主動語態的動詞錯誤寫成被動語態；把必須用被動語態的動詞錯誤寫成主動語態。

中文： 這個委員會由九個委員組成。

問題： *The committee is consisted of nine members.

處理 1： The committee **consists of** nine members.

處理 2： The committee **is composed of** nine members.

處理 3： The committee **is made up of** nine members.

中文： 飛行員的粗心造成了幾百個人死亡。

問題 1： *The pilot's carelessness was resulted in hundreds of deaths.

處理： The pilot's carelessness **resulted in** hundreds of deaths.

比較： The pilot's carelessness **caused** hundreds of deaths.

問題 2： * Hundreds of deaths were resulted from the pilot's carelessness.

處理： Hundreds of deaths **resulted from** the pilot's carelessness.

比較： Hundreds of deaths **were caused by** the pilot's carelessness.

中文：校車駛向路邊停靠，學生們慢慢下車。

問題：*The school bus was pulled over and the students got off the bus slowly.

處理：The school bus **pulled over** and the students got off the bus slowly.

比較 1： The police officer **pulled over** his truck.

　　　　= The police officer **pulled** his truck **over**.

比較 2： The police officer **pulled him over** for speeding.

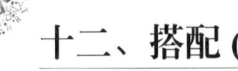

十二、搭配 (collocition)

　　廣義而言，搭配是一種固定組合，就是習慣上一個單詞或片語會固定與某個詞彙一同出現。搭配是形成片語的重要原則之一。有些搭配只要合乎邏輯即可，例如 by bus, after seven tonight, in the morning, blue sky, white clouds 等；有些是可以預測的，例如「J 是字母表的第十個字母」，那麼字母 (letter) 和字母表 (alphabet) 的一同出現是可以預測的，"J is the tenth letter of the English alphabet."；有些會有特殊的語法限制，例如樂器名稱常與定冠詞 the 同現，例如 (play) the piano, (play) the violin 等，例如球類活動名稱常與零冠詞同現，例如 play baseball, play football 等；有些會有特殊的語義限制，例如 consist mainly of（主要是由……組成），consist entirely of（全部由……組成）；或例如面有菜色/面帶病容，用綠色 look green；臉色蒼白，用灰白 look pale；困窘羞愧，用紅色 go red；有些名詞或形容詞常與固定的動詞一同出現，例如認罪 plead guilty，洗衣服 do the laundry，按處方買藥 fill a prescription等。寫英文作文，要時時以搭配為念，尤其是名詞與動詞的搭配以及名詞與形容詞的搭配。搭配是平常一點一滴累積的成果，馬虎不得。

1. 動詞+名詞的搭配

do homework 做功課	make coffee 煮咖啡
do chores 做日常家事	make a decision 做決定
do the dishes 洗碗	make an effort 努力
do the laundry 洗衣服	make a mistake 犯錯
do 100 kilometers 旅行 100 公里	make progress 進步
do one's best 盡最大努力	make a contribution 貢獻

deliver an address 演講

擴增 → deliver a televised address 發表電視演說

make a speech 演講

擴增 → make a successful speech 做了一次成功的演講

give a talk 演講

擴增 → give a series of talks on global warming 就地球暖化舉行系列演講

---

gain weight/time 發胖／爭取時間

lose weight/ten pounds 減肥／體重減輕十磅

take pictures/prescribed medication 照相／吃藥

shoot a film/the ball 拍攝電影／投籃

send invitations/e-mails/messages 發請帖／寄電子郵件／發信息

2. 形容詞+名詞的搭配

a big/huge/large/small number (of something) 很多／很多／很多／很少

a small favor/mistake 小忙／小錯誤

strong voice/tea 洪亮的聲音／濃茶

heavy wind/rain/drinker/smoker/loss/traffic

強風／大雨／酒癮很大的人／煙癮很大的人／嚴重虧損／車輛很多

light food/jacket/music/traffic/rain/breeze

輕食／薄夾克／輕音樂／車輛稀少／細雨／微風

thick slice/hair/beard/forest/accent/sweater

厚片（土司）／濃密的頭髮／濃密的鬍鬚／茂密的森林／濃重的口音／厚毛衣

從以上的例子與討論，我們可以深深感受到搭配的力量與重要性。從現在開始，我們不應該只背單字，我們要向前邁進一步，我們要記片語，要記習慣上會固定組合的單詞或片語。

十三、逗號連接 (comma splice)

逗號連接是一種錯誤，是用逗號連接二個獨立子句。二個獨立子句必須用（逗號加上）連接詞或是用分號來完成合乎語法的連接。逗號連接是臺灣學生寫英文作文時，很容易犯的一個錯誤，因為中文很少用或根本不用分號連接句子。只要用一點點心，就能避免逗號連接，不是嗎？

逗號連接： *He studied very hard, he did not pass the exam.

修改 1： He studied very hard, **but** he did not pass the exam.

修改 2： He studied very hard**; however,** he did not pass the exam.

修改 3： He studied very hard**;** he did not pass the exam.

逗號連接： *The cheerleaders practiced very hard, they won the national championship.

修改 1： The cheerleaders practiced very hard**, and** they won the national championship.

修改 2： The cheerleaders practiced very hard**;** they won the national championship.

修改 3： The cheerleaders practiced very hard**; therefore,** they won the national championship.

修改 4： The cheerleaders practiced very hard**; as a result,** they won the national championship.

三節格律法的句子、平衡句、比較短的句子，常使用逗號連接。

練習 7

1. 下列的句子，有些有「文法上」的錯誤。請將它們圈選出來，然後加以訂正。
正確的句子，只要在句子後面寫上「正確」即可。

例：I cannot stop love you.

答：I cannot stop loving you.

(1) I want go home.

(2) I want to go home.

(3) The security guard forced my roommate leave.

(4) The security guard forced my roommate to leave.

(5) The security guard forced my roommate leaving.

(6) Enough! Stop to call her names in front of her peers.

(7) I double-checked the schedule to avoid to make any mistakes.

(8) Students spend too many hours to surf the Internet.

(9) Slow and steady win the race.

(10) The fact that the homeroom teacher is late to class is surprised.

(11) Those who are interesting in the program can sign up before Friday.

(12) I am sure of that the San Antonio Spurs will win the championship.

(13) There has a night club at the corner of the street.

(14) The answer keys of the exercises are including in the handbook.

(15) Many a boy and many a girl are at the party.

2. 請依照組合關係，判斷下列各句是單句、合句、複句或複合句。

例：I love you.

答：單句

(1) Nice people come and go.

(2) Talented singers come and talented singers go.

(3) Walking in the park, I met my shrink.

(4) If you should have any comment, please feel free to tell me.

(5) You return the key to me and leave my room immediately or I'll call the police.

(6) Her wife sells and buys second-hand furniture.

(7) If you have a valid driver's license and if you have car insurance, then you can rent a car from us.

(8) The woman who has been nominated for the award is my fiancee.

(9) You can take the written exam and/or you can write a term paper.

(10) I always enjoy listening to soft music and reading a good novel when I am alone or when I am waiting for my friend.

3. 請按照第 7 章第 2 節的七個基本句型，判斷下列各句屬於哪一種句型。

例：I finished my homework with her help.

答：SVO

(1) My ex-husband is the secretary-general of the association.

(2) The maid laid the clean sheet on the bed.

(3) We are going downtown.

(4) I teach young kids basic English.

(5) My boyfriend is ambitious and determined.

(6) Young people were singing and shouting.

(7) I love you from the bottom of my heart.

(8) Can we give the invitation to you in person?

(9) Please put the key back as soon as possible.

(10) Your team just broke the record.

4. 請提供一個相同的結構，使下列的單詞、片語或句子形成一個「適當的」平行結構。請特別考量「語義」、「節奏」、「詞序」。必要時，請參考詞典。

例：salt and _____ （（胡）椒鹽）

答：pepper

(1) the poor and the _____ （貧困人士）

(2) ladies and _____ （各位來賓）

(3) now or _____ （稍縱即逝）

(4) friends and _____ （親戚朋友）

(5) hot and _____ （辛辣）

(6) hustle and _____ （熙攘喧鬧）

(7) drink and _____ （酒後駕車）

(8) the true, the good, and the _____ （真善美）

(9) law and _____ （法治）

(10) checks and _____ （制衡）

(11) track and _____ （田徑運動）

(12) trial and _____ （反複試驗）

(13) wax and _____ （興衰）

(14) rise and _____ （興衰；起伏）

(15) hit and _____ （肇事逃逸）

(16) slow and _____ （慢而穩）

(17) social, political, and _____ reforms （社會、政治與經濟改革）

(18) head and _____ above the rest （出類拔萃）

(19) an investor and _____ （投資者兼探索家）

(20) I came, I saw, I _____. （我來之，見之，克之。）

5. 請依下列各句的文意，在空格內填入一個適當的對等連接詞。

例： I have a bike _____ I don't want to lend it to you.

答： but

(1) You leave the little boy alone _____ I will call security.

(2) I love your daughter very much _____ I decide to marry her.

(3) I am really sorry. I can _____ speak _____ read English.

(4) Can we meet twice a week? Mondays _____ Wednesdays?

(5) Can we meet once a week? Mondays _____ Wednesdays?

(6) _____ you can stay in your room and play computer games _____ you can go shopping with us.

(7) The entrepreneur is rich _____ he leads a frugal life.

(8) _____ only will we win the game _____ also we will break the record.

(9) For lunch, we can choose between cheeseburgers _____ beef noodles.

(10) _____ that I love English less, _____ that I love Chinese more.

6. 請依下列各句的文意，在空格內填入一個適當的從屬連接詞。

例： I was late _____ I missed the train.

答： because

(1) I have lived with my grandparents in Hawaii _____ I was three

years old.

(2) _____ you drink and drive, and _____ you

get caught, you will be fined NT$60,000.

(3) The students went surfing _____ it was dark and cold.

(4) The movie star was on a diet _____ she can lose weight.

(5) The movie star was on a diet _____ she should be overweight.

(6) A lion is a carnivore _____ a sheep is a herbivore.

(7) _____ I was young, I used to play the piano well.

(8) Her parents do not care if she is an A student _____ she is

happy in college.

(9) To be straightforward, I was _____ you are.

(10) "_____ there is a will, there is a way."

7. 請依下列各句的文意，在空格內填入一個適當的連接副詞。

例：I missed the train; _____, I was late.

答：therefore

(1) It was dark and cold; _____, the students went surfing.

(2) I did not set my alarm clock; _____, I was late for the interview.

(3) Hurry up; _____, we will surely miss the train.

(4) The train was delayed; _____, we were late for the rehearsal.

(5) We have a backup copy; _____, we did not lose any information.

(6) He did not have a driver's license; _____, he was drunk.

(7) The people living in the area have changed; _____, the

language they use has changed.

(8) According to the evening news, the danger of infection has not decreased; _____

_____, it has increased.

(9) The player took drugs; _____, she was disqualified from the game.

(10) No official order has been given; _____, the soldiers did not take any action.

8. 請利用形容詞子句，將下列各組句子合併。必要時，請作適當的調整。

例：He published a new book. The book is about gay marriage.

答：He published a new book which is about gay marriage.

(1) I know the woman.

The woman is the CEO of my company.

_____

_____

_____

(2) I know the woman.

Every man in my office loves the woman.

_____

_____

_____

(3) I know the woman.

Everyone in my office is proud of the woman.

_____

_____

_____

(4) I know the woman.

The woman's son is the CEO of my company.

_____

_____

(5) The retired professor published a book.

The book is about migratory birds.

_____

_____

(6) The retired professor published a book.

She discussed migratory birds in the book.

_____

_____

(7) My father gave me a guitar on my sixteenth birthday.

He bought the guitar in Spain.

_____

_____

(8) They are shooting a film on the campus.

The Parent-Teacher Association protests the film.

_____

_____

(9) My father gave me a guitar on my sixteenth birthday.

   The strings of the guitar are made of precious nylon.

   The color of the nylon is black.

_____

_____

_____

(10) I came across a beautiful woman in the carnival.

   The woman is from India.

   The woman was wearing a silk sari.

   The sari was purple and gold.

_____

_____

_____

9. 請將下列的句子形成名詞子句。

例： Did she tell you my secret?

答： if/whether she told you my secret

(1) Can your son fly a jet plane?

_____

_____

(2) Have you taken drugs before?

_____

_____

_____

(3) When will you return the books to the library?

_____

_____

(4) Does your husband work for the CIA?

_____

_____

(5) Social networking plays an important role in our future success.

_____

_____

_____

10. 下列的句子都有「懸擺修飾語」的問題，請加以修正。

例： Jogging in the track, a bullet pierced my girlfriend's left lung.

答： Jogging in the track, my girlfriend had her left lung pierced by a bullet.

(1) Swimming in the pool, the tile cut my right ankle.

_____

_____

(2) Bound in leather, my grandfather gave me an old dictionary.

_____

_____

_____

(3) To get a refund, both the receipt and the proof of purchase must be enclosed.

_____

_____

(4) To become a professional football player, constant practice is needed.

_____

_____

(5) Before climbing the mountain, our food supply must be double-checked.

_____

_____

_____

11. 下列的句子都有「誤置修飾語」的問題，請加以修正。

例：My best friend and I used to enjoy a first-run film with a large bucket of popcorn.

答：With a large bucket of popcorn, my best friend and I used to enjoy a first-run film.

(1) At the age of three, my grandfather took me to Hong Kong Disneyland.

_____

_____

(2) We nearly walked ten miles to buy some water to drink.

_____

_____

_____

(3) The little boy who walked onto the podium confidently bowed to the audience.

_____

_____

_____

(4) The new LED TV was put in the living room which was bought last night.

_____

_____

_____

(5) My husband took my car to the body shop that needed to be repaired.

_____

_____

_____

12. 請在下列各題的空格內填入一個單詞，以達到「押尾韻」的修辭格式。

例：_diligent_ and _____

答：intelligent

(1) an _able_ and _____ director

(2) a _gorgeous_ but _____ woman

(3) a _gorgeous_ and _____ hostess

(4) a _competent_ and _____ contestant

(5) an _investor_ and _____

(6) _poetic_ and _____

(7) _intensive_ and _____

(8) _intelligent_ and _____

(9) _peaceful_ and _____

(10) _safety_ and _____

13. 請在下列各題的空格內填入一個單詞，以達到「押頭韻」的修辭格式。

例：*slow* and _____

答：steady

(1) *pride* and _____

(2) *now* or _____

(3) *clean* and _____

(4) *fast* and _____

(5) *bed* and _____

(6) *friends* and _____

(7) *friend* and _____

(8) *wax* and _____

(9) *peaceful* and _____

(10) *rock* and _____

14. 下列的句子都有「不當省略」的問題，請加以修正。

例：Today's temperature is even higher than yesterday.

答：Today's temperature is even higher than yesterday's.

(1) My suitcase is larger than you.

_____

_____

_____

_____

_____

_____

_____

(2) This year's corn harvest is not as good as last year.

_____

_____

(3) The number of run-aways is larger than drop-outs.

_____

_____

(4) They are enthusiastic and supportive of the new plan.

_____

_____

(5) We are told not to dispose the used batteries.

_____

_____

(6) Your daughter is as diligent if not more diligent than my.

_____

_____

(7) "My dog barks a lot." "Me too."

_____

_____

(8) My wife always has and will remember to pay the bills on time.

(9) My daughter is taller than any girl on her team.

(10) I love you more than Jennifer.

15. 下列的句子都有「代名詞指涉模稜兩可」的問題，請加以修正。

例：Betty told Bella that she had been set up.

答：Betty said to Bella, "I was set up."

(1) When a writer has finished her essay, you need to edit it carefully.

(2) My son told his father that he needed to buy a new cell phone.

(3) My roommate is a famous photographer and he enjoys showing it to me.

_____

_____

(4) My new friend talked endlessly about his trip to Paris, and this was boring.

_____

_____

(5) If a foreign student wants to participate in the field trip, she can sign up for which by next Tuesday.

_____

_____

第 8 章

組織

一個段落有三大要求：一致、連貫、發展。「發展」跟我們這個章節要討論的「組織」關係密切，幾乎是同義詞。根據「評分說明」，「組織」這個項目的評分標準，特優等級與優等級的文章組織必須達到「重點分明，有開頭、發展、結尾，前後連貫，轉承語使用得當」。

重點分明

重點分明就是每一段要有一個主題句 (topic sentence)，這個主題句清楚地呈現該段落的重點，也就是段落的中心思想。簡單地說，作者利用主題句清楚明白地告訴讀者他的觀點，因此我們強烈建議考生用主題句開始一個段落。

第二節 有開頭、有發展、有結尾

一、開頭

記住「起、承、合」的「起」，就會記得用一個主題句開門見山，開始一個段落。主題句可長可短，可以短如「我愛狗」，可以長如「從小我生長在臺灣南部海邊的一個小魚村，有一次我在岸邊的堤防散步，一不小心掉到海裡，有一隻狗跳到海裡救了我，從此我愛上了狗」。我們建議不要寫太短、太廣泛或太長、太詳細的主題句，十五個單詞左右是一個不錯的標準。

二、發展

發展就是「起、承、合」的「承」。承就是作文寫作常講到的支撐句，用來支撐主題句。你先用主題句導出你的主張和論點，接著你必須回應讀者心中的問題和疑惑。你必須要提出具有說服力的證據來讓讀者認同。什麼是具有說服力的證據呢？一般而言，考生可以用事實、資料、定義、舉例、闡明、解釋等做為佐證。事實就是可以查證的資訊，例如「哈佛大學位於美國東部麻薩諸塞州劍橋市，以法學院著稱」，「美國的國旗又名星條旗，上面有 13 道紅白相間的寬條，這 13 道寬條象徵美國最初建國時期的 13 個殖民地。左上角有一個藍色長方形，藍色長方形上面有 50 顆白色的五角星。每一顆五角星代表了美國的一個州」。

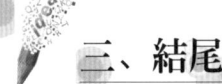

三、結尾

結尾就是結論，通常是最後一句。沒有結尾就是文章沒有寫完。沒有寫完的文章會被扣分，所以考試的時候一定要預留足夠的時間來寫英文作文。如果寫的是故事，就要讓故事有結束，例如，「最後，我匆匆忙忙跳下計程車，飛也似地衝進教室，卻發現今天不用上課」，「（我詢問了 Apple Store 的店員一大串諸如價格、記憶體容量、配備、保固等方面的問題，她也很耐心地一一回答。）最後，我問她要如何操作 iPad 的時候，她滿臉疑惑地看著我的手機說：『就跟你操作你的 iPhone 一樣。』」。

第三節　前後連貫

「起、承、合」的承，指的就是前後連貫。同一段的句子如果能像魚鱗或是像屋頂上的瓦片一樣，一鱗接一鱗，一片接一片，條理清晰，流暢緊湊，就會是很高明的前後連貫。更明確地說，從作者的角度而言，思緒要源源不絕，不要無故或突然中斷；從讀者的角度而言，「讀起來」有如順水推舟，順暢無阻。例如「我家門前有小河，後面有山坡，山坡上面野花多，野花紅似火。」，「古之學者必有師。師者，所以傳道受業解惑也。人非生而知之者，孰能無惑？惑而不從師，其為惑也終不解矣。」，以及前面提過的「美國的國旗……。」等。以上是利用修辭格「頂真/聯珠」作前後連貫的一些實例，值得我們學習。

我們也可以有信心地利用形容詞子句來進行二個相同指涉的名詞片語的前後連貫，例如「這個委員會由七位**委員**組成，每一位**委員**都是來自美國疾病管制局的**病毒學家**。**病毒學**是研究與治療病毒所引起的疾病的學問。」，「一個英語單詞由**字根、字首、字尾**組合而成，**字根**是單詞的基礎形式，常表示單詞的主要語義。**字首**又名首綴，是黏在字根前面的詞綴。**字尾**又名尾綴，是黏在字根後面的詞綴。」等。另外一個常用而且好用的前後連貫方式，是從屬連接，因為從屬連接可以清楚呈現二個子句的邏輯關係，例如「因為是颱風夜，又下著大雨，所以這場演唱會取消了。」，「雖然是颱風夜，又下著大雨，但是還是有成千上萬的歌迷湧入演唱會的現場。」等。還有一個常用的前後連貫的方式，就是利用轉承語。

第四節　轉承語使用得當

　　轉承語 (transition word or phrase)，常稱為轉折詞，有時候稱為連接副詞，是一個單詞，例如 thus, however 或是一個片語，例如 as a result, in conclusion 放在一個句子的前面，用以表示跟前一個句子的邏輯關係，例如在上一節討論「前後連貫」的最後二個例子中，我們用「因為……所以」、「雖然……但是」來呈現「適當的」邏輯關係。同樣地，英語允許我們利用轉承語達到相同的目的。例如「颱風夜，又下著大雨，**因此**這場演唱會取消了。」（...; **therefore,** [　] ...），「颱風夜，又下著大雨，**然而**還是有成千上萬的歌迷湧入演唱會的現場。」（...; **however,** [　] ...）等。使用轉承語就像開車時的換擋，換擋換的好，當然車子開得很順，開車的人（作者）和坐車的人（讀者）都很舒適安全。

　　有三點補充說明：

　　第一，基本上，轉承語是副詞，不要與對等連接詞、從屬連接詞搞混。第二，轉承語常前接一個分號來承接前一個句子，同時後接一個逗號來引導後面的句子。第三，前後二個句子的邏輯關係會決定轉承語的選用。有關轉承語的分類，請參考附錄 2。

第五節　三種文體：議論文、記敘文、描述文

　　接下來，我們要討論如何組織一篇文章。一般而言，一篇文章有三段，如果全篇是十到十二個句子的篇幅，那我們建議採取 1：3：1 的組織，也就是第一段寫 2~3 句作為「導論」，第二段寫 6 句作為「討論」，第三段寫 2~3 句作為「結論」。一般的作文，我們根據篇幅要求不同，可以做等比例的調配。但是，針對考試，我們建議考生同學寫二段，我們可以採取 2：3 的組織，也就是第一段寫 4 句作為「啟」，第二段寫 6 句作為「承合」。當然 2：3 這個比率只是一個原則。對非以英語為母語的同學來說，寫得愈多犯錯的機會也相對愈多。別忘了，文章長度超過 120 個單詞並不會加分。然而，我們必須承認，最近幾年大考中心所公佈的學測指考英文作文佳作，篇幅都大大地超過 120 個單詞。

　　「組織」是將文章的內容作合理的安排，因此在英文作文的培訓過程，「內容」和「組織」是相輔相成的二個重要元素。我們在第 9 章第 5 節關於內容的討論裡面，將學測指考常考的「主題」，依照出現的頻率多寡排序如下：

(1)「解釋說明」；(2)「經驗」；(3)「故事、情節發展」；(4)「提出具體的做法」；(5)「舉例」；(6)「因果」；(7)「影響啓示」。

為了方便討論，我們將上述的主題歸納成三種文體：議論文 (argument)、記敘文 (narration)、描述文 (description)。概略而言，我們將「解釋說明」，「提出具體做法」，「舉例」，「因果」，「影響啓示」歸為議論文；將「故事、情節發展」歸為記敘文；將「經驗」歸為描述文。我們以二段，四句加六句的模式，將三種文體的組織討論如下。

一、議論文好比辯論

作者透過分析與評估，提出自己對特定人事物的看法，然後提供足夠的、可靠的證據來說服讀者。議論文強調的是事實。

（一）議論文的第一段

「主題句」—「定義句」—「數據句」—「如下句」〔請參考 9.7〕

我們以「節約用電」為主題，第一段的四個句子，組織如下：(1) 由於科技的進步，我們舒適便利的生活幾乎離不開電。(2) 舒適便利的生活包括有手機、電視、捷運、高鐵、空調等。(3) 根據統計，台灣平均每人用電量高居世界第 14 位，用電之凶是亞洲之冠。(4) 我們必須省電，有效的省電方法討論如下：……

另外以「尊重隱私」為主題，第一段的四個句子，組織如下：(1)「不自由，毋寧死。」（"Give me liberty or give me death."）同理，「沒有隱私，活著等於行屍走肉（動物園的人類）」。(2) 隱私是一個人有不受他人監視自己行為的自由。(3) 根據一項由某某學會在 2012 年所做的調查，臺灣高中生有高達 78% 的受訪者認為自己的隱私受到侵犯。(4) 我們一定要尊重他人的隱私，具體做法建議如下：……

（二）議論文的第二段

「方法／步驟句 1」—「方法／步驟句 2」—「方法／步驟句 3」—「效果句 1」—「效果句 2」—「結論句」〔請參考 9.7〕

以「節約用電」為主題，第二段的六個句子，全篇的第(5)句到第(10)句，組織如下：(5)

第一個省電方法是冷氣機溫度設定在攝氏 27 度，並且有效利用隔熱設備。(6) 第二個省電方法是有效利用太陽能。(7) 第三個省電方法是關閉暫時不用的電腦、影印機、列表機等。(8) 省電的第一個好處／效果是可以節省電費。(9) 省電的第二個好處／效果是可以有效減少浪費地球有限的資源。(10) 結論是有電當思無電之苦，想要長久享用電的好處，就要善待它─節約用電。

　　以「尊重隱私」為主題，第二段的六個句子，組織如下：(5)（第一個作法。）尊重隱私首要尊重個人選擇的自由。個人可以選擇什麼事情要給誰知道的權利。(6)（第二個作法。）隱私權受到挑戰就像是選擇的自由受到侵害。我們應該像捍衛自由一樣來捍衛隱私權。「不自由，毋寧死。」(7)（第三個作法。）尊重隱私就是尊重差異性，尊重不同族群的語言、文化傳統與生活方式。(8)（第一個好處／效果。）尊重別人就是尊重自己。(9)（第二個好處／效果。）尊重隱私就是不容許個人資料被濫用。(10)（結論。）我們要保護自己的隱私也要尊重別人的隱私，所以我們應該提倡尊重隱私權。

二、記敘文好比講故事

　　作者合理地串連時空，引人入勝地依序報導過去發生的事件，例如吳樂天開講《廖添丁》。記敘文以報導 5W1H 為重心，也就是「人 (who)、地 (where)、事 (what)、物 (which)、時 (when)、原因 (why)、方式 (how)」。

（一）記敘文的第一段

　　「主題句」─「實例鋪陳句」─「背景資料句」─「時空串連句」〔請參考 9.7〕

　　記敘文第一段的四個句子要如何安排呢？可以選用一句格言來當「主題句」，例如「活到老，學到老」，「助人為快樂之本」，「有志者，事竟成」等，或是利用介紹一個特定的「人、地、事、物」來當「主題句」，例如「我的游泳教練」、「墾丁國家公園」等。第二句舉一個實例來做鋪陳。第三句介紹所列舉的實例的背景資料。第四句將時空合理串連。也就是以「主題」─「實例」─「背景」─「串連」作為典型組織。

　　我們以「助人」為主題，第一段的組織如下：(1) 諺語：「助人為快樂之本」，幫助別人讓我們覺得自己不只是「接受」，也有能力「付出」。(2) 我們班上有一位女同學 Judy 行動不便，必須坐輪椅。(3) 有一天班導師告訴全班同學說 Judy 要請二個星期的假，因為她要動手術。(4) 原來 Judy 患有天生腦性麻痺，急需動手術治療，但是家裡很窮。

另外以「畢業旅行」為主題，第一段的組織如下：(1) 我們是臺北 ABC 高中 2014 級的學生，我們畢業旅行選擇去墾丁。(2) 墾丁有全臺灣最美麗的海灘。(3) 墾丁位於臺灣南部，是世界聞名的度假勝地。(4) 因為明年我們要考學測，因此畢聯會決定我們在 2013 年的暑假舉行畢業旅行。

（二）記敘文的第二段

「鋪陳句」—「時空句 1」—「時空句 2」—「時空句 3」—「效果句」—「結論句」
〔請參考 9.7〕

記敘文第二段的六個句子要如何安排呢？組織安排的原則是按時空的邏輯排序。在作法上可以有底下不同選擇：一、前而後的順序，二、後而前的倒序，三、內而外的漣漪，四、外圍內的收網，五、順時鐘方向的連續，六、逆時鐘方向的接龍，七、以中心點為準，八、以左上角為準，凡此等等。

以「助人」為主題，第二段的組織如下：第 (5) 句做鋪陳。例如，我們開班會決定全班同學輪流幫助 Judy。第(6)～(8)句舉三個實例。例如，(6) 我們輪班到醫院陪她，幫她複習功課。(7) Judy 出院後，我們班的男生輪班幫她推輪椅。(8) 我們舉辦義賣活動，募款捐助 Judy。第 (9) 句做成效，例如，Judy 非常感謝我們同學的關懷與幫助。第 (10) 句做結論，例如，Judy 接受電視節目的專訪，當下，她一面流著眼淚，一面笑著說：「我真幸福」。

以「畢業旅行」為主題，第二段的組織如下：第(5)句做鋪陳，例如，這是一次四天三夜的快樂畢業旅行。第(6)～(8)句介紹三個行程，例如，(6)第一天在高雄。行程安排：中午是佛陀紀念館，下午是西子灣，晚上是六合夜市。(7)第二天在墾丁。大家在海灘盡情玩樂，被陽光親吻，被海水沐浴。(8)第三天在大鵬灣。有人玩水上摩托車，有人玩滑水，有人玩風帆。大家都玩瘋了。第(9)句做成效，例如，第四天是賦歸，個個累壞了，一路睡回臺北。第(10)句做結論，例如，這次的畢業旅行讓我見識到平常印象中的書呆子原來是那麼的陽光、豪放。真棒。

當然，如果主題是如何辦好一次畢業旅行的話，我們可以將第二段的六個句子，調整組織如下：第(5)句做鋪陳，例如，我們全班分成三個小組，有效地分工合作。第(6)～(8)句介紹三個小組的權責，例如，(6)介紹總務組：負責交通、住宿、飲食、保險等。(7)介紹財務組：負責收支、會計、申請補助與贊助等。(8)介紹活動組：負責規劃行程、活動、趣味競賽、攝影等。第(9)句做成效，例如全班同心協力，發揮團隊精神。第(10)句做結論：平常印象中的書呆子、分數的奴隸，辦起事來，居然是「使命必達」，創新又有效率。

三、描述文好比畫圖/攝影

作者透過文字，生動地描繪、記錄人事物的細節，例如徐志摩的《康橋的早晨》。人事物的細節包括外表、動作、聲音、形狀、顏色、味道、感覺等。概略而言，描述文就像在細緻地陳述個人的生活「體驗」。

（一）描述文的第一段

「介紹人物句」—「時空典故句」—「特徵句」—「原因句」〔請參考 9.7〕

描述文第一段的四個句子可以這樣組織：(1)介紹文章的主題，也就是我們要描述的人地事物等，簡稱為「介紹人物句」，例如「陽明山的夜空」。(2)提供關於主題的有趣的時空資訊與歷史典故，簡稱為「時空典故句」。(3)提供主題與眾不同的特徵或重要性，簡稱為「特徵句」。(4)提供主題會讓人難以忘懷的原因，簡稱為「原因句」。

我們以「我的英文老師」為主題，第一段的組織如下：(1)我的英文老師 Julia 是位美國人。(2)她在 2011 年到臺灣師大學中文。(3)Julia 的家鄉是加州納帕市，家裡種葡萄。(4)我們班都很喜歡上她的英語會話課，因為她臉上總是帶著燦爛的笑容。

底下，我們引用 Doubleday (1997) 出版，Mitch Albom 所著之 *Tuesdays with Morrie*《最後十四堂星期二的課》這本小說一開始（第 3~4 頁），作者對他老師 Morrie Schwartz 的描述。

"He is a small man who takes small steps, as if a strong wind could, at any time, whisk him up into the clouds. In his graduation day robe, he looks like a cross between a biblical prophet and a Christmas elf. He has sparkling blue-green eyes, thinning silver hair that spills onto his forehead, big ears, a triangle nose, and tufts of graying eyebrows. Although his teeth are crooked and his lower ones are slanted back--as if someone had once punched them in--when he smiles it's as if you'd just told him the first joke on earth."

作者利用四個句子，一百個單詞 (24+18+23+35) 描述他老師的小個子、小步伐、穿上博士袍像是聖經裡的先知、耶誕節裡的小精靈，眼睛的顏色，斑白稀疏的頭髮，大耳朵，三角鼻，灰白的眉毛，參差不齊的牙齒、向內傾斜的下排牙齒、誇張的笑容等。我們見證了作者成功地利用了「比喻象徵」的修辭格，尤其是顏色和形狀。〔請參考 10.5〕

（二）描述文的第二段

「時空特徵句 1」—「時空特徵句 2」—「時空特徵句 3」—「時空特徵句 4」—「收尾句 1」—「收尾句 2」〔請參考 9.7〕

在討論描述文的第一段的組織的時候，我們建議(1)～(4)句依序為「介紹人物句」，「時空典故句」，「特徵句」，「原因句」。其實，我們也可以變通，將第一段鎖定在描述主題的一個特色，第二段鎖定在描述主題的另一個特色，例如，第一段描述日月潭的地理位置，全潭的面積，湖面的周圍等，第二段描述日月潭的形狀，潭水，朝霧，夕陽等。

描述文第二段的組織跟第一段的組織大同小異，區別只是聚焦的重點不同，例如第一段描述你英文老師的背景：美國加州納帕人，來臺灣學中文，二十幾歲，笑容甜美等。在寫第二段的時候，你可以把鏡頭換一個角度，例如描寫老師的身材、頭髮、面貌、個性等。

底下，我們引用 Doubleday (1997) 出版，Mitch Albom 所著之 *Tuesdays with Morrie*《最後十四堂星期二的課》第二章第三段（第 5 頁）作者描述他的教授每個禮拜三晚上的戶外活動。

"He used to go to this church in Harvard Square every Wednesday night for something called 'Dance Free.' They had flashing lights and booming speakers and Morrie would wander in among the mostly student crowd, wearing a white T-shirt and black sweatpants and a towel around his neck, and whatever music was playing, that's the music to which he danced. He'd do the lindy to Jimi Hendrix. He twisted and twirled, he waved his arms like a conductor on amphetamines, until sweat was dripping down the middle of his back...."（4 句，90 個單詞）

我們再次見證了作者熟稔地運用了時空、燈光、聲音、形狀、動作（跳舞、扭擺）、顏色、人物（學生、Hendrix、指揮家），巧妙地利用「比喻象徵」的修辭格，細膩生動地描述他的老師跳舞時的生龍活虎（扭擺身子、擺動手臂、汗流浹背），成功地讓讀者身歷其境地渾然投入。

描述文第二段的首句和尾句，可能的話，可以加上一點反差、幽默的元素，例如溫柔可愛的英文老師曾經是 2009 年加州空手道亞軍，目前是臺北市市刑警大隊的武術教練；跳舞時渾然忘我的瘋狂老頭是「知名的社會學教授，有豐富的教學經驗，寫過幾本備受尊崇的好書。人們卻當他是個老怪物。」

第六節　三種文體的組織（二段十句）表格簡示

	文體	議論文	記敘文	描述文
第一段	第1句	主題句	主題句	介紹人物句
	第2句	定義句	實例鋪陳句	時空典故句
	第3句	數據句	背景資料句	特徵句
	第4句	如下句	時空串連句	原因句
第二段	第5句	方法/步驟句之一	鋪陳句	時空特徵句之一
	第6句	方法/步驟句之二	時空句之一	時空特徵句之二
	第7句	方法/步驟句之三	時空句之二	時空特徵句之三
	第8句	效果句之一	時空句之三	時空特徵句之四
	第9句	效果句之二	效果句	收尾/反差幽默句之一
	第10句	結論句	結論句	收尾/反差幽默句之二

　　有一點必須再次加強說明。四句加六句 (2:3) 的分配、十個句子的組織安排、每一句的內容等只是提出概略的原則，其目的是讓考生同學在時間緊迫，壓力又大的情況下，能夠從容淡定以對。同學儘可能將組織的概念內化，多寫二句或少寫一句都沒差。一定要遵照各段的提示撰寫，而且文長至少 120 個單詞。

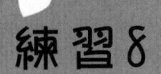

練習 8

1. 近年來，學測指考的英文作文要求考生寫幾個段落？

2. 近年來，學測指考的英文作文最常要求考生寫的是哪三種文體？

3. 如果你準備寫一篇由十個句子組成的二段式的文章，一般而言，你會如何分配這些個句子？ 也就是說你第一段會寫幾個句子？ 第二段會寫幾個句子？ 如果是十二個句子呢？

4. 如果你準備寫一篇由 150 個單詞左右組成的二段式的文章，你會如何分配這150 個單詞？ 也就是說你第一段會寫幾個單詞？ 第二段會寫幾個單詞？ 如果是120 個單詞呢？

5. 根據本章節的討論，「議論文」文體的第一段可以如何安排？ 「記述文」文體的第一段可以如何安排？ 「描述文」文體的第一段可以如何安排？

6. 根據本章節的討論，「議論文」文體的第二段可以如何安排？「記述文」文體的第二段可以如何安排？「描述文」文體的第二段可以如何安排？

_____

_____

_____

_____

7. 英文作文的主題是「節能減碳」(conserving energy and reducing carbon emission)，請你用英文寫出三個「方法/步驟句」。

_____

_____

_____

_____

8. 英文作文的主題是「一次安寧醫院之旅」(a visit to a hospice)，請你用英文寫出三個「時空句」。

_____

_____

_____

_____

9. 英文作文的主題是「我最珍愛的一張賀卡」(my most cherished greeting card)，請你用英文寫出三個「時空特徵句」。

_____

_____

_____

_____

第 9 章

內容

第一節　內容的重要性

　　「內容」與「組織」是學測指考英文作文分項式評分指標，五項裡面占分比率最高的二項，各占 5 分 (25%)，稱得上是考高分的主要關鍵。

　　根據「評分說明」，「內容」這個項目的評分標準在於「內容是否切題」與「內容是否充分完整」。特優等級與優等級的作答內容必須滿足三大要求：「主題（句）清楚切題，並有具體、完整的相關細節支持」。

　　「內容」是一篇文章所談論的主題、觀點、故事或敘述。作答的時候，只要按照試題的提示與注意事項，言之有物就可以拿到「內容」這個項目不錯的分數。這裡的言之有物指的是所談論的主題、觀點、故事或敘述要清楚切題，支撐句所提供的舉例、原因、說明、經驗、發展、做法等必須具體、完整、明確、詳細。清楚切題是不含糊地、不拐彎抹角地把你的觀點，尤其是重要的觀點，利用主題句明白交代。具體就是要合乎邏輯、要有真憑實據，完整就是徹頭徹尾，明確就是明白正確，詳細就是詳盡仔細。

　　一個普遍的問題是，考生一看到作文題目時，常有不知所措、腦中感到一片空白的情況。通常是一、無法以有限的詞彙完整表達自己的想法，二、無法建構具有邏輯性的架構，三、沒有豐富的生活經驗可以「精彩」敘述。高中生的基本詞彙有 5000 到 7000 個單詞，足夠寫出考試所要求的內容。在結構上，本書已經詳實提供基礎英文作文的文章組織發展的邏輯架構，但是文章內容豐富與否與個人生活經驗息息相關，而且每個人的生活經驗需要長時間的累積。

　　一般而言，高中生的生活經驗差異不大，但是透過閱讀卻可以累積大量不同的他人的人生經驗，因為每一個故事就是一個人的部分生活經驗，因此每次閱讀完一篇文章或故事，就像是體驗到一個人的生活，或瞭解到一個人對事情的看法。同樣地，看電影、看電視也可以增加生活的經驗。生活的個人體驗非常獨特、非常珍貴，但是卻非常耗時。因此，在經驗累積無法超越時間的限制的現實情況下，有時候透過有層次的自我冥想，也常常可以類推出生活的經驗。

　　總之，廣讀與精讀「正確的」英語語言輸入，毋庸置疑地可以有效、快速地增進英文寫作能力。

底下，我們舉二個實例來進一步說明。

　　仔細觀察 102 學測英文作文的連環圖片的內容之後，我們收集、整理了以下的訊息：我們先幫故事的主人翁取個名字叫做 George。(1) 從第一幅圖片，我們可以確認 George 低著頭坐在捷運車廂的博愛座上面，旁邊坐著一位戴眼鏡白髮蒼蒼的老太太，表情似乎有點不高興。車廂內人多有點擁擠，有三個人站著，其中有一位是老先生，一支手拄著手杖，一支手抓著吊環就站在 George 前面。George 沒有禮讓座位給老先生。(2) 從第二幅圖片，我們可以知道 George 是頭髮較黑，身穿 77 號球衣的男孩子。另外有一個身穿 3 號球衣的男孩子。George 當天上午打籃球摔傷了右腳踝。(3) 第三幅圖片告訴我們的訊息如下：現在車廂裡有三個人沒有座位而站著：George 和另外二個人，一男一女，那個男的背著背包。George 沒有座位，他一手拄著拐杖，一手抓著吊環，無奈地站著。博愛座上坐著一位年輕女子，輕鬆愉快地在看書，旁邊坐著一位打著圍巾拄著手杖的男人，看起來像是在閉目養神。(4) 第四幅圖片只有一個大大的問號。

　　切題的重點整理如下：

1. 中學生身份的 George「不應該地」在車廂內的博愛座卡了一個座位。
2. 車廂內人多擁擠，有一位老先生沒有座位，拄著手杖站在 George 前面。
3. 車廂內的人認為 George 一個年紀輕輕的學生為什麼坐在博愛座而且不讓座給老人家。
4. George 看起來有點尷尬。
5. 這一天的車廂內人多擁擠，George 沒有座位。
6. 一位年輕女子坐在博愛座上，George 有一點不高興。
7. 這一天上午 George 跟朋友打球摔傷了右腳踝。

　　不切題的細節整理如下：（可以捨棄不用）

1. 博愛座是保留給老年人、孕婦、行動不便、攜帶幼童的人坐的。
2. 拄著手杖的老先生禿頭留有八字鬍。
3. 跟 George 一起打球的男生戴眼鏡，球衣號碼是 3 號，旁邊還有幾個小朋友在打球。
4. 站在 George 旁邊的男生戴眼鏡、背著背包。
5. George 的包包是側背的。
6. 坐在博愛座的女生穿裙子留辮子，額頭左邊別著一支髮夾。
7. 坐在博愛座的另外一個人是男生，打著圍巾，手裡拿著一支手杖。

故事內容編排

第一幅圖片:

(1) George is a high school student.

(2) George goes to school by MRT.

(3) The MRT car was crowded.

(4) Several people did not have seats.

(5) Those people, including an old man, had to stand in the crowded car.

(6) George seated himself on one of the priority seats in the car.

(7) George did not offer the seat to the old man.

第二幅圖片:

(8) This morning George was playing basketball with his friend.

(9) David had his right ankle twisted.

第三幅圖片:

(10) As usual, the car/MRT was crowded.

(11) George did not have a seat.

(12) George was on crutches.

(13) The young girl was sitting and reading a book in comfort on the priority seat.

(14) George was not happy with the girl.

如果不會寫 George 拄的拐杖 (crutches)，也不知道 crutches 要用單數或是複數，就放棄不寫(12)句。

假想第四幅圖片的情景:

(15) Suddenly, the girl sitting on the priority seat noticed George.

(16) She offered her seat to George.

(17) George thanked the girl for her kindness.

(18) George had a smile on his face.

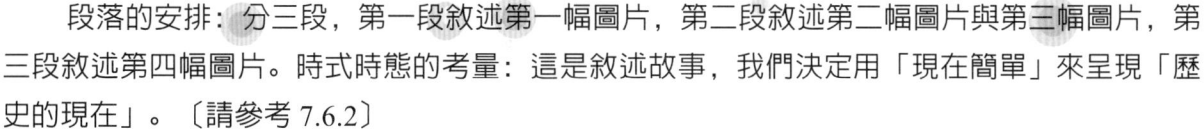

第二節 文法、句構與修辭

段落的安排：分三段，第一段敘述第一幅圖片，第二段敘述第二幅圖片與第三幅圖片，第三段敘述第四幅圖片。時式時態的考量：這是敘述故事，我們決定用「現在簡單」來呈現「歷史的現在」。〔請參考 7.6.2〕

組織

我們決定分成三段，寫 10 個句子，每個句子 12~15 個單詞。第一段寫三個句子，第二段寫四個句子，第三段寫三個句子。我們要用「長短句交互使用」的技巧。我們想要用對等連接、從屬連接、分詞構句、設問等句構與修辭。

句子合併

(1) George is a high school student.（6 單詞；短句）

(2) He goes to scholl by train *everyday*.（7 單詞；短句；累計 13 單詞）

(3)+(4)：The train is always so crowded that many people do not have seats.（13 單詞；中句；累計 26 單詞）

(5)+(6)+(7)：George is sitting on one of the priority seats, but he does not offer the seat to the old man who *was* standing with his hand holding a walking stick.（30 單詞；長句；累計 56 單詞）

(8)+(9)：This morning George is playing basketball and has his right ankle twisted.（12 單詞；中句；累計 68 單詞）

He goes to the hospital.（5 單詞；短句；累計 73 單詞）

He is wearing a cast.（5 單詞；短句；不會「石膏」這個單詞，也不知道「打」石膏，動詞要用 "wear"，放棄本句。

(10)+(11)+(12)：On his way home, the train **was** crowded as usual, and George has no *sit*; as a result, George has to stand with a twisted ankle.（26 單詞；長句；累計 99 單詞）

(13) George notices that the young girl is sitting and reading a book in comfort on the priority seat.（18 單詞；中句；累計 117 單詞）

(14) George is not happy with the girl.（7 單詞；短句；累計 124 單詞）

(15)+(16) Suddenly, the girl sitting on the priority seat *noticed* George and *she* offered her seat to George with **courtecy**.（19 單詞；中句；累計 143 單詞）

(17)+(18) With a smile on his face, George **thanked** the girl for her kindness .（13 單詞；中句；累計 156 單詞）

檢查修改

1. 發現全文並未一致使用「現在簡單」。

2. 有些單詞拼錯了：sit 改為 seat；courtecy 改為 courtesy；everyday 改為 every day。

3. 加了一個片語 because of her indifference（因為她的冷漠）。

4. 換了一個片語：~~the old man~~ → the senior citizen。

5. 加了一個「設問」作結尾：Is the world full of love and thoughtfulness?

6. 做了一些修改：~~has his right ankle twisted~~ → has twisted his right ankle；將誤置修飾語 on the priority seat 移動；Is → Isn't。

準備交卷的 150 個單詞左右的文章如下：

George is a high school student. He goes to school by MRT everyday. The train is always so crowded that many people do not have seats. Sitting on one of the priority seats, George does not offer his seat to the old man who is standing with his hand holding a walking stick.

This morning George is playing basketball and has his right ankle twisted. He goes to the hospital. On his way home, the train is crowded as usual, and George has no seat; as a result, George has to stand with his ankle twisted. George notices that the young girl is sitting and reading a book in comfort on the priority seat. George is not happy with the girl her indifference.

Suddenly, the girl sitting on the priority seat notices George and offers her seat to George with courtesy. George thanked the girl for her kindness with a smile on his face. Is the world full of love and thoughtfulness?

初步修改：（刪除線或斜體字型代表修改）

~~**George is a high school student.**~~ George goes to school by MRT *every day*. The train is always so crowded that many people do not have seats. Sitting on one of the priority seats, George does not offer his seat to the ~~**old man**~~ *senior citizen* who is standing with his hand holding a walking stick.

This morning George is playing basketball and *has twisted* his right ankle **twisted**. He goes to the hospital. On his way home, the MRT is crowded as usual, and George has no seat; as a result, *poor* George has to stand with **his** *a* twisted ankle. George notices that the young girl on the priority seat is sitting and reading a book in comfort. George is not happy with the girl *because of* her indifference.

Suddenly, the girl **sitting on the priority seat** noticed George and she offers her seat to *him* with courtesy. **With a smile on his face**, George thanked the girl for her kindness. *Isn't* the world full of love and thoughtfulness?

完整修改後的文章

George goes to school by MRT every day. The train is always so crowded that many people do not have seats. Sitting on one of the priority seats, George does not offer his seat to the senior citizen who is standing with his hand holding a walking stick.

This morning George is playing basketball and has twisted his right ankle. He goes to the hospital. On his way home, the train is crowded as usual, and George has no seat; as a result, poor George has to stand with a twisted ankle. George notices that the young girl on the priority seat is sitting and reading a book in comfort. George is not happy with the girl because of her indifference.

Suddenly, the girl *notices* George and she offers her seat to him with courtesy. With a smile on his face, George thanks the girl for her kindness. Isn't the world full of love and thoughtfulness?

還有三分鐘的時間，再仔細默念校對一遍。一切 OK？OK！停筆。

跟學測相比較，指考的英文作文簡單多了。第一，有段落的限制，規定寫二段。第二，指示簡要明確。考生只要跟著「一個口令，一個動作」去完成任務即可。我們來試試看：

主題: 游泳

A 如何進行
A1 學校游泳池、經濟、方便、安全、省時
A2 跟好友 David
A3 每星期三個晚上
A4 泳褲、泳帽、蛙鏡、耳塞、大毛巾

B 原因
B1 經濟（一期三個月 1200 元）、方便（在校園）、安全（有救生員）、省時
B2 可以跟好朋友在一起，可以互相切磋
B3 可以請教救生員
B4 可以看到心中的女神 Julia（對她有好感，暗戀）

C 影響
C1 可以紓緩壓力、減肥、保持身材
C2 良好的習慣（不上網、不打電玩、不熬夜）
C3 身心健康
C4 與好友互相鼓勵，對未來樂觀，充滿信心和期待

組織: 主題是游泳，下分二個子題: 如何進行與原因、影響。如何進行、原因、影響各寫出四點。如果每一點個寫一個 10~15 單詞的句子，全文就會有 120~180 單詞。

詞彙: 「方便」有一點挑戰，想改用 "simple"；「救生員」"lifeguard" 不會，改用「教練」"coach"；「蛙鏡」不會寫，避開不談；「切磋」就用 "learn skills from each other"；「暗戀」想用 "fall in love with her in secret"；「紓壓」就用 "release stress"。

文法、句構與修辭: 長短句交互使用，加強語氣的重複，句子合併，平行結構，分詞構句，虛主詞，倒裝句，押韻，比喻等。

造句

A 如何進行

(1) I like to exercise.

(2) Swimming is my favorite exercise.

(3) Usually I go swimming at the swimming pool in my school.

(4) I usually go swimming with my friend, David.

(5) I go swimming three times a week.

(6) To go swimming, many things such as a pair of swimming trunks, a swimming cap, ear plugs, a towel are needed.

B 原因

(7) It is economic, convenient, safe, save time to go swimming in the school swimming pool. Only NT$1200 every semester.

(8) I have my best friend as my company.

(9) We learn from each other.

(10) We can ask the coach to teach us advanced skills.

(11) I can see my idol, Julia.（我想表達的是「女神」。我想嘗試用「校園女神」"campus goddess"）。

C 影響

(12) Swimming is good for releasing the stress, for losing weight, to keep in shape.

(13) Because of swimming, I do not stay up surfing the internet, playing video games.

(14) I am healthy.

(15) With my friend's encouragment, I feel a lot of expectations.

句子合併

(1)+(2) I enjoy a number of exercises and swimming is my favorite.（11 單詞；短句）

(3)+(4)+(5) I usually go swimming with my best friend, David, three nights a week in the school swimming pool.（18 單詞；中句；累計 29 單詞）

(6) To go swimming, *many equipments (equipment)* such as a pair of swimming trunks, a swimming cap, ear plugs, a towel are needed.（21 單詞；長句；累計 50 單詞）

(7) I like going swimming in the *scholl (school)* swimming pool because it is *economic (economical)*, convenient, safe, and *time-saving (economical)*.（17 單詞；中句；累計 67

單詞）

(8) +(9) And it is always fun to have my best friend, David, as my company; in addition, we can learn different strokes from each other.（24 單詞；中句；累計 91 單詞）

(10) It is even better that sometimes we can ask the coach to teach *our (us)* skills.（15 單詞；中句；累計 106 單詞）

(11) I *can not* deny that I hope to meet Julia, my idol, at the pool.（15 單詞；中句；累計 121 單詞）

(12) Swimming is good for releasing the stress, losing weight, and getting in shape.（13 單詞；短句；累計 134 單詞）

(13)+(14) Because of swimming, I am healthy and I stop staying up surfing the Internet and/or playing computer games.（18 單詞；中句；累計 152 單詞）

(15) What is more important is that with David's company and *encouragment (encouragement)*, I *feel my future optimistic (feel optimistic about my future)*.（16 單詞；中句；累計 168 單詞）

檢查修改

1. 發現有「懸擺修飾語」，(6)更改為 To go swimming, *I* need basic equipment such as swimming trunks, swimming caps, ear plugs, *and* towels.

2. (6)句的 equipment 不能用複數形。

3. (7)句的 school 拼寫錯了。economic 和 economical 搞混了，economical 好像也可以表示節約時間，因此決定不寫 time-saving。根據平行結構的詞序排列原則，將 economical, convenient, safe 改為 safe, convenient, and economical。〔請參考 10.2〕

4. (8)句的 as my 改為 for。

5. (10)句的 teach our skills 改為 teach us skills；仔細思考之後 teach 決定利用「類轉」better，當動詞用。〔請參考 10.7〕

6. (11)句的 can not 改成 cannot。hope 改成 desire。

7. (12)句 the stress 的 the 決定刪除。

8. (12)句的 releasing 改成 relieving。

9. (15)句的 encouragment 拼寫錯了。

10. 文章有點長，準備再做一些刪減。

準備交卷的 150 個單詞左右的文章如下：（刪除線或斜體字型代表修改）

I enjoy *a number of* exercises and swimming is my favorite. I usually go swimming with my best friend, David, three nights a week in ~~the school my~~ *my school's* swimming pool. To go swimming, I need some basic equipment such as *a pair of* swimming trunks, *a* swimming *caps*, ear plugs, and *a towels*.

I like going swimming in my school's swimming pool because it is safe, convenient, and economical. And it is always fun to have my best friend, David, as ~~my~~ for company; in addition, we can learn different strokes from each other. It is even better that sometimes we can ask the coach to better our skills. I cannot deny that I desire to meet Julia, my ~~idol~~ *campus goddess*, at the pool. Swimming is good for ~~releasing~~ relieving stress, losing weight, and getting in shape. Because of swimming, I am healthy and I have stopped staying up surfing the Internet and/or playing computer games. What is more important is that with David's company and encouragement, I feel optimistic about my future.

交卷前的修改

I enjoy a *variety* of exercises and swimming is my favorite. I usually go swimming with my best friend, David, three nights a week in my school's swimming pool. To go swimming, I need some basic equipment such as swimming trunks, swimming caps, ear plugs, and towels.

I like going swimming in my school's swimming pool because it is safe, convenient, and economical. And it is always fun to have David for company; in addition, we can learn different strokes from each other. It is even better that sometimes we can ask the coach to better our skills. I cannot deny that I *also* desire to meet Julia, my campus goddess, at the pool. Swimming is good for relieving stress, losing weight, and getting in shape. Because of swimming, I am healthy and I have stopped staying up surfing the Internet and/or playing computer games. What is more important is that with David's company and encouragement, I feel optimistic about my future.

修改後的文章

I enjoy a variety of exercises and swimming is my favorite. I usually go swimming with my best friend, David, three nights a week in my school's swimming pool. To go swimming, I need some basic equipment such as swimming trunks, swimming caps, ear plugs, and towels.

I like going swimming in my school's swimming pool because it is safe, convenient, and economical. And it is always fun to have David for company; in addition, we can learn different strokes from each other. It is even better that sometimes we can ask the coach to better our skills. I cannot deny that I also desire to meet Julia, my campus goddess, at the pool. Swimming is good for releasing stress, losing weight, and getting in shape. Because of swimming, I am *strong and healthy. And now* I have stopped staying up surfing the Internet and/or playing computer games. What is more important is that with David's company and encouragement, I feel optimistic about my future. 〔臨時加上 strong，同時把 because of ... 的長句切分成二個短句。〕

還有二分鐘的時間，再默念校對一遍。一切 OK？OK！停筆。

真的有心按表操課的話，要寫 150 個單詞的文章，好像沒有想像中的難啊！

第三節　三段：導論+討論+結論

現在，讓我們回到本章的主題：「內容」。一般來說，如果沒有規定寫幾段的話，我們建議將一篇文章分成三個部分：導論、討論、結論。

導論等於「起」，討論等於「承」，結論等於「合」。導論就是開場白，通常是用一至三個句子切入第一段的主題。以下分成六大主題，並舉例說明如何「起」一篇文章。

1. 游泳對身心有益，是一個很好的運動。
2. 酒駕必須全面遏阻，因為酒駕肇禍奪去太多無辜又寶貴的生命，很多家庭也因而破碎。
3. 我們必須節能減碳，地球暖化的速度以及所造成的危害程度已經不允許我們等閒視之，如果地球不能住了，我們還能去哪裡。
4. 販賣有毒的食物跟蓄意殺人沒有兩樣，事實上等於謀殺，必須將販賣有毒食物的個人與/或公司繩之以法，處以重刑。
5. 校園霸凌沒有容忍的餘地，今天會在校園霸凌自己的同學，明天就會霸凌自己的同事，後天就會作奸犯科，傷害他人。
6. 電視與/或網路節目必須分級，因為社會形態的改變，很多未成年人很容易被有些節目裡面的性和暴力的成分影響。

第四節　二段：導論+討論與結論

　　除非有明確的規定，為了考試，我們建議將第二部分「討論」和第三部分「結論」合成一段，也就是第二段。別忘了，最近十年的指考只要求寫二段。第二段比第一段好寫，因為主題不外乎下一節的內容。

第五節　主題

1. 解釋說明（學測 97，93，92：比率 **3/10**），（指考 101，100，99，98，97，96，94，93，91：比率 **9/10**）
2. 經驗（指考 101，100，99，98，97，96，95，93，92：比率 **9/10**）
3. 故事、情節發展（學測 100，99，96，95，94，93：比率 **6/10**）
4. 提出具體的做法（學測 101，98，97：比率 3/10）；（指考 100，98，94，91：比率 **4/10**）
5. 舉例（學測 92，91：比率 **2/10**）；（指考 99：比率 **1/10**）
6. 因果（學測 98，94：比率 **2/10**）；（指考 101：比率 **1/10**）〔嚴格來說，「因果」可以併入「解釋說明」。〕
7. 影響啟示（指考 95：比率 **1/10**）等。

　　如果時間有限，請問聰明的您，會依序先練習進而學會哪一類型的主題呢？

　　底下，我們來討論如何寫，而且如何寫好二段的培訓。別忘了練習畫樹狀圖，每一個小框框幾乎等於一個句子；一個句子大約是 10~15 個單詞。

一、解釋說明

　　竅門：所論述的解釋要簡要明白，讓讀者首肯，要通俗、有說服力。

　　主題：爬山既是一種有益健康的休閒活動也是一種很好的團體運動。爬山稱得上是一種專業運動，因為要爬得安全、要爬得享受，需要豐富的經驗、專門的知識與強壯的體力。爬山讓

我們接觸大自然。爬山讓我們培養團隊精神，讓我們增進跟山友的默契，讓我們認識山嶽的美麗與生態。

詞彙

有益健康	be good for one's health
豐富的經驗	abundant experience
專門的知識	expertise, expert knowledge, special knowledge
強壯的體力	athletic ability, physically strong
接觸	get in touch with
曬太陽	be kissed/be bathed/to bask in sunshine
詳盡的規劃	detailed plan
耐力	stamina, endurance
團隊精神	teamwork
默契	coordination
生態	ecology

提醒：我們的基本原則是只用有把握的單詞和片語。不會的單詞或片語就不要勉強自己。我們可以改用別的單詞或片語代替，例如「豐富」就改用 "rich, a lot of, a great deal of"；「專門的」就改用 "professional"；「曬太陽」就改用 "enjoy sunshine, enjoy myself in the sun"；「默契」就改用 "help each other smoothly and successfully" 等。另外，文章不需要寫太長，又不會加分，要學會捨得削減，寫大約 150 個單詞，也就是 10 個句子左右就可以喊卡了。底下各篇的造句，以此類推。

造句

1. 大家都知道爬山對身體好。

   Everyone knows that mountain climbing is good for our health.

2. 爬山，又名登山，是一種健康的個人休閒活動，也是一種很好的團體運動。

   Mountain climbing or mountaineering is a healthy personal hobby and it is a good group activity.

3. 爬山稱得上是一種戶外運動，因為要爬得安全，要爬得享受，需要豐富的經驗、專門的知識與強壯的體力。

Mountain climbing is an outdoor sport because if we want to maintain safety and enjoyment, we need abundant experience, expert knowledge, and athletic ability.

4. 爬山讓我們接觸大自然。

It enables us to get in touch with nature.

5. 爬山讓我們呼吸新鮮的空氣、沐浴太陽、享受流汗。

It lets us breathe fresh air, be bathed in sunshine, and enjoy sweating.

6. 爬山讓我們練習詳盡的規劃、鍛鍊體力和耐力。

It lets us plan a detailed plan and it strengthens our strength and stamina.

7. 爬山讓我們培養團隊精神，讓我們增進跟山友的默契，讓我們認識山嶽的美麗與生態。

It develops teamwork among us mountaineers; it improves our coordination; it introduces us to the beauty and the ecology of mountains.

8. 爬山好，爬山真好。

Mountain climbing is cool and nothing is cooler.

結合成二段式短文

I Love Mountain Climbing

Generally speaking, everyone knows that mountain climbing is good for our health. As far as I am concerned, mountain climbing is not only a healthy personal hobby but also a good group activity. In essence, mountain climbing is a professional sport because if we want to maintain safety and enjoyment, we need abundant experience, expert knowledge, and athletic ability.

Mountain climbing enables us to get in touch with nature, letting us breathe fresh air, be bathed in sunshine, and enjoy sweating. In addition, it lets us plan a detailed plan and it strengthens our strength and stamina. It develops teamwork among us mountaineers; it improves our coordination; it introduces us to the beauty and the ecology of mountains. Mountain climbing is cool and nothing is cooler.

主題：酒駕常釀成車禍，車禍常導致無辜人員的傷亡。政府必須採取有效措施遏阻酒駕。

詞彙

也就是說 / 易言之	put differently, in other words

平均	on average
快速攀升	rocket, suddenly increase a lot
採取（有效）措施	take (effective) measures
遏阻酒駕	ban/stop drunk driving
廣告	commercial, advertisement
塑造	create
高尚的	noble
社交行為	social activity
規定	rule, prescribe, stipulate
裝設	be equipped with
自動酒測器	automatic alcohol testing instrument, breathalyzer, a device/instrument for testing alcohol content〔利用 for testing alcohol content「後位修飾」device, instrument 儀器〕
規定的含量	prescribed level
重傷	severe injury
法辦	be brought to justice, be punished by law
吊銷	revoke, suspend
求處重刑	be severely punished by law
悲劇	tragedy
天災	natural calamity/disaster
人禍	man-made disaster
全力	with all our efforts

造句

1. 根據昨天的電視報導，台灣一年因車禍喪命的有二千多人。

   According to yesterday's TV news report, in Taiwan more than 2000 people were killed in car accidents a year.

2. 其中因酒駕而導致死亡的有 439 人。

   Among them, 439 people were killed in accidents due to drunk driving.

3. 也就是說，平均每天就有 1.2 人死於因為酒駕所釀成的車禍。

Put differently, on average 1.2 people were killed per day because of accidents resulting from drunk driving.

4. 這個數字太恐怖了，而且這個數字每一年都在快速攀升。

   This figure is terrifying and it skyrockets every year.

5. 政府必須採取有效措施遏阻酒駕。

   The authorities concerned must take effective measures to stop drunk driving.

6. 建議如下：〔請參考 9.7.4〕

   Some of my suggestions are as follows:

7. 規範酒類廣告的時間和方式。

   We have to standardize the time and the styles for commercials for alcoholic drinks.

8. 很多酒類廣告將喝酒塑造成高尚的社交行為，因此許多喝酒的人認為自己是「上等人」。

   Many such commercials portray drinking as a noble social activity; as a result, many drinkers regard themselves as "classy".

9. 規定所有汽車必須裝設「自動酒測器」，它是一種呼吸酒精值測試儀器。駕駛者酒測值一旦超過標準，汽車無法啟動。

   The traffic rules stipulate that every car must be equipped with an "automatic breathalyzer," a breath alcohol testing instrument. If a driver has a blood alcohol content (BAC) level that is higher than the prescribed level, the car will not start.

10. 如因酒駕造成車禍而導致他人重傷或死亡，駕駛者一律法辦。

    If the accidents resulting from drunk driving lead to severe injuries or deaths, the drivers are brought to justice.

11. 除吊銷駕照之外，還要具體求處重刑。

    Their driver's licenses will be revoked and they will be severely punished by law.

12. 酒駕釀成的悲劇不是天災，不是意外。酒駕事故是人禍，是必須全力遏阻的人禍。

    Tragedies resulting from drunk driving are neither natural calamities nor accidents. They are man-made disasters which must be banned with all our efforts.

    如果字數太多，我們必須考慮刪除一些相對來講比較不重要的句子。

結合成二段式短文

No More Drunk Driving

Drunk drivers are murderers on highways. According to yesterday's TV news report, more than 2000 people were killed in car accidents a year. Among them, 439 people were killed in accidents due to drunk driving. Put differently, on average 1.2 people were killed per day because of accidents resulting from drunk driving. This figure is terrifying and it skyrockets every year. The authorities concerned must take effective measures to stop drunk driving. Some of my suggestions are as follows:

First, we have to standardize the time and the styles for commercials for alcoholic drinks. Many such commercials portray drinking as a noble activity; as a result, many drinkers regard themselves as "classy." Second, we need to make traffic rules which stipulate that every car must be equipped with an "automatic breathalyzer," a breath alcohol testing instrument. If a driver has a BAC (blood alcohol content) level that is higher than the prescribed level, the car will not start. Third, if the accidents resulting from drunk driving lead to severe injuries or deaths, the drivers are brought to justice. Their driver's licenses will be revoked and they will be severely punished by law. Tragedies resulting from drunk driving are neither natural calamities nor accidents. They are man-made disasters which must be banned with all our efforts.

二、經驗

竅門：你的描述必須逼真又尋常，好像隨時會發生在讀者身上一樣。另外一個技巧就是讓人覺得幽默、覺得不可思議。

主題：不會講日語卻在銀座迷了路。

詞彙

自助旅行	go backpacking
地鐵	subway
迷住	be charmed by
不知不覺地	unconsciously, before I know it
迷路	get lost
真夠倒楣的！	Just my luck!
沒電	out of power

偶遇	come across
硬著頭皮	force oneself to
肢體語言	body language
外事警察	Foreign Affairs Police Officers
警察局	the police station
筆錄	statement
擠滿了	be jammed/crowded/packed with
SNG 採訪車	SNG vans

造句

1. 去年夏天我和我的未婚夫去日本自助旅行。

   I went backpacking in Japan with my fiancé last summer.

2. 第一天的下午，我獨自一人搭地鐵從東京去銀座。

   On the first afternoon, I took the subway by myself from Tokyo to Ginza.

3. 我未婚夫生病了。

   My fiancé was not feeling well.

4. 一下地鐵，我被銀座的景色給迷住了。

   I was completely charmed by everything in Ginza as soon as I got off the subway.

5. 不知不覺地發現自己迷路了。

   I got lost before I knew it.

6. 真夠倒楣的！我的手機電池沒電。

   Just my luck! The battery of my cell phone was out of power.

7. 我陷入困境因為我把飯店的名字和電話號碼儲存在手機裡面。

   I was stuck since I had stored the information of the hotel in my cell phone.

8. 我恨不得能碰到警察。

   I wished I would come across a police officer.

9. 我硬著頭皮用肢體語言比手畫腳，請附近 Seven 裡面的老外打電話向外事警察求助。

   I forced myself to use body language to communicate with a foreigner in the nearby 7-Eleven, trying to ask him to make a phone call to the Foreign Affairs Police Officers for help.

10. 大約 20 分鐘左右，二名外事警察到了，接我到派出所。

    In about 20 minutes, two police officers arrived and they drove me to the police station.

11. 做完筆錄之後，外事警察用警車送我回飯店。

    Having finished the statement, the police officers drove a police car to take me back to the hotel.

12. 天哪！飯店門口擠滿了電視記者，還有幾輛 SNG 採訪車。

    My goodness! The gate of the hotel was jammed with reporters and there were SNG vans.

13. 我未婚夫等了八個小時。

    My fiancé waited for eight hours.

14. 不見我回飯店，他很擔心，所以請飯店櫃檯向警方通報「人口失蹤」。

    As I had not returned to the hotel, he was so worried that he asked the front desk to file a "missing persons" notice with the police.

15. 我只想拜託外事警察用警車載我回警局。

    I just wanted the police officers to take me back to the police station.

結合成二段式短文

A Moment of Embarrassment

My fiancé and I are high school teachers and we have a common hobby--backpacking. I went backpacking in Japan with my fiancé last summer. On the first afternoon, because my fiancé was not feeling well, I took the subway by myself from Tokyo to Ginza. I was completely charmed by everything in Ginza as soon as I got off the subway. Suddenly, I got lost before I knew it. Just my luck! The battery of my cell phone was out of power. I was stuck since I had stored the information of the hotel in my cell phone.

I wished I could come across a police officer. I forced myself to use body language to communicate with a foreigner in the nearby 7-Eleven, trying to ask him to make a phone call to the Foreign Affairs Police Officers for help. In about 20 minutes, two police officers arrived and they drove me to the police station. Hoving finished the paperwork, the police officers drove a police car to take me back to the hotel. My goodness! The gate of the hotel was jammed with reporters and there were SNG vans. My fiancé waited for eight hours. Not seeing me returning to the hotel, he was so worried that he asked the front desk to file a "missing persons" notice with the police.

I was so embarrassed that I just wanted the police officers to take me back to the police station.

主題: 尷尬

竅門: 讓人感同身受的類似經驗; 讓人感到好笑或幽默的經驗。

詞彙

沈默	silence
耐心	patience
尷尬	be embarrassed, embarrassment
補習班	cram school, bushiban
加州洛杉磯	Los Angeles, California
碰到	come across
賣弄	show off
抓住機會	seize a chance
自我介紹	introduce myself
急著要	could not wait to
留	wear, have
鬍鬚	beard
想當然地認為	assume that, take ... for granted
把……誤認為	mistake ... for
犯錯	make a mistake
愚蠢的	foolish, stupid
歇斯底里地	hysterically
差點	nearly
昏倒	faint

造句

1. 我在一家外語補習班補英語, 補了有六個星期。

   I have been learning English in a local cram school for six weeks.

2. Daphne 老師是從加州洛杉磯來的美國人。

   My teacher, Daphne, is an American from Los Angeles, California.

3. 上個星期天早上我在麥當勞碰到我的老師。

Last Sunday, I came across Daphne in the McDonald's.

4. 我想賣弄我的英語。

I wanted to show off my English.

5. 不等老師開口,我就急著自我介紹。

Before Daphne could say anything, I hurried to introduce myself.

6. 我沒讓老師有機會講話,又急著要認識老師身邊的男士。

Daphne did not have a chance to talk and I could not wait to meet the man sitting next to Daphne.

7. 那位男士留著鬍鬚。

The man had a beard.

8. 我想當然地認為他大約三十幾歲,一定是老師的老公。

I took it for granted that he must be in his 30s and that he was my teacher's husband.

9. 我犯了個愚蠢的錯誤,我居然把老師的兒子當成是老師的丈夫。

I made a foolish mistake: I mistook Daphne's son for her husband.

10. 老師和她「丈夫」笑歪了。我差點昏倒。

My teacher and her "husband" were laughing hysterically and I nearly fainted in embarrassment.

結合成二段式短文

An Awkward Silence

If silence is golden, then patience is silver. I am a high school student and I have been learning English in a local cram school for six weeks. My teacher, Daphne, is an American from Los Angeles, California. Last Sunday, I came across Daphne in the McDonald's in downtown Tainan. I was anxious to show off my English so I seized every possible chance.

Before Daphne could say anything, I hurried to introduce myself. Daphne did not have a chance to talk and I could not wait to meet the man sitting next to Daphne. The man had a beard. I took it for granted that he must be in his 30s and that he was my teacher's husband. I said: "Hi. I know you are Daphne's husband. My name is Dakang. Nice to meet you." My teacher and "her husband" were laughing hysterically and I nearly fainted in embarrassment. I realized that I had made a foolish mistake: I mistook Daphne's son for her husband.

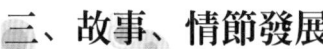

三、故事、情節發展

竅門：講故事要合乎邏輯，要按照時間、情節的順序發展。必要的時候，要誇張，要讓讀者熱淚盈眶或是開懷大笑或是如釋重負。

主題：（第一、第二和第三幅圖畫的情節。）一個下著大雨的冬天清晨，我才下公車，看到一位老婆婆一個人氣喘吁吁地在推著腳踏車，車上堆滿了回收物。我跟同學小真冒著雨幫助老婆婆，把回收物推到了回收廠，老婆婆拿到 100 元，非常高興，我們也替她高興，這時候，小真的手機響了，是班長麗心打來的，老師在問我們怎麼沒到學校參加英語演講比賽，老師很生氣……。

詞彙

大雨	heavy rain
清晨	early morning
下公車	get off the bus
氣喘吁吁	pant
推著腳踏車	push the bicycle
堆滿了	be loaded with
回收物	recyclable materials
堆積如山	mountains of
回收廠	recycling plant
英語演講比賽	English speech contest

情節發展：聽完電話，我們心情很緊張，擔心會被老師處分。於是趕緊跟老婆婆說再見。我們匆匆忙忙搭計程車趕到學校。我們全身濕透地衝進教室，誠實地跟老師說明原委。老師不但沒有責備我們，還當全班同學的面讚揚我和小真。雖然全身又濕又冷，我的心卻是熱哄哄的。

詞彙

老婆婆	elderly woman
趕緊，匆匆忙忙	in a hurry, rush
搭計程車	to take a taxi
歇斯底里地	hysterically
加快速度	speed up
自願做	volunteer
迫切地	urgently
全身濕透地	be soaked to the skin
衝	dash
責備	blame
令你們感到驚訝	much to your surprise
讚揚	praise

1. 我和小真趕緊跟老婆婆說再見。

   Xiaozhen and I said good-bye to the elderly woman in a hurry.

2. 我們匆匆忙忙搭計程車趕到學校。

   We rushed to take a taxi to school.

3. 我們歇斯底里地一直叫司機加快速度。

   We hysterically kept ordering the driver to speed up.

4. 我們自告奮勇幫助別人。

   We volurteered to help people.

5. 現在我們迫切需要別人幫助。

   Now we urgently need someone to help us.

6. 我們心裡擔心會被老師處分。

   We were worried that we might be punished by the teacher.

7. 我們全身濕透地衝進教室。

   Soaked to the skin, we dashed into the classroom.

8. 我們誠實地跟老師說明原委。

   We told the whole story to the teacher honestly.

9. 老師沒有責備我們。

   The teacher did not blame us.

10. 令我們感到驚訝的是，老師還當全班同學的面讚揚我和小真。

    Much to our surprise, the teacher praised us in front of the class.

11. 雖然全身又濕又冷，我的心卻是熱哄哄的。

    Although I was wet and cold, I felt warm and encouraged.

12. 世界真奇妙啊！

    What a wonderful world!

結合成二段式短文

To Be or Not to Be

... Checking our watches, Xiaozhen and I said good-bye to the elderly woman in a hurry. We were so late for school. After we had double-checked the cash in our wallets, we rushed to take a taxi to school. We hysterically kept ordering the driver to speed up. We were worried that we might be punished by the teacher. It was the end of the world for us, who volunteered to help people and who now urgently needed someone to help us.

Soaked to the skin, we dashed into the classroom. We told the whole story to the teacher honestly. The teacher did not blame us because the elderly woman had asked her neighbor to call our school to thank us. Much to our surprise, the teacher praised us in front of the class. Although I was wet and cold, I felt warm and encouraged. What a wonderful world!

主題：（第一、第二和第三幅圖畫的情節。）跟往常一樣，你帶著你的寵物狗 Lady 到你們家附近的公園散步。公園裡有很多人在散步、玩耍，也有幾個人在遛狗。正當你跟 Lady 準備回家的時候，有一位穿著制服的中年婦女，走到你面前，指責你沒有清理你的寵物狗的排泄物。她是環保署的公園稽查員，她不聽你的任何解釋，堅持給你一張 1200 元的罰單。......

詞彙

寵物狗	pet dog
玩耍	have fun
遛狗	walk one's pet dog
穿著制服	wearing a uniform
中年婦女	middle-aged woman

指責你	blame you for ...
清理	clean up
排泄物	waste matter, dog's excrement
環保署	Environmental Protection Administration
公園稽查員	Park Patrol Officer
罰單	ticket
罰鍰	fine

情節發展：請參考造句。

詞彙

鎮靜地	calmly
請求	request
閉路電視	closed circuit television (CCTV)
監視器	surveillance camera
查證	verify
無辜	innocence
氣呼呼的	very angry, with a long face
一五一十地／詳細地	in detail
同情	sympathize with
被冤枉	be made a scapegoat, an unfair treatment
抱著	hold ... in one's arms
道歉	apologize
強調	emphasize
啼笑皆非	between tears and laughter

造句

1. 雖然我很生氣，但是我很鎮靜地請求那位公園稽查員（答應我將事發地點旁邊的監視器錄下來的錄影帶帶回去）查證，因為我是無辜的。

Although I was very angry, I calmly requested the park patrol officer to verify my innocence.

2. 她答應了。

She promised to do so.

3. 我們互相記下了對方的電話號碼。

We wrote down each other's phone number.

4. 回到家後，我媽看到我氣呼呼的，就問我發生了什麼事。

Seeing me come home with a long face, my mother asked me what had happened to me.

5. 我一五一十地告訴我媽事情的經過。

I told my mom everything in detail.

6. 我媽知道我被冤枉了，十分同情我的遭遇。

She sympathized with me because of my unfair treatment.

7. 我回到房間，抱著 Lady 哭了很久，哭到睡著了。

I went to my room, held Lady in my arms, and cried. I fell asleep with tears in my eyes.

8. 第二天，我媽叫醒我，說有我的電話。

The next morning, my mom woke me up. There was a phone call for me.

9. 是那位公園稽查員打來的，她等不及要跟我道歉。

It was from the park patrol officer, who could not wait to apologize.

10. 她昨晚仔細地看了相關的錄影帶，Lady 真的被冤枉了。她對我很抱歉。她一再強調我不用繳罰款。

Last night, she carefully watched the tapes in question. Lady had been made a scapegoat. She was so very sorry for me. And she kept emphasizing that I did not need to pay the fine.

11. 我拿著電話，又想哭，又想笑。謝天謝地！

With the phone in my hand, I was lost between tears and laughter. Thank goodness!

結合成二段式短文

Fair Defense or Unfair Offense

... Although I was very angry, I calmly requested the park patrol officer to verify my innocence. She promised to do so. We wrote down each other's phone number.

Seeing me come home with a long face, my mother asked me what had happened to me. I told my mom everything in detail. She deeply sympathized with me for my unfair treatment.

I went to my room, held Lady in my arms, and cried. I fell asleep with tears in my eyes. The next morning, my mom woke me up. There was a phone call for me. It was from the park patrol officer, who could not wait to apologize. Last night, she carefully watched the tapes in question. Lady had been made a scapegoat. She was so very sorry for me. And she kept emphasizing that I did not need to pay the fine. With the phone in my hand, I was lost between tears and laughter. Thank goodness!

四、提出具體做法

竅門：做法就是解決之道。要讓讀者認同的解決之道必須明確、具體、可行，切記打高空、打空炮彈。

主題：提高英文寫作能力與好友互相鼓勵如何精進英文寫作能力，期盼學測指考英文作文能夠考高分。

詞彙

高二學生	second-year students in high school
英文程度	English proficiency, command of English
文法還不錯	good at English grammar
學年	academic year
模擬考	practice test
非選擇題部分	non-multiple choice section
決心	be determined to
制訂	work out
影印	photocopy
社論	editorial
朗讀	read aloud
定義	definition
發音	pronunciation
衍生詞	derivative

用法	usage
搭配	collocation
例句	sample sentence
能背誦	by heart
靈活地	flexibly
句構	sentence structure
批改	grade
校對	proofread
有恆	persevere in doing something

造句

1. 我和我的好友 David 是國立高中的高二學生。

 My best friend, David, and I are in the second year of a national high school.

2. 我們的英文程度一般，基本文法還不錯。

 Our English proficiency is no better than average. We are good at English grammar.

3. 學校上星期，高二下最後一個星期，舉行了一次模擬考。

 Last week, the last week of the academic year, a practice exam was held by our school.

4. 我們二個人英文科非選擇題的部分，成績都不理想。我們不高興。

 Neither of us did well in the non-multiple choice section. And we were not happy.

5. 請教學校英文老師後，我們決心要提升英文作文能力。

 After consulting with our English teacher, we are determined to better our proficiency in English Composition.

6. 我們制訂了一套計畫。

 We have worked out a plan.

 (1) 每個星期的一、三、五午休時間或放學後，到圖書館影印當天某某英文報的社論，二個人輪流朗讀。

 During the lunch break or after school on Mondays, Wednesdays, and Fridays, we will go to the school library, photocopy the editorial of the day in the AAA English newspaper, and read the article aloud.

 (2) 在每篇社論中挑選 20 個生字與／或片語。

 We are supposed to select 20 new words and/or phrases used in the article.

(3) 在下一次到圖書館之前，也就是每個星期的二、四、週末，要先用英英詞典查好這
20 個生字的定義、發音、衍生詞、用法、搭配、例句等。

The day before our next trip to the library, that is Tuesdays, Thursdays, and weekends, we are responsible for looking up definitions, pronunciations, derivatives, usages, collocations, sample sentences, and the like.

(4) 從社論選一個喜歡的例句，把這個例句背起來。

We select from the editorial one sample sentence which we like and try to learn it by heart.

(5) 要利用每一個生字造一個至少 10 個單詞長的句子。

For each new word, we have to use it to make a sentence of no fewer than 10 words.

(6) 將造好的 20 個英文句子交給英文老師批改。

We then ask our English teacher to grade the 20 sentences.

(7) 每個星期日，以星期三的社論或是請老師出題，寫一篇與社論相同或相似的主題的
英文作文。

Every Sunday, we are supposed to write an essay on the topic which is given by our teacher or which is the same as or similar to that of the Wednesday's editorial.

(8) 文章至少 120 個單詞。

Our essay must be no fewer than 120 words.

(9) 文章至少要用到這個星期學會的 60 個生字裡面的五個。

In our essay, we need to use at least five of the 60 new words we have learned this week.

(10) 文章至少要靈活運用到這個星期學會的 60 個句子結構裡面的三個。

In our essay, we need to use flexibly at least three of the 60 sentence structures we have learned this week.

(11) 將寫好的文章先自行檢查校對後再交給英文老師批改。

Before we ask our English teacher to grade the essay for us, we need to proofread it first.

(12) 我們有信心如果持之以恆，明年的學測指考英文作文一定考高分。

We are confident that this plan will work if we persevere in doing it. We are so positive that we shall get good grades in the coming entrance exams.

結合成二段式短文

A Simple Formula for Better English

My best friend and I are in the second year of a national high school. Our English proficiency is no better than average. We are good at English grammar. Last week, the last week of the academic year, a practice exam was held by our school.

Neither of us did well in the non-multiple choice section. And we were not happy. After consulting with our English teacher, we are determined to better our proficiency in English Composition. We have worked out a plan as follows:

1. During the lunch break or after school on Mondays, Wednesdays, and Fridays, we will go to the school library, photocopy the editorial of the day in the AAA English newspaper, and read the article aloud.
2. We are supposed to select 20 new words and/or phrases used in the article.
3. The day before our next trip to the library, that is Tuesdays, Thursdays, and weekends, we are responsible for looking up definitions, pronunciations, derivatives, usages, collocations, sample sentences, and the like.
4. We select from the editorial one sample sentence which we like and try to learn it by heart.
5. For every new word, we have to use it to make a sentence of no fewer than 10 words.
6. We then ask our English teacher to grade the 20 sentences.
7. Every Sunday, we are supposed to write an essay on the topic which is given by our teacher or which is the same as or similar to that of the Wednesday's editorial.
8. Our essay must be no fewer than 120 words.
9. In our essay, we need to use at least five of the 60 new words we have learned this week.
10. In our essay, we need to use at least three of the 60 sentence structures we have learned this week.
11. Before we ask our English teacher to grade the essay for us, we need to proofread it first.
12. We are confident that this plan will work if we persevere in doing it. We are so positive that we shall get good grades in the coming entrance exams.

主題：減肥

竅門：身材苗條體態輕盈是王道，二十一世紀不是肥仔胖妹的世紀。減肥只憑決心是不夠的，要有可行的方法，討論如下。

詞彙

驕傲地	proudly, with pride
說謊	tell a lie
嫉妒	be jealous of
苗條	have a slim figure
羞愧	be ashamed of
決心	be determined to
減肥	to lose weight
要求	requirement
節食	be on a diet
規定飲食	a prescribed diet
公尺	meter
熬夜	stay up
營養師	dietitian
量身訂做	custom-made
埋頭於/專注於	bury oneself in
上網	surf the Internet
打電玩	play video games
空格	box
一排	row
笑臉貼紙	smiley sticker
處罰	penalty, punish
六分之一	one-sixth
窈窕淑女	a fair and graceful lady
夢想實現	a dream come true
公分	centimeter
公斤	kilogram

造句

1. 我是高中生。

　　I am a high school student.

2. 我可以驕傲地告訴別人我的真實年齡，可是談到體重，我不得不說謊，以少報多。

I can always proudly tell people my real age, but when it comes to my weight, I have to lie to them, giving false figures.

3. 我好嫉妒班上的其他同學，個個身材苗條。

I am very jealous of my classmates who have slim figures.

4. 我的體重讓我羞愧，讓我失去信心，讓我不想去學校。

I am ashamed of being overweight as it makes me lose confidence so I feel unwilling to go to school.

5. 我決心減肥。

I am determined to lose weight.

6. 我的減肥方法是六個要求：只喝水、只吃規定飲食、天黑後不吃東西、每天慢跑 3000 公尺、不熬夜、為期 12 個月。

My plan to lose weight has six requirements: Drink only water, eat only the prescribed diet, eat nothing after sunset, jog 3000 meters every day, do not stay up, and make sure the plan lasts 12 months.

(1) 每天喝 2000cc 的水，不碰其他飲料。

I drink 2000cc of water per day; I drink no other drinks.

(2) 請營養師幫我量身設計一套規定飲食。

I have asked a dietitian to design a custom-made diet for me.

(3) 天黑後不吃東西，想辦法把自己埋頭於練習英文寫作。

I eat nothing after sunset, burying myself in learning English writing.

(4) 每天傍晚跟麻吉骨感美女小莉到公園慢跑 3000 公尺。

Every evening, my close friend Bony Lily and I go for a 3000-meter jog in the park.

(5) 每天晚上 11:30 準時就寢，絕不熬夜上網、打電玩。

I go to bed at 11:30 p.m. sharp, never staying up surfing the Internet nor playing video games.

(6) 畫一張大大的日曆，有 365 個空格，有 53 排，每排 7 個空格，每成功一天就在空格上貼上一個笑臉貼紙鼓勵自己。

I have made a huge calendar made of 365 boxes; these boxes are divided into 53 rows, each of which has seven boxes. Every successful day wins a smiley sticker, which is to be stuck in the designated box.

(7) 每個星期檢查空格，絕不容許過去的日子有任何空格。如果有，一個空格就罰自己週末加跑 3000 公尺。

I make a weekly check, allowing no empty boxes. If there are empty boxes, I will jog 3000 meters for each on the weekend.

(8) 14 個月過去了，你知道我「瘦了」幾公斤嗎?

Fourteen months have passed and can you guess how many kilograms I "have lost"?

(9) 我很滿意，我比起 14 個月前的體重少了六分之一。

I am very satisfied because I have lost one-sixth of the weight I was fourteen months ago.

(10) 我還要繼續努力，我要成為窈窕淑女的夢一定會實現。

I will persevere in carrying out my project to realize my dream--to become a fair and graceful lady.

(11) 你相信嗎? 我老爸，165 公分，79 公斤，比我瘦，從上個月也跟我們一起慢跑減肥了喔!

Believe it or not, my father, who is 165 centimeters, 79 kilograms, and thinner than I am, has joined us in the jogging project since last month.

結合成二段式短文

Call Me Slim and Sexy

(I am a high school student. I can always proudly tell people my real age, but when it comes to my weight, I have to lie to them, giving false figures. I am very jealous of my classmates who have slim figures. I am ashamed of being overweight as it makes me lose confidence so I feel unwilling to go to school. And, I am determined to lose weight.)

My plan to lose weight has six requirements: Drink only water, eat only the prescribed diet, eat nothing after sunset, jog 3000 meters every day, do not stay up, and make sure the plan lasts 12 months.

1. I drink 2000cc of water per day; I drink no other drinks.
2. I have asked a dietitian to design a diet for me.
3. I eat nothing after sunset, burying myself in learning English writing.
4. Every evening, my close friend Bony Lily and I go for a 3000-meter jog in the park.
5. I go to bed at 11:30 pm sharp, never staying up surfing the Internet nor playing video games.
6. I have made a huge calendar made of 365 boxes; these boxes are divided into 53 rows, each of which has seven boxes. Every successful day wins a smiley sticker, which is to be stuck in the designated box.

7. I make a weekly check, allowing no empty boxes. If there are empty boxes, I will jog 3000 meters for each on the weekend.

8. Fourteen months have passed and can you guess how many kilograms I have lost?

9. I am very satisfied because I have lost one-sixth of the weight I was fourteen months ago.

10. I will persevere in carrying out my project to realize my dream--to become a fair and graceful lady.

11. Believe it or not, my father, who is 165 centimeters, 79 kilograms, and thinner than I am, has joined us in the jogging project since last month.

I have never been more proud of myself.

五、舉例

竅門：比較空洞抽象的主題往往需要具體明確的例子來支撐。最有信服力的例子通常是身邊的人物，日常的生活作息，男女老幼耳熟能詳的點點滴滴。簡單一句話，舉例越通俗越能讓讀者感同身受。

主題：闡釋閱讀的重要性。以你或他人的經驗為例，敘述閱讀所帶來的好處。

詞彙

「活到老，學到老」	"It's never too late to learn."
對聯	couplet
高貴	noble
鼓勵的	inspiring
佃農	tenant farmer
大蒜	garlic
家貧如洗	as poor as a church mouse, very poor, extremely poor
寒暄	exchange a few words in greeting
白話文	vernacular Chinese
天書	double Dutch
奇跡似地	magically, miraculously

社區	community
長青大學	college for senior citizens
中國文學	Chinese literature
仁義	benevolence and virtue

造句

1. 很多人都贊同「活到老，學到老」。

   Many people agree that it is never too late to learn.

2. 我曾經在台中火車站附近的一家書店看到門口的對聯寫著：「貧者因書而富，富者因書而貴」。

   On the doors of a bookstore near Taichung Railway Station I once saw a couplet which read "With books, the poor become rich and the rich, noble."

3. 這二句話講得很好，很鼓勵人。

   I like the couplet. The words are so inspiring.

4. 我爺爺年輕時是佃農，在鄉下種大蒜。

   When he was young, my grandfather was a tenant farmer, growing garlic in the country.

5. 我爺爺家貧如洗，沒有念書的機會。

   My grandfather was as poor as a church mouse. It was impossible for him to go to school.

6. 有一天，我爺爺送我爸去學校的時候，校長跟我爺爺寒暄了幾句。

   One day, my grandfather accompanied my father to his school. The principal and my grandfather exchanged a few words in greeting.

7. 臨走前，校長送我爺爺一本白話文版的《論語》。

   Before they said goodbye to each other, the principal gave him a copy of The Analects of Confucius translated into vernacular Chinese.

8. 我爺爺告訴我說校長送了他一本天書。

   My grandfather told me that the principal had given him a double Dutch.

9. 我爺爺不認輸，一定要讀完、讀懂這本天書。

   My grandfather refused to give up; he was determined to finish reading The Analects of Confucius.

10. 從此，我爺爺就經常到圖書館自修。

    Thereafter, my grandfather would go to the library to self-study.

11. 藉著詞典以及圖書管理員的幫助，我爺爺奇跡似地讀完也讀懂了天書。

With the help of dictionaries and assistance of the librarians, my grandfather miraculously completed reading and figured out this double Dutch.

12. 從此，我爺爺有空就借書回家閱讀，有時候也會要我陪他去書店買書。

Ever since then, my grandfather has borrowed books from the library and sometimes he would ask me to accompany him to buy books.

13. 閱讀成為我爺爺生活中重要的一部分。

Reading has become an important part in his life.

14. 我爺爺現在是社區長青大學的老師。他教「中國文學」。

My grandfather is now a teacher in the community college for senior citizens. He teaches Chinese Literature.

15. 我爺爺常常帶著微笑跟我說：「乖孫子，我雖不富有，但是我一點都不覺得窮，因為我的書櫃擺滿了好書，我的心充滿了仁義。」

With a gentle smile on his face, he often enjoys telling me: "My beloved grandson, I am not rich, but I never regard myself as poor at all because my bookcases are filled with good books and my heart is filled with kindness and virtue."

結合成二段式短文

Where There Is a Will, There Is a Way

Many people agree that it is never too late to learn and my grandfather is no exception. On the doors of a bookstore near Taichung Railway Station I once saw a couplet which read "With books, the poor become rich and the rich, noble." I like the couplet. The words are so inspiring.

When he was young, my grandfather was a tenant farmer, growing garlic in the country. My grandfather was as poor as a church mouse. It was impossible for him to go to school. One day, my grandfather accompanied my father to his school. The principal and my grandfather exchanged a few words in greeting. Before they said goodbye to each other, the principal gave him a copy of The Analects of Confucius translated into vernacular Chinese. My grandfather told me that the principal had given him a double Dutch. My grandfather refused to give up; he was determined to finish reading The Analects of Confucius. Thereafter, my grandfather would go to the library to self-study. With the help of dictionaries and assistance of the librarians, my grandfather miraculously completed reading and figured out this double Dutch. Ever since then, my grandfather has borrowed books from the library and sometimes he would ask me to accompany him to buy books. Reading has become an important part in his life. My grandfather is now a teacher in the community college for senior citizens. He teaches Chinese Literature. With a gentle smile on his face, he often enjoys telling me: "My beloved grandson, I am not rich, but I never regard myself as poor at all because my bookcases are filled with good books and my heart is filled with kindness and virtue."

六、因果

　　因果是針對一個存在的事件或情況，說明其發生的原因，廣義來說，因果算是一種解釋說明。要處理「因果」類型的英文作文，可以先敘述一個事件或情況（通常試題的提示會點出來），接著對該情況表達自己的主見，然後提出它之所以發生的原因。當然，作者列舉的原因必須合乎邏輯，要合情合理。

　　主題：很多學生上課常常打瞌睡，而且這些學生下課休息時一定趴在桌上「休息」。如果是用投影片上課的科目，這些學生幾乎會從開始上課一直「休息」到下課。請寫一篇至少 120 個單詞的文章，說明這種上課「打瞌睡」的原因。（注意：提示並沒有要求你提出解決的方法，千萬不要離題。）

詞彙

打瞌睡	doze off
家訓	parental instruction, family motto
嘆了口氣說	say with a sigh
現象	phenomenon
補習班	cram school, buxiban
校慶	anniversary
園遊會	campus carnival
慈善義賣	charity bazaar
凡此等等	etc., to name just a few, and the like
應酬活動	social engagement
更不用說	let alone, not to mention
使人成癮的	addictive

無法抗拒的	irresistible
心輔室	Counseling Office
民調	survey, poll

造句

1. 我母親是國中英文老師，已經教了 15 年。

 My mom has taught English in a junior high school for 15 years.

2. 昨天晚上我們在聊天的時候，我媽問我我在學校上課的時候會不會常常打瞌睡。

 Last night while we were chatting, my mom asked me if I often dozed off in class.

3. 我們家的家訓是「誠實乃上上策。」

 The motto of my family is "Honesty is the best policy."

4. 我不想讓我媽傷心，所以就沒有全說實話。

 I did not want to let her down so I did not tell her the whole truth.

5. 我告訴我媽說我「偶爾」會在上課的時候打瞌睡。

 I told my mom that I would "sometimes" doze off in class.

6. 我媽大大地嘆了口氣說她教的三個班 92 個學生裡面，每個星期差不多有 40 個學生會在上課的時候打瞌睡。

 My mom said with a heavy sigh, "Among the 92 students in my three classes, about 40 students a week would doze off in class."

7. 我媽想知道這種現象發生的原因。

 My mom wanted to know the reasons why such a phenomenon existed.

8. 我以「當事人」的身份坦白告訴我媽以下的原因。

 As one of the "criminals," I told my mom the following reasons:

(1) 學校與／或補習班老師每天給的功課太多了，不到半夜是做不完的。

 We have too many assignments from the teachers of our school and/or the cram schools every day. It is impossible to finish all of them before midnight.

(2) 學校主辦的活動很多，如迎新、送舊、校慶、園遊會、各種比賽、慈善義賣等。

 The school hosts many activities such as welcome parties, farewell parties, anniversaries, campus carnivals, a variety of contests, charity bazaars, to name just a few.

(3) 學生也有很多個人的應酬活動，如同學生日派對、班遊、逛街、看電影，更不用說是有人一個星期打工 20 個小時。

Likewise, students have a number of social engagements: birthday parties, class outings, shopping, watching films and the like, let alone the weekly 20-hour shifts for some students.

(4) 另外一個最主要的原因是會讓人沉迷上癮的電玩。它們令人無法抗拒。根據我們學校心輔室上學期所做的民調，約有七成的學生每天打電玩超過四個鐘頭。

Another major reason is addictive video games. They are irresistible. According to the survey conducted last semester by the Counseling Office of our school, about 70% of the students spent more than four hours a day playing video games.

> ## 結合成二段式短文

> ### They Are Busy and Tired
>
> My mom has taught English in a junior high school for 15 years. Last night while we were chatting, my mom asked me if I often dozed off in class. The motto of my family is "Honesty is the best policy." Nevertheless, I did not want to let her down so I did not tell her the whole truth. I told my mom that I would "sometimes" doze off in class. My mom said with a heavy sigh, "Among the 92 students in my three classes, about 40 students a week would doze off in class." My mom wanted to know the reasons why such a phenomenon existed. As one of the "criminals," I told my mom the following reasons:
>
> First, we have too many assignments from the teachers of our school and/or the cram schools every day. It is impossible to finish all of them before midnight. Second, the school hosts many activities such as welcome parties, farewell parties, anniversaries, campus carnivals, a variety of contests, charity bazaars, to name just a few. Likewise, students have a number of social engagements: birthday parties, class outings, shopping, watching films and the like, let alone the weekly 20-hour shifts for some students. Last, another major reason is addictive video games. They are irresistible. According to the survey conducted last semester by the Counseling Office of our school, about 70% of the students spent more than four hours a day playing video games.

七、影響、啓示

影響、啓示是一個人或一群人的一句話或一個行為對另外一個人或一群人的想法或行為

所產生的結果。簡單地說，啓示就是激勵。影響有正面的，也有負面的，但是啓示通常是正面的。考試的時候，就以某人的某一句話或某一個行為對你的影響和激勵去鋪陳論述就對了。時空人物等儘可能具體確實，如此更能說服、感動讀者。

　　主題：你在英文老師的推薦之下，在 YouTube 觀賞了前美國蘋果公司執行長賈伯斯先生 (Steve Jobs) 於 2005 年 6 月 12 日，對美國史丹福大學畢業生演講的錄影片段。他的二句話，四個字對你有所影響啓發。你要寫一篇文章跟讀者分享這四個字：Stay Hungry. Stay Foolish.（求知若飢，虛心若愚。）

詞彙

從小	since childhood
自私	selfish
自滿	complacent
更明確地說	to be more precise
掌上明珠	the apple of someone's eye
成績頂尖	get straight A's, an A student
琴棋書畫	music, chess, calligraphy, and painting, all artistic accomplishments
精通	be good at, excel in
推薦	recommend
錄影片段	video clip
史丹福大學	Stanford University
畢業典禮演講	commencement address, graduation speech
演講	make a speech, deliver an address
當時的	then
總裁，首席執行長，CEO	chief executive officer
謙虛地	humbly
膚淺	shallow
無知	ignorant
求知若飢	Stay hungry.
虛心若愚	Stay foolish.

企業家	entrepreneur
思想開明的	liberal
心胸寬闊的	open-minded
有遠見的	far-sighted
決心	decide to, be determined to, resolve to
自大	arrogance
擁抱	hug, embrace
謙虛	humble, humility
平凡	ordinary
貢獻	devoted, devotion

造句

1. 從小我就是一個自私、自滿、驕傲的女孩。

   Ever since childhood, I have been a proud, selfish, and complacent girl.

2. 更明確地說，從小我就是一個自私、自滿、驕傲的「公主」。

   To be more precise, I have been a proud, selfish, and complacent "princess."

3. 我一直是我的父母和師長的掌上明珠。

   I have always been the apple of my parents' and my teachers' eyes.

4. 我人長得美麗，學業成績頂尖，而且琴棋書畫樣樣精通。

   I am beautiful; I am an A student; I excel in music, chess, calligraphy, and painting--all artistic accomplishments.

5. 我是女王，而且同學都聽我發號施令。

   I am the queen and my classmates are my followers.

6. 一直到我看了英文老師向我推薦的賈伯斯先生 (Steve Jobs) 於 2005 年，對美國史丹福大學畢業生演講的錄影之後，我才知道我的膚淺和無知。賈伯斯先生當時是蘋果公司的首席執行長。

   Not until I watched the video clip recommended by my English teacher did I realize how shallow and ignorant I have been. It was the 2005 Stanford University commencement address delivered by Steve Jobs, the then CEO of Apple and Pixar Animation.

7. 在他這場演講的一開始，賈伯斯先生說他大學沒有畢業。

   He began the address with the sentence "... I never graduated from college."

8. 他用二句話作為他這場演講的結束，就是「求知若飢，虛心若愚」。

He ended the address with two sentences written in only four words: "Stay hungry. Stay foolish."

9. 當然，世界上或許有比他更成功的企業家、政治家、科學家、教育家等。

Of course, there may be entrepreneurs, statesmen, scientists, educators who are more successful than he.

10. 賈伯斯先生的胸襟和遠見是相當罕見的。

Very few people are as open-minded and far-sighted as he is.

11. 從當下開始，我決心要永遠脫掉自私、自大、驕傲的面具。

Influenced and inspired by his address, I decide/resolve to remove forever my masks of pride, selfishness, and arrogance.

12. 我要又飢又愚，我要擁抱謙虛，我要跟朋友和家人平凡快樂地享受生活。

I am determined to stay hungry and to stay foolish; I will embrace humility and enjoy a happy and ordinary life with my friends and family.

結合成二段式短文

Modesty Brings Benefit

Ever since childhood, I have been a proud, selfish, and complacent girl. To be more precise, I have been a proud, selfish, and complacent "princess." I have always been the apple of my parents' and my teachers' eyes. I am beautiful; I am an A student; I excel in music, chess, calligraphy, and painting--all artistic accomplishments. I am the queen and my classmates are my followers.

Not until I watched the video clip recommended by my English teacher did I realize how shallow and ignorant I have been. It was the 2005 Stanford University commencement address delivered by Steve Jobs, the then CEO of Apple and Pixar Animation. He honestly and humbly began the address with the sentence "... I never graduated from college." He ended it with two sentences written in only four words: "Stay hungry. Stay foolish." Of course, there may be entrepreneurs, statesmen, scientists, educators who are more successful than he, but very few people are as far-sighted and open-minded as he is. Influenced and inspired by his address, I resolve to remove forever my masks of pride, selfishness, and arrogance. I am determined to stay hungry and to stay foolish; I will embrace humility and enjoy a happy and ordinary life with my friends and family.

第六節 處理「內容」的四個原則

我們來做一個總結。在處理「內容」的時候，我們要鎖定四個基本原則：邏輯、具體、細膩、幽默。

一、邏輯

邏輯主要是安排時空的順序與事件的連貫，例如講故事的時候，情節的先後順序必須合乎一般人的認知，也就是要切合實際。例如，臺灣以前很少過萬聖節，現在臺灣過萬聖節時，本地人的小孩很少有挨家逐戶要糖果吃的「不給糖吃就搗蛋」的風俗 (trick or treat)，但是卻幾乎都有化裝或怪裝舞會。因此，如果要描述臺灣的萬聖節活動，就應該淡化「不給糖吃就搗蛋」的風俗。

要記述臺灣一年十二個月的代表性活動時，可以按照月份聯想到「新年元旦—春節—元宵節—情人節—媽祖遶境—清明節—母親節—端午節—畢業典禮—暑假開始、出國旅遊—暑假結束／中原普渡—繳學費—中秋節—國慶升旗—萬聖節化裝舞會—聖誕節—跨年」來安排順序。

底下，我們來欣賞美國「歌唱音樂全能藝人」Stevie Wonder 在 1984 年自己作曲、作詞、製作、演唱的一首膾炙人口，得獎無數的單曲唱片 "I Just Called to Say I Love You" 的歌詞。歌詞從新年 (New Year's Day) 按照時間的順序，配合著代表性的活動、時令等，一直「唱」到聖誕節 (Christmas)。這是 Stevie Wonder 生涯中最成功的單曲之一。歌詞中的粗斜體字代表一年中的每個月份。

"I Just Called to Say I Love You"

No ***New Year's Day*** to celebrate

No ***chocolate covered candy hearts*** to give away

No first of ***spring***

No song to sing

In fact here's just another ordinary day

No *April* rain

No **flowers** bloom

No wedding Saturday within the month of *June*

But what it is, is something true

Made up of these three words that I must say to you

I just called to say I love you

I just called to say how much I care

I just called to say I love you

And I mean it from the bottom of my heart

No summer's high

No warm *July*

No harvest moon to light one tender *August* night

No *autumn* breeze

No falling leaves

Not even time for birds to fly to southern skies

No *Libra* sun

No *Halloween*

No *giving thanks* to all the *Christmas* joy you bring

But what it is, though old so new

To fill your heart like no three words could ever do

I just called to say I love you

I just called to say how much I care, I do

I just called to say I love you

And I mean it from the bottom of my heart

...

二、具體

　　具體是對於所提供的例子、想法、資訊、步驟等，要真實明確，不要含糊籠統，例如，將「一個企業家曾經在一所大專院校的正式場合的講話」改為「前蘋果公司執行長賈伯斯先生於

2005 年 6 月 12 日，對美國史丹福大學畢業生的演講」，將「一位有名又有錢的女藝人」改為「世界第一位女性非洲裔美國億萬富翁，同時也是年薪最高、最受觀眾喜愛的著名脫口秀節目主持人」。具體的事實和資訊會讓讀者首肯認同。所以，我們平常就要養成規律的閱讀習慣，以儲存豐沛的事實和資訊，臨時抱佛腳很難累積廣且深的事實、資訊。

三、細膩

「細膩」就是對於人、地、事、物的形式、情況的描述，例如，顏色、材質、外表、年齡、職業、頭銜、興趣、習慣、專長等，儘量做到細緻詳盡，當然也不能過於細膩，要適可而止。作者可以將「一支手機」改寫成「一支造型優美，紅色的 SONY Xperia 智慧型手機」，將「有一天上午」改寫成「2013 年初夏，一個又熱又濕的星期六上午」。「細膩」運用在敘述與描述特別有加分的功用。

四、幽默

「幽默」主要是在敘述的時候，讓讀者體驗出言語和故事的趣味性。檢驗一篇文章是否加入了「幽默」的元素，一個驗收標準就是讀者是否覺得文章的故事和敘述有趣好笑，例如，「有一位六十幾歲的老婆婆在火車站的候車大廳傷心地哭著，車站服務台的小姐走過去，關心地問老婆婆發生了什麼事，老婆婆說她今天早上被媽媽訓了一頓，因為她忘了給奶奶泡咖啡」。或是「小海他們家養的金魚昨天被水淹死了」。或是「你的室友是一個不折不扣的『宅女』。今天晚上她打扮美美的，一邊吹著口哨，一邊叮嚀妳，她晚上不回宿舍了，不用等她。你好奇地問她要去哪裡。她淡定地回答說：『老娘要去和我未來的前夫約會！』」等這一類不尋常的誇張或邏輯。幽默可以活化我們的文章，讓讀者讀的津津有味，回味無窮。

第七節　常用句型

一、主題句

1. 初學者宜將主題句作為每一段的首句。
2. 主題句必須是一個完整的句子。
3. 主題句必須表達整個段落的中心思想。

4. 主題句不可過於籠統，也不要過於詳盡。

5. 主題句的長度在 15 個單詞左右。

6. 例句：

(1) I am convinced that using English-English dictionaries is one of the most essential elements for mastering the English language. （19 單詞）

我深信使用英英詞典是精通英語的最重要元素之一。

(2) Successful business people over the world believe that social networking has played an important role in their careers. （21 單詞）

全世界的成功企業家相信社群網站在他們的事業扮演一個重要的角色。

二、定義句

1. 先介紹被定義的人物所歸屬的上義詞。上下義關係是指「一般」和「具體」的關係，例如「狗」是「動物」的下義詞；反之，「動物」是「狗」的上義詞。「顏色」是「紅色」的上義詞，故「紅色」是「顏色」的下義詞。

2. 用形容詞子句修飾該上義詞，以突顯被定義的人物的特徵。這個特徵使得被定義的人物不同於同一個集合裡面的其他元素。例如「心理學家」不同於「學家」這個上義詞集合裡面的「人類學家」、「語言學家」、「物理學家」等。

3. 利用定義句的句型：By definition，a 被定義的人物 is a 上義詞 who/which ...。

4. 例句：

(1) By definition, "a drunk driver is someone who drives after drinking more than the amount of alcohol that is legally allowed."〔註：引用自 *Collins COBUILD English Dictionary for Advanced Learners*, 第三版，第 475 頁〕

酒醉駕駛者的定義是喝了比法定許可含量還要多的酒精之後開車的人。

(2) By definition, paparazzi are "photographers who follow famous people in order to take photographs they can sell to newspapers."〔註：引用自 *Longman Dictionary of Contemporary English*, 第五版，第 1261 頁〕

狗仔隊的定義是跟蹤名人，對他們拍照，然後將照片賣給報紙的攝影師。

三、數據句

1. 引述完成報告的時間、單位與方式。

2. 確切的統計資料。

3. 相關的人物。

4. 相關的敘述。

5. 利用數據句的句型：According to a 2008 survey conducted by XYZ, ...。

XYZ = 完成報告的單位。

6. 例句：

(1) According to a 2011 study conducted by XYZ, about 88% of the high school students in Taiwan spent an average of 20 hours playing video games every week.

根據 XYZ 在 2011 年所做的一項研究，臺灣大約有 88% 的高中生一個星期平均花二十個小時打電玩。

(2) According to a recent study by XYZ, more than 200 million cups of pearl milk tea were sold last year at night markets across the island.

根據 XYZ 最近所做的一項研究，臺灣全島的夜市去年賣了二億杯以上的珍珠奶茶。

四、建議句：如下句、方法句、步驟句

1. 利用轉折詞 as far as ... is concerned，提出理由、方法或步驟。

2. 利用動詞片語 are as follows 或 are discussed below 介紹第二段要討論的理由、方法或步驟。

3. 建議句稱得上是用來連接第一段和第二段的橋樑句。

4. 例句：

(1) As far as I am concerned, some of the best ways to master English listening comprehension are as follows:

就我而言，精通英語聽力的幾個最好的方法，討論如下：

(2) As far as preventing drunk driving is concerned, some of the effective measures are discussed below:

就防止酒駕而言，幾個有效的措施，討論如下：

(3) The most important steps you can take to prevent car thefts are suggested below:

防止汽車失竊的最重要的步驟，建議如下：

五、效果句

1. 利用動詞片語 lead to，前接方法或步驟，後接效果。

2. 句型：方法或步驟 can lead to 效果。

3. 例句：

(1) Energy conservation measures can effectively lead to decreasing the waste of the earth's limited resources.

節能措施能夠有效減少浪費地球有限的資源。

(2) The first effective step which leads to preventing drunk driving is to punish drunk drivers severely.

防止酒駕的第一個有效的步驟是嚴厲懲罰酒駕者。

六、實例鋪陳句、舉例句

1. 舉例句具有強力的說明作用。
2. 舉例句具有前後連貫的支撐作用。
3. 句型： ... 人物, for example....

      ... 人物. They include....

4. 例句：

(1) There are varieties of pop music, for example, jazz, blues, and rhythm and blues.

流行音樂有很多種類，例如爵士、藍調與節奏藍調。

(2) A good coffee shop is made up of a number of elements. They include reasonable price, excellent service, and select music.

一家好的咖啡館具備許多元素，例如合理的價位，一流的服務，精心挑選的音樂。

七、分類句

1. 將主題人事物作出明確的分類。
2. 依據讀者熟悉的標準作分類。
3. 利用分類句的句型：

According to 標準，主題人事物 can be divided into the following categories:

Based on 標準，主題人事物 can be classified into the following types:

4. 例句：

(1) According to different functions, voluntary services can be divided into the following three categories.

根據不同的功能，志願性的服務可以分成下列三種：

(2) Based on various services, charity organizations can be classifieded into the following types:

依據不同的服務內容，慈善團體可以分成下列幾種：

八、背景資料句

1. 介紹主題人物的背景。
2. 背景資料包羅萬象，儘可能挑選重要的、有趣的、獨特的特徵，讓主題人物與眾不同，讓讀

者對主題人物印象深刻。

3. 利用同位語的句型：...名詞 i, 名詞 i, ...

　　名詞 i= 指涉相同的人物。

4. 例句：

　　(1) The principal, a husky man in his early fifties, stood up and began his address with confidence.

　　　　校長，五十出頭，身體壯碩，站起來很有信心地開始演講。

　　(2) My roommate, an eighteen-year-old girl from Canada, majors in business administration.

　　　　我的室友是一位十八歲的加拿大女孩，她主修企管。

九、時空串連句

1. 介紹時空背景並且有效串連。

2. 時空背景務必合乎邏輯。

3. 標示時間的單詞：before, after, during 等。

　　標示空間的單詞：before, behind, above, below, next to 等。

4. 配合利用「現在簡單式態」表示「歷史的現在」。〔請參考 7.6.2〕

5. 例句：

　　(1) Just as we arrive at Kenting National Park, it begins pouring.

　　　　就在我們到達墾丁國家公園的時候，天空下起了傾盆大雨。

　　(2) Let me describe my school dormitory room. The north side of my room.... Turning east in this tiny room.... The south side of the room... The west side of the room....

　　　　讓我來介紹我住的學校宿舍的房間。房間的北面……。轉向這個小房間的東面……。房間的南面……。房間的西面……。〔順時鐘方向〕

　　(3) I am standing on the arch bridge of Cheng-Kung Lake on Kuang-Fu campus. To my right are the relics of the Little West Gate and the building of the Department of Chinese Literature; in front of me is the building of the Department of Foreign Languages and Literature; to my left is the picturesque Banyan Garden; behind me is Yun-Ping Hall, the Administration Center of NCKU.

　　　　我站在光復校區成功湖的拱橋上面。我的右手邊是小西門的遺跡和中文系系館。我的正前方是外國語文學系系館。我的左手邊是美麗如畫的「榕園」。我的後面是「雲平大樓」，它是成大的行政中心。〔逆時鐘方向〕

十、因果句

1. 說明一個現象或問題的原因與／或結果。

2. 承接一個現象或問題，引導解決的方案與步驟。

3. 句型： 因 lead to/result in/be responsible for/cause 果

   果 result from/because/because of/be caused by 因

4. 因果句與效果句有點類似，前者因果並重，後者偏重效果。

5. 例句：

   (1) Unsafe sexual behavior may lead to sexually transmitted diseases and unwanted pregnancies.

      不安全的性行為可能導致性病和意外的懷孕。

   (2) It is scientifically proven that stress can result in both physical and psychological illnesses.

      科學上證明壓力會導致生理與心理疾病。

十一、若則句

1. 用來提出因應之道和結果成效。

2. 可以連續使用。

3. 句型： If ... then ...

   If ..., if ..., and if ..., then ...

4. 例句：

   (1) If there are enough qualified English teachers and if there are suitable teaching materials for young children, then we can have a first-class English program.

      如果有足夠的合格的英語老師，而且有適合兒童的教材，那麼我們就會有一流的英語課程。

   (2) If we can "stay hungry," if we can "stay foolish," and if we can respect expertise, then we will become professionals.

      如果我們能夠「求知若飢」，如果我們能夠「虛心若愚」，如果我們能夠尊重專業，那麼我們將來會成為專家。

十二、結論句

1. 常常是段落的最後一句。

2. 用來重申作者的看法和立場。

3. 利用轉承語 in conclusion, in summary。

4. 例句：

(1) In summary, a team of fully-fledged doctors and nurses, state-of-the-art equipment and technology, and modern administration can make our hospital everlasting.

　　總之，訓練有素的醫護團隊，最先進的設備和技術，以及現代化的管理，能使得我們的醫院永續經營。

(2) In conclusion, regular and constant practice is the key to success in English writing.

　　總之，經常且有恆的練習是英文寫作成功的關鍵。

練習 9

1. 底下有三個「主題」：(1)資訊就是力量，(2)成功的元素，(3)如何辦一場令人難忘的畢業晚會，請用英文為每個主題寫二句主題句。

2. 底下有三個「單詞」：(1) volunteer（志工），(2) expertise（專門知識），(3) bullying（霸凌），請用英文為每個單詞寫一句定義句。

3. 底下有二個「主題」：(1)逛夜市，(2)吃便當，請用英文為每個主題寫一句數據句。

4. 底下有二個「主題」: (1)培訓英語聽力，(2)減肥，請用英文為每個主題寫一句如下/方法/步驟句。

_____

_____

_____

_____

5. 底下有二個「主題」: (1)時間管理，(2)面對挑戰，請用英文為每個主題寫一句效果句。

_____

_____

_____

_____

6. 底下有二個「主題」: (1)課外活動，(2)業餘愛好，請用英文為每個主題寫一句舉例句。

_____

_____

_____

_____

7. 底下有二個「主題」: (1)詞典，(2)音樂，請用英文為每個主題寫一句分類句。

_____

_____

_____

_____

8. 底下有二個「主題」：(1)我的游泳教練，(2)一位醫院志工，請用英文為每個主題寫一句背景資料句。

9. 底下有二個「主題」：(1)一次班遊，(2)我們學校的禮堂，請用英文為每個主題寫一句時空串連句。

10. 底下有二個「主題」：(1)體重過重，(2)學業成績退步，請用英文為每個主題寫一句因果句。

11. 底下有二個「主題」：(1)防止校園霸凌，(2)永遠的綠色地球，請用英文為每個主題寫一句若則句。

12. 底下有二個「主題」：(1)永遠的好朋友，(2)遠離壓力，請用英文為每個主題
　　寫一句結論句。

_____

_____

_____

_____

13. 請分別以(1)「助人為快樂之本」，(2)「活到老，學到老」，(3)「有志者，事
　　竟成」為主題，各寫一篇至少 120 個單詞的文章。文章請分二段。

　　（請參考本章節的範文。）

_____

_____

_____

_____

_____

_____

_____

_____

_____

_____

_____

_____

_____

_____

第 10 章

修辭

　　修辭就是修飾詞藻，作說者利用適當的技巧，也就是修辭格，使自己的想法、論點透過文字傳達聲音旋律，靈活地充分表達意境，而且使文字變得更有說服力，進而感動閱聽者。底下，我們選擇幾個初學者必備的英語修辭格，讓讀者能舉一反三、靈活運用，讓句子結構更富於變化，讓文章更出色。

第一節　重複

　　重複指的是加強語氣的重複，是利用同樣的句型，利用同樣的句構的修辭格。易學又好用，算是修辭基本功的第一招。

"... **we shall fight** on the beaches, **we shall fight** on the landing grounds, **we shall fight** in the field and in the streets, **we shall fight** in the hills ..." 〔來源：邱吉爾 Winston Churchill's report on the Miracle of Dunkirk (An excerpt), 4 June 1940〕

We will make you a popular singer, **we will make** you a super star, and **we will make** you rich and famous.

第二節　平行

　　平行指的是對應一致，是將二個以上語義屬性相同的人事物，利用同樣的結構排列的修辭格。運用平行結構，依序有四個考量：結構相同、語義相關、節奏和諧、詞序排列。〔請參考7.4.2〕

一、結構相同

　　結構相同指的是句子和句子，子句和子句，片語和片語，單詞和單詞，形容詞和形容詞，介系詞片語和介系詞片語等。中文的「松、竹、梅」，「人蔘、貂皮、烏拉草」，「友直、友諒、友多聞」，「傳道受業解惑」是結構相同，也是語義相關的例子。

sex, drugs, and rock and roll
（三個名詞）

to read comprehensively, to think critically, and to write effectively

（三個不定詞片語）

listening, speaking, reading, and writing

（四個 V-ing）

You need food, they need shelter, and we need respect.

（三個獨立句子）

I believe that you need freedom, that you need privacy, and that you need independence.

（三個名詞子句）

二、語義相關

語義屬性相同的元素才可以利用平行結構連接。

students, staff, and faculty
學生與教職員（教職員生）

a football game, a beauty contest, and an alumni dinner
一場足球比賽，一場選美，一場校友餐會

The cell phone can play music, can take photos, and can be used as a remote control.
這款手機可以播放音樂、可以照相、還可以當遙控器。

三、節奏和諧

節奏和諧主要是尾韻 (end rhyme) 與頭韻 (alliteration)。尾韻指的是二個單詞末尾母音及其後隨的子音必須相同。頭韻指的是二個單詞用相同的字母或聲音開頭。

尾韻

act**ive** and innovat**ive**
積極創新

protec**tion** and decora**tion**
保護與裝飾

confid**ent** and independ**ent**
自信又獨立

We are devoted to social and judicial reforms.
我們致力社會與司法改革。

頭韻

head, heart, hands, and health
手腦身心 /（頭心手健康）

smooth and successful
順利成功

peaceful and prosperous
平安昌盛

Slow and steady wins the race.
緩慢穩定贏得勝利。

參考

A friend in need is a friend indeed.
患難見真交。

Well begun is half done.
好的開始是成功的一半。

Birds of a feather flock together.
物以類聚。

四、詞序排列

　　本章節所討論的詞序排列，專指由 and 連接的並列結構，特別是「二項式結構」: A and B (hustle and bustle) 或是重疊詞: A-B (hip-hop)。其中 A 和 B 是二個相同的語法結構。詞序排列有兩個考量，一個是語義，也就是邏輯或事實，例如:「尊卑」,「好壞」,「先後」;另一個是節奏，也就是聲音和諧，例如: 敵友 friend and foe。

　　就節奏而言，基本判斷原則是音節數目較多的元素擺後面 (hot and spicy; fast and furious);音節數目相同時，重讀音節母音響度較高的元素擺後面 (clean and clear; hip-hop);音節數目相同且重讀音節母音相同時，重讀音節母音前面或後面的子音響度較高的元素擺後面 (hustle and bustle; teeny-weeny)。其他條件相同情況下，開音節，也就是字尾沒有子音關閉的元素擺後面

(friend and foe; tic-tac-toe)。

響度高低的等級：後母音 [ɑ, o] 等 > 前母音 [æ, e] 等；低母音 [ɑ, æ] 等 > 高母音 [u, i] 等；滑音 [w, j] > 流音 [l, r] > 鼻音 [m, n, ŋ] > 摩擦音 [v, z] 等 > 阻塞音 [b, d, g] 等。聲帶振動的摩擦音 [v, ð, z, ʒ]、阻塞音 [b, d, g]、塞擦音 [dʒ]，分別高於聲帶不振動的摩擦音 [f, θ, s, ʃ]、阻塞音 [p, t, k]、塞擦音 [tʃ]。〔請參考 11.13；附錄 6。〕

當然，作者可以自由創作，但是有時候要注意約定俗成的原則。

1. 依照「邏輯／事實」排列詞序：

drink and drive 酒駕

hit and run 肇事逃逸

build-operate-transfer (BOT) 建造，營運，轉移

washed, dried, and folded 洗滌、烘乾、折疊

signed, sealed, and delivered 已成定局（經簽名蓋章完畢的）

2. 依照「節奏」排列詞序：

pride and prejudice 傲慢與偏見

sense and sensibility 感性與理性

fast and furious 飆速飛馳

checks and balances 制衡

law and order 法治

ladies and gentlemen 各位來賓（女士們、先生們）

boys and girls 各位同學

slow and steady 緩慢穩定

track and field 田徑運動

deaf and blind 又瞎又聾

friends and relatives 親戚朋友

參考與比較

friends and family（節奏）

family and friends（約定俗成）

家人與朋友

day and night（節奏）

night and day（約定俗成）

夜以繼日；日以繼夜

staff and faculty（節奏）

faculty and staff（約定俗成）

教職員

students and faculty（節奏）

faculty and students（約定俗成）

師生

第三節 三節格律法

（節錄自書林 (2013) 出版，蔣炳榮所著之《簡明當代英文法》第 284~285 頁）

　　三節格律法「…… 是一個句子由三個獨立子句或片語形成，而這三個獨立子句或片語的重要性、緊湊性、長度等會逐漸增強或減弱。廣義而言，三節格律法是不用 and 連接的三個平行的結構。最典型的例子是凱撒大帝 (Julius Caesar) 於西元前 47 年向羅馬元老院報捷時講的 Veni, vidi, vici，英文翻譯為 "I came, I saw, I conquered."（我來，我見，我征服。）」

> "But in a larger sense, we cannot dedicate--we cannot consecrate--we cannot hallow-this ground."
>
> 「但是，就更大的意義而言，我們無法致力、無法奉上、無法成就這塊土地的神聖。」

> "of the people, by the people, for the people"
>
> 「民有、民治、民享」

> "Faster, Higher, Stronger"
>
> 「更快、更高、更強」
>
> 註：奧林匹克格言 (the Olympic Motto)，原文為拉丁文 "Citius, Altius, Fortius"。

> He is calm; he is clever; he is confident.
>
> 他冷靜、他聰明、他有自信。

"Friends, Romans, countrymen"
「各位朋友，各位羅馬人，各位同胞」

My friend will always squeeze me, tease me, please me.
我朋友總是會擁抱我、逗弄我、取悅我。

第四節　聯珠

聯珠，又名頂真，是將一個句子結尾的一個字或詞，重複用在下一個句子的開頭，使尾首連接。記住「我為人人，人人為我」、「時勢造英雄，英雄造時勢」，就會記得頂真。

Choose what you love; love what you choose.
選你所愛，愛你所選。

God loves people; people love God.
神愛世人，世人愛神。

We are living in a new era, an era of virtual reality.
我們活在一個新的時代，一個虛擬現實的時代。

Are you ready for the "cruel" society, a society full of dangers and challenges?
你準備迎接這個「殘酷的」社會，這個充滿危險和挑戰的社會了嗎？

My husband is a gentleman, a gentleman with a sense of humor.
我老公是個正人君子，有幽默感的正人君子。

第五節　比喻象徵

比喻象徵，是利用動物、植物、顏色、形狀等自然現象的特質來呈現人物特點的修辭格，可以讓閱聽者感受這種特質並產生共鳴。最常用也最好用的比喻修辭格是「明喻」，就是用 like 或 as 後接一個閱聽者熟悉的動物、植物或自然現象來做比喻。記住「行如風，立如松，坐如鐘」，就會記得比喻象徵。擬人化也是常用的一種比喻象徵。〔請參考附錄 1〕

The train is moving **as slowly as a turtle**. (明喻)

The walls in the room are **as white as snow**.（明喻）

"Justice rolls down **like waters**, and righteousness **like a mighty stream**."（明喻）

Can you hear the **whisper** of the wind?（擬人化）

My girlfriend has gone away and the moon was **shedding tears** for me.（擬人化）

第六節　雙重否定

　　雙重否定就是用否定副詞 not, never 等，後接一個具有否定語義的單詞或片語。從字數的比較而言，肯定的敘述來的精簡。從句構要富於變化的角度而言，一篇文章中穿插一、二個雙重否定，特別是用來表達作者個人觀點的時候，這種「突兀」的邏輯，可以算是一種加分。

It is **not uncommon** for university students to have school loans.

大學生申請就學貸款並不少見。

For respectable judges to break the law is **not impossible**.

值得人們尊敬的法官會犯法並不是不可能。

Not unnaturally, the general was greatly sad by his son's sudden death.

那位將軍因為兒子突然去世而十分悲傷，這也是人之常情。

第七節　設問

　　設問，又名修辭疑問，是利用問句的語氣、句型來做加強語氣的聲明。記住「太陽會從西邊出來嗎？」等於加強語氣的聲明「太陽絕不會從西邊出來。」，就會記得設問。考試時，最後一句利用設問來結束，也是一種好的選擇。

Is that a reason for students to cheat in the exam?

= Surely that is not a reason for students to cheat in the exam.

這個當然不是學生考試可以作弊的理由。

Has the government taken good care of us laborers?

= The government has not taken good care of us laborers.

政府沒有照顧到我們勞工。

How can you have an affair with your secretary?

= Stop having an affair with your secretary.

不要再和你的秘書搞婚外情！

第八節　類轉

　　類轉就是詞性轉換，將一個單詞末加上詞綴就從原來常用的一種詞類轉換成另外一種不常用的詞類。常用到的類轉模式是將一個常作名詞用的單詞，轉換成動詞。記住前英國首相邱吉爾的名言："To jaw-jaw is always better than to war-war."（嘮嘮叨叨好過打打殺殺。），就會記得類轉。類轉像是一種創作，抓到機會又有把握就好好表現一番，不必猶豫。

一、名詞轉換成動詞

The security guard **eyed** the visitors with suspicion.

警衛懷疑地打量著那些遊客。

Mr. Walker has **headed** our department for over twenty years.

Walker 先生負責我們這個部門已經二十多年了。

Who is going to **chair** the meeting of the investigation?

誰會主持這個調查會議?

Her research **evidenced** my experiments.

她的研究證明了我的實驗。

二、形容詞轉換成動詞

For the past two decades, no other players have **bettered** her record.

過去這二十年沒有其他選手可以超越她的紀錄。

The customs officers ordered the singer to **empty** her suitcase.

海關人員命令那位歌手把皮箱的東西全部倒出來。

Like a magician, my little sister successfully **stilled** the big dog.

好像在變魔術似的，我小妹成功地讓那隻大狗平靜了下來。

My brother shouted: "Don't **dirty** my new suit."

我哥激動地喊道:「別弄髒我的新西裝!」

第九節 倒裝

「倒裝」就是「非順裝」。當代英語的順裝詞序是 S-V-O (主詞-動詞-受詞)。廣義而言,一個句子的動詞或受詞出現在主詞前面就是倒裝結構,通稱為「倒裝句」。常用的動詞在主詞前面的「倒裝句」句構,討論如下:

一、句構變形

> 順裝: 主詞-be 動詞/助動詞 be, have, do/情態助動詞 will, can ... -動詞 ...
> 倒裝:
> ⇨ ... be動詞-主詞 ...
>   ... 助動詞 be, have, do/情態助動詞 will, can ... -主詞-動詞 ...

1. 主詞 -be 動詞 ...

   ⇨ ... be 動詞-主詞 ...

   A new toy is inside the box.
   ⇨ Inside the box is a new toy.

2. 主詞 -be 動詞 -V-ing/V-en ...

   ⇨ ...V-ing/V-en 助動詞 be -主詞-...

   The director is standing next to the mayor.
   ⇨ Standing next to the mayor is the director.

   My fiancée was so embarrassed that she was speechless.
   ⇨ So embarrassed was my fiancée that she was speechless.

3. 主詞-助動詞 have - V-en ...

   ⇨ ... 助動詞 have - 主詞 -V-en

The exhibition has never attracted so many visitors.

⇨ Never has the exhibition attracted so many visitors.

4. 主詞 -V ...

   ⇨ ... 助動詞 do -主詞-V

My grandmother rarely wears a lot of jewelry.

⇨ Rarely does my grandmother wear a lot of jewelry.

5. 主詞-情態助動詞 will, can ... -V ...

   ⇨ 情態助動詞 will, can ... -主詞-V

My daughter will never see you again.

⇨ Never will my daughter see you again.

二、使用「倒裝結構」的時機

1. 否定詞在句首。

Never can we live without the computer.

No sooner had we got off the bus than it began pouring.

Under no circumstances can you tell him my secret.

否定詞：barely, hardly, neither, never, no, nor, not, rarely, scarcely, seldom等。

2. 副詞 only 在句首。從屬子句由 only 引導時，主要子句要用倒裝結構。

Only if you apologize for your rude behavior will I forgive you.

Only with her husband by her side does the woman poet feel secure.

3. 補語，通常是地方副詞，在句首。

Sitting next to me was a flight attendant.

比較：There was a flight attendant sitting next to me.

North of the Great Lakes lies Canada.

Behind the department store are two parking lots.

4. 由 had, should 或 were 引導的非真條件子句。

Were I a submarine, I would take you to the bottom of the sea.

Had he made the room reservation, we would not have slept in the rest area.

Should you need a letter of reference (= if you need a letter of reference), please feel free to tell me.

練習10

1. 請利用「重複」修辭格式將下列的句子改寫與／或擴增。

例： I love you.

答： I love you; I love you; I always do.

(1) We shall fight against drunk driving.

_____

_____

(2) If people believe that our civil servants are integral.

_____

_____

2. 請利用「平行」修辭格式完成下列的句構以形成一個有至少 15 個單詞的句子。

例： government of the people

答： Every statesman believes that government of the people, by the people, for the people shall never perish from the earth.

(1) a computer is used to

_____

_____

(2) I have been jogging for five years because

_____

_____

3. 請在空格上填入一個單詞或片語以形成押頭韻與/或押尾韻的平行結構。

例： political and _____ reforms

答： educational

(1) a peaceful and _____ New Year

(2) a hot and _____ summer night

(3) to make you cool and _____

(4) away from the hustle and _____ of Christmas shopping

(5) will make you healthy and _____

(6) big, bright, and _____ eyes

(7) man, money, and _____

(8) the 5 Cs of a diamond: carat, _____, clarity, _____
_____ and _____

(9) for your safety and _____

(10) the 3 Ps that make English so popular: person, people, and _____

4. 請在空格上填入一個單詞，使得結構達到具有「比喻象徵」的修辭格式。必要時，請參考詞典。

例：as sharp as a _____ （非常機靈）

答：razor

(1) the _____ of someone's eye （掌上明珠）

(2) as busy as a _____ （非常忙碌）

(3) as clean as a _____ （非常乾淨）

(4) as _____ as a church mouse （一貧如洗）

(5) as mute as a _____ （靜悄悄的）

(6) as rcd as a _____ （面色紅潤的）

(7) as white as a _____ （臉色蒼白）

(8) head and _____ above the rest （出類拔萃）

(9) the _____ is the limit （一切都有可能做到）

(10) born with a silver _____ in one's mouth （生於富貴之家）

(11) make a _____ out of a molehill （小題大做）

(12) read somebody like a _____ （瞭若指掌）

(13) lend me your _____ （請聽我說）

(14) a peaches-and-_____ complexion （白裡透紅的膚色）

(15) a _____ of strength （可信賴的人）

5. **請在空格上填入一個單詞，使得結構達到具有「類轉」的修辭格式。必要時，請參考詞典。**

例：The president went abroad. Who is going to _____ the meeting now?

答：chair

(1) I saw a few high school kids _____ around the singer's affairs. （四處打聽）

(2) At midnight, the visitors were _____ toward a local bar. （前往）

(3) A group of local people _____ the imported sports car in admiration. （仔細打量）

(4) At last, the little boy _____ his toy to the librarian. （遞）

(5) Her young sister successfully _____ her way to the stage. （朝……擠去）

(6) The witness _____ something but nobody in the court could figure it out. （用口型默示；嘴動而不出聲地說）

(7) It is not fair to ask the public to _____ the loss of National Health Insurance. （承擔）

(8) A large part of her story has been _____ down by the director. （淡化）

(9) Her son _____ Hamlet in the 2013 Graduation Drama Performance. （擔任主角）

(10) While the girl was waiting in the office, she unconsciously _____ _____ her necklace. （撥弄）

第 11 章

中譯英導論

　　學測指考的中譯英大題，有二個子題，每題 4 分，共 8 分。作答說明簡單明確：「請將以下中文句子譯成正確、通順、達意的英文。」考生除了英文要好，中文也要有相當的水準，必須要能確實看懂每題平均 25~30 個字的中文句子。理論上，翻譯是比寫作還要高階的語言成就，因為作者必須「精通」二種語文。我們在前面提過，母語是國語、台語等的非英美人士的「英文好」＝講好英語 + 寫好英文 + 流暢通順的中英對譯，因為很多英語測驗，包括「全民英檢」，都要考翻譯，所以在臺灣的英語教學所培訓的英語能力除了聽說讀寫之外，還要納入翻譯，至少是中譯英。

　　中譯英是遣詞用字、文法句構、語義、修辭、音韻和寫作等各種層面的綜合「創作輸出」，經常還必須考慮到所謂習慣用法、固定語式和中英二種語文的特徵與同異之處。這是相當具有挑戰性的測驗方式，不是嗎？

　　幸運的是，100~102 學年度的學測與 99~101 學年度的指考中譯英試題「好像」有一定的脈絡可循。主題「似乎」可以預測。學測是夜市、觀光，台灣製作的影片，高房價；指考是出生率快速下滑，核電廠爆炸，核能安全，綠色能源，對人體有害的包裝食品。因此，就考試論考試，考生讀者在考試前的三個月或者是平常，就應該關心家事國事天下事，不但要熟悉當時的熱門議題，而且要整理歸納那些熱門議題的英語對應語。臺灣有幾家本地出版的英文或雙語的報紙和雜誌，要收集相關的熱門議題和對應語，算不上是太困難的事情。再說，中譯英「評量的重點在於考生能否能運用熟悉的詞彙與基本句型將中文翻譯成正確達意的英文句子，所測驗之句型為高中生熟悉的範圍，詞彙亦控制在大考中心詞彙表四級內之詞彙，中等程度以上的考生，如果能使用正確句型並注意用字、拼字，應能得理想的分數。」（請參考附錄 7「評分說明」）

　　底下，僅就中譯英常用到的部分，將中英文不同之處列舉整理，讓考生讀者在參加考試碰到相關題型時，能有所依據處理應對，而且有正確的大方向可以著手，進而順利達到目標。要達到預期的目標（「正確、通順、達意」），我們建議採取以下的步驟。第一，確實把題目看清楚弄明白，例如是核電廠爆炸，不是核能爆炸，更不是核子武器；是出生率快速下滑，不是出生率超低；是包裝食品，不是垃圾食品。第二，經由遣詞造句，用適當的句型翻譯成正確達意的英文。第三，避免逐字而且按照中文的詞序來處理英文，因為中英文的句構有差異而且詞序也不一樣。

　　列舉要訣，討論如下：〔＝號左邊是中文的處理方式，＝號右邊是英文的處理方式。〕

第一節 ……的+N = N+後位修飾；前位修飾+N

中文採用名詞前位修飾；英文採用名詞前位修飾與/或名詞後位修飾。

名詞前位修飾是修飾語置於所修飾的名詞前面；名詞後位修飾是修飾語置於所修飾的名詞後面。常用的修飾語有（單詞）形容詞、介系詞片語、分詞片語、形容詞子句等。

都會區的高房價（102 學測） *high* house prices *in city areas*
對社會的嚴重影響（102 學測） *serious* effects *on society*
對人體有害的成分（101 指考） ingredients (*that are*) *harmful to human bodies*
包裝上的說明（101 指考） instructions *on the package*
臺灣的夜市（100 學測） *Taiwan's* night markets (the) night markets *in Taiwan*
來自不同國家的觀光客（100 學測） tourists/visitors *from many different countries*
年輕性感美麗的啦啦隊員 *young, sexy, and beautiful* cheerleaders
在月光下跳舞的臺灣原住名 Native Taiwanese *dancing in the moonlight* Native Taiwanese *who are dancing in the moonlight*
在爆炸中身亡的馬拉松跑者 the marathon runners *killed in the explosion* the marathon runners *who were killed in the explosion*

第二節　著／在／正 = 進行時態；了／過／已經 = 完成時態

中文利用時間副詞與/或語尾助詞表示動詞的時式與時態；用「過」、「著／在／正」、「了／已經」分別表示「經驗貌」、「進行貌」與「完成貌」；英文（除了利用時間副詞之外）動詞必須作相關的時式、時態等屈折變化。

產生了嚴重的影響（102 學測）
have had serious effects
have caused serious effects
正推出新的政策（102 學測）
is launching new policies
is introducing new policies
已經引起（100 指考）
has caused
has resulted in
正尋求（100 指考）
are seeking
are looking for

其他時式時態和情態助動詞或從屬連接詞的合用：

太陽東升西落。
The sun **rises** in the east and **sets** in the west.
我們以前禮拜日常去上教堂。
We **used to go** to church on Sundays.
她們明天要去紐約。
They **will go** to New York tomorrow.
我們一定要奮戰到底。
We **shall fight** to the end.
當時我們的父母在廚房聊（著）天；我們在客廳下（著）棋。
Our parents **were chatting** in the kitchen while we **were playing chess** in the living room.

總經理從來沒有犯過類似的錯誤?

The general manager **has never committed** similar mistakes?

我最小的妹妹做完報告後跟她男朋友去看電影。

My youngest sister **had finished** the report **before** she **went** to the movies with her boyfriend

My youngest sister **went** to the movies with her boyfriend **after** she **had finished** the report.

到了明年夏天我在該小學任教就滿三十年。

I **will have taught** in the elementary school for thirty years by next summer.

蘋果成熟的時候,我女兒就要出嫁。

My daughter **will be married when** the apples are ripe.

 第三節 總稱單數 = a N; the N; Ns

(狗 = a dog, the dog, dogs;玫瑰 = a rose, the rose, roses;電腦 = a computer, the computer, computers)

中文沒有不定冠詞 a 或 an 接名詞表「總稱單數」(同種類全體)的用法;。其他的用法中,a 或 an 都被處理成 "one" 的同義字。英文的不定冠詞可以表示:(1) 動物、植物和器具的「總稱單數」;(2) 下定義;(3) 等於 every/per;(4) 等於 the same 等用法。

狗是忠實的動物。

A dog is a faithful animal.

(用不定冠詞 a/an 和單數形的可數動物名詞合用,表「總稱單數」。)

玫瑰代表愛情。

A rose is a symbol of love.

(用不定冠詞 a/an 和單數形的可數植物名詞合用,表「總稱單數」。)

智慧型手機是非常有用的工具。

The smart phone is a very useful tool.

(用定冠詞 the 和單數形的可數器具名詞合用,表「總稱單數」。)

心理學家是研究人類思維的人。

A psychologist is **a person** who studies the human mind.

(下定義的句型,請參考 9.7.2)

物以類聚。

Birds of **a** feather flock together. (a = the same)

一星期二次；一個晚上新台幣 2,000 元；每小時 100 公里

twice **a** week; NT$2,000 **a** night; 100 kilometers **an/per** hour (100KPH)

(a = every; per)

人體	human bodies
說明	instructions
房價	house prices
都會區	city areas
高中學生	high school students
＊非動物、非植物和非器具的名詞可以用零冠詞的複數形名詞表「總稱單數」。	

第四節　V+V = V+to V; V+V-ing; V+ (and +) V

　　中文容許有二個限定動詞接連出現的句構，而英文不容許，必須用限定動詞後接非限定動詞的句構。中文的動詞沒有外形上的屈折變化；英文的非限定動詞，有四種外型上的屈折變化：不定詞 (to v)、現在分詞 (v-ing)、過去分詞 (v-en)、原形動詞 (v)。

週末他們喜歡去露營。 On weekends they **like going camping**.
他無法避免犯同樣的錯誤。 He cannot **avoid making** the same mistakes.
你看起來很困惑。 You **look confused**.
我看見你母親把帶子交給記者。 I **saw** your mother **give** the tape to the reporter.
我看見你母親（在）把帶子交給記者。 I **saw** your mother **giving** the tape to the reporter.
大家一塊來享受樂子。 **Come** (and) **join** us and **have** fun.〔請參考 7.6.3〕

去弄一點吃的。
Go (and) **get** something to eat.

 第五節 人稱代名詞或重複名詞片語 = WH

中文沒有關係代名詞或引導名詞子句的 that，必須利用人稱代名詞或「重複名詞片語」的方式來表達，英文用關係代名詞（wh 字詞）形成關係/形容詞子句或用重複名詞片語的方式來表達，利用 that 引導名詞子句。〔請參考 7.5.2-3。請比較 11.1〕

我們認為安全的包裝食品（101 指考）
packaged food (**which/that**) we consider safe
對人體有害的成分（101 指考）
ingredients (**which/that are**) harmful to human bodies
玉山是東亞第一高峰，以生態多樣聞名。（100 指考）
Mt. Jade is the highest mountain in East Asia, **which** is known for its diverse ecology.
Mt. Jade is the highest mountain in East Asia, and **it** is known for its diverse ecology.
許多臺灣製作的影片（101 學測）
many films (**which** were/have been) produced in Taiwan
拍攝這些電影的地點（101 學測）
the locations **where/in which** these films were shot
安全、乾淨又不昂貴的綠色能源（100 指考）
safe, clean and inexpensive green energy（名詞前位修飾）
green energy **which** is safe, clean and inexpensive（名詞後位修飾）
一個你可以終生享受的嗜好（97 學測）
a hobby (**which**) you can enjoy all your life
不抽煙的人（95 指考）
those **who** do not smoke
專家警告我們不應該再將食物價格低廉視為理所當然。（名詞子句；97 指考）
Experts/Specialists (have) warned us (**that**) **we should no longer take low food prices/low-priced food for granted**.

警方通知她，她兒子在車禍中死了。

The police informed her **that her son had died in the car accident**.

邁阿密熱火隊會贏得冠軍這是大家都知道的事。

That the Miami Heat will win the championship is known to everyone.

我們不相信部長會把機密檔案賣給媒體。

We do not believe **that the Minister will sell the classified documents to the media**.

我們的原則是人生而平等。

Our principle is **that all men are created equal**.

我們的原則，人生而平等，應該受到每一位政治領袖的尊重。

Our principle **that all men are created equal** should be respected by every political leader.

第六節　從屬連接

雖然……（但是）= although[...], [...] 或

= [...] although [...]

因為……所以 = because/since/as[...], [...]或

= [...] because/since/as [...]

　　中文必須用從屬子句在前，主要子句在後的「掉尾句」。英文除了用掉尾句之外，也可以用主要子句在前，從屬子句在後的「鬆散句」。中文的「雖然……但是……」，「因為……所以……」是「片語連接詞」，可以成組使用。英文的 although, but, because, so 是個別獨立的單詞連接詞，不可以成組使用。英文只能用一個從屬連接詞，來連接二個句子，形成一個複句；如果要連接三個句子，就需要用二個連接詞，以此類推。〔請參考 7.3.2；7.5〕

---

*雖然*遭到許多癮君子的反對，這對不抽煙的人的確是一大福音。（95 指考）

Although many chain/heavy smokers are against it, this is indeed/definitely good news for non-smokers/those who do not smoke.

雖然 Lily 生來又瞎又聾，*但*她從來不氣餒。（93 學測）

Although Lily was born deaf and blind, she never felt discouraged.

比較：Lily never felt discouraged *although* she was born deaf and blind.

　　　　Lily was born deaf and blind, *but* she never felt discouraged.

*如果*我們只為自己而活，就不會真正地感到快樂。（96 學測）

If we live only for ourselves, we will not feel *really/truly* happy.

If we lived only for ourselves, we would not feel *really/truly* happy.

We will not feel *really/truly* happy *if* we live only for ourselves.

---

*當*我們開始為他人著想，快樂之門自然會開啟。（96 學測）

When we *begin/start* to think for/of others, the *door/gate* to happiness will open naturally.

The *door/gate* to happiness will open naturally *when* we begin/start to think for/of others.

人類對外太空所知非常有限，*但*長久以來我們對它卻很感興趣。（94 學測）

Human beings have a very limited knowledge of outer space, *but* we have long been very interested in it.

Human beings have a very limited knowledge of outer space; *nevertheless*, we have long been very interested in it.

---

*如果*天氣放晴的話，我們去爬山。

If it clears up, we will go mountain climbing.

We will go mountain climbing *if* it clears up.

在他到達*之前*，記得把車子洗好。

Before he arrives, remember to have the car washed.

Remember to have the car washed *before* he arrives.

---

*因為*重感冒，所以她化裝舞會缺席了。

Because she had a bad cold, she was absent from the masquerade ball.

She had a bad cold *so* she was absent from the masquerade ball.

She had a bad cold; *therefore*, she was absent from the masquerade ball.

這位電影明星*雖然*很有錢，*但是*他生活簡樸。

Although the movie star is very rich, he lives a frugal life.

The movie star is very rich, *but* he lives a frugal life.

The movie star is very rich; *however*, he lives a frugal life.

The movie star is very rich; *nevertheless*, he lives a frugal life.

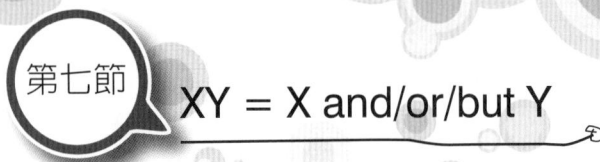

XY = X and/or/but Y

　　中文的並列或對比結構僅由並列或對比的二個元素 (X, Y) 組成；在英文中，這二個並列或對比的元素必須用對等連接詞 and 或 or 或 but 或連字號（-）連接形成。〔請參考 10.2.4〕

往返臺灣南北兩地（96 指考）
travel **back and forth** between the south and the north of Taiwan
travel **back and forth** between northern Taiwan and southern Taiwan

生死	life and death
來回	back and forth; to and fro
買賣	sell and buy
利弊	pros and cons
血肉之軀	flesh and blood
法治	law and order
制衡	checks and balances
熙攘喧鬧	hustle and bustle
是非	right and wrong/right or wrong
成敗	success or failure
真假	true and false
稍縱即逝	now or never

對等連接

[ ]，[ ]。=[ ], and/or/but[ ]. 或 =[ ];[ ].
〔獨立句子，獨立句子。〕=〔獨立句子，and/or/but 獨立句子〕
=〔獨立句子；獨立句子〕

中文可以一口氣寫好幾個獨立句子，常以逗號連接。英文二個獨立子句必須用逗號加上連

接詞來做連接，或用分號連接。

大部分的學生不習慣自己解決問題，他們總是期待老師提供標準答案。（98 學測）

Most students are not used to solving problems by themselves**;** they always expect their teachers to provide (them with) standard answers.

Most students are not used to solving problems by themselves, **and** they always expect their teachers to provide (them with) standard answers.

科技讓我們的生活更舒適，然而它也被利用來犯罪。（93 指考）

Technology makes our lives more comfortable, **but** it is also used to commit crimes.

Technology makes our lives more comfortable; **however/nevertheless**, it is also used to commit crimes.

 第九節　非限定動詞結構

[ ], V...... = **[ ],** 非限定動詞結構或
　　　　　　 = 非限定動詞結構，**[ ].**
非限定動詞結構是由 **v-ing, v-en, to v** 所引導的結構。
〔完整的句子＋動詞......〕=〔完整的句子＋（,）＋非限定動詞結構〕或
　　　　　　　　　　　　 =〔非限定動詞結構，完整的句子〕

　　中文可以在一個完整的句子後面緊接著用一個動詞片語來延續前面的敘述，常表示目的或結果。英文不允許一個句子出現二個限定動詞，因此必須利用對等連接或從屬連接來處理。而且從屬子句可以經由縮減變形成為非限定動詞結構。〔請參考 7.6.5〕

政府正推出新的政策，**以滿足**人們的住房需求。（102 學測）

The government is launching new policies **to meet** people's housing needs/needs of houses.

To meet people's housing needs/needs of houses, the government is launching new policies.

Wanting to meet people's housing needs/needs of houses, the government is launching new policies.

大家在網路上投票給它，**要讓它**成為世界七大奇觀之一。（98 指考）

People are voting for it on the Internet, **hoping** to make it one of (the) Seven Wonders of the World.

People are voting for it on the Internet **to make** it one of (the) Seven Wonders of the World.

To make it one of (the) Seven Wonders of the World, people are voting for it on the Internet.

除了用功**讀書獲取**知識外（98 學測）

in addition to **studying** hard **to acquire** knowledge

第十節　這件事情/也就是 = 虛詞 it

　　中文常用「這件事情」來代替冗長的主詞或受詞；英文用虛詞 "it" 來代替冗長的主詞或受詞（that〔　〕或 (for ...) to v）。另外，英文用 **it** 將要強調的部分移至句首來形成分裂結構。〔請參考 **7.5.3**〕

一般人都知道閱讀對孩子有益。（95 學測）

It is generally known *that reading is good for children*.

地球是圓的這件事情是真的。

It is true *that the earth is round*.

學英語的中國學生使用英英詞典這件事情是重要的。

It is important *for Chinese EFL students to use English-English dictionaries*.

我自己立下一個規定：晚飯後不喝咖啡。

I myself have made *it* a rule *not to drink coffee after dinner*.

哥倫布在 1492 年發現新大陸。

Columbus discovered America in 1492.

It was **Columbus that**/who discovered America in 1492.（分裂結構）

It was **America that** Columbus discovered in 1492.（分裂結構）

It was **in 1492 that** Columbus discovered America.（分裂結構）

參考：美式英語常用 wh-詞代替 that。

第十一節　搭配 (collocation)

　　中文與英文一樣都有嚴謹的字詞間的搭配。尤其是動詞和名詞之間；動詞、形容詞和介系詞之間。〔請參考 7.6.12〕

高房價（102 學測）

high house prices

參考： 價錢昂貴 / 便宜 high/low price

　　　 數量多 / 寡 large/small number

　　　 絕大 / 微弱多數 vast/narrow majority

食物價格低廉（97 指考）

low food prices; **low**-priced food; (the) **low** cost of food

---

騎腳踏車（99 學測）

riding bicycles/bicycle-riding

開汽車

drive a car

開飛機

fly a plane

彈奏樂器（97 學測）

play a musical instrument/play musical instruments

犯罪（93 指考）

commit crimes

犯錯

make a mistake

自殺

commit suicide

kill oneself

正在做有氧運動

doing aerobic **exercises**

正在做一系列的實驗

conducting a series of **experiments**

正在做一項調查	正在做評論
undergoing an **investigation**	**making** a **comment**

控告（某人某事）

to **charge** someone **with/against** something

to **accuse** someone **of** something

to **file** a lawsuit **against** somebody

遵守規定

to **abide by** the rules

to **comply with** the rules

這個委員會由高中生組成。（由……組成）

The committee **consists of** high school students.

The committee **is composed** of high school students.

The committee **is comprised of** high school students.

The committee **is made up of** high school students.

 第十二節　部分詞 (partitive)

片 / 件 / 塊 / 則 = **piece**

群 = **crowd/flock/herd/school**

中文和英文一樣都有相當靈活的部分詞或量詞來精準量化名詞。

成千上萬（99 學測）

hundreds and **thousands** of

hundreds of **thousands** of

millions of

一種交通工具

a **means** of transportation（99 學測）

一句忠告	a **piece** of advice	一件傢俱	an **item** of furniture
一塊肥皂	a **box/cake/bar** of soap	一陣咳嗽／大笑	a **fit** of coughing/laughter
一群粉絲	a **crowd** of fans	一群足球隊員	a **team** of football players
一群牛／狼	a **herd** of cattle/wolves	一群海豚	a **school** of dolphins
一群罪犯／少年	a **gang** of criminals/youths	一窩小狗／小貓	a **litter** of puppies/kittens
一群記者	a **flock** of reporters	一群蜜蜂／蒼蠅	a **swarm** of bees/flies
一條牛仔褲／熱褲	a **pair** of jeans/jorts	一片煙霧	a **cloud** of smog
一團疑雲	a **cloud** of suspicion	一片水域	a **body** of water
麻疹發作	an **attack** of measles	流感侵襲	an **attack** of the flu

 第十三節 聲調與響度研判二項式結構的詞序

聲調（平前仄後；聲調質低的在前，高的在後）研判中文詞序 = 響度（音節數目少的在前，多的在後）研判英文詞序〔請參考 10.2.4；附錄 6〕。有趣的是，中文的複詞與英文的二項式結構的詞序常常相反。

食宿（二聲—四聲）	bed and breakfast（1 個音節-2 個音節）
辛辣（一聲—四聲）	hot and spicy（1 個音節-2 個音節）
親（戚朋）友（一聲—三聲）	friends and relatives（1 個音節-3 個音節）
（胡）椒鹽（一聲—二聲）	salt and pepper（1 個音節-2 個音節）
田徑（運動）（二聲—四聲）	track and field（1 個音節-2 個音節）
買賣（三聲—四聲）	sell and buy（1-1 再比較響度）
（又）瞎（又）聾（一聲—二聲）	deaf and blind（1-1 再比較響度）
老少（三聲—四聲）	young and old（1-1 再比較響度）
真假（／對錯）（一聲—三聲）	true or false（1-1 再比較響度）
敵友（二聲—三聲）	friend and foe（1-1 再比較響度）
往返（三聲—三聲）	back and forth（1-1 再比較響度）
熙攘（喧鬧）（一聲—三聲（一聲—四聲））	hustle and bustle（2-2 再比較響度）

第十四節　……的 = 連字號形容詞

英文利用連字號形容詞來形成名詞前位修飾。

一份長達八百頁的報告

an **800-page** report ← a report which has/consists of 800 pages

一份長達二十多萬字的起訴書

an **over-two-hundred-thousand-word** indictment ← an indictment which has/consists of over two hundred thousand words

一個五歲大的幼稚園學生

a **five-year-old** kindergarten student ← a kindergarten student who is five years old

（比較：兩個五歲大的小孩 two five-year-olds）

一個現買現賺的便宜貨

a **you-buy-and-you-save** good deal ← a good deal in which you buy and you save money

不滿意就退錢的保證

a **money-back** guarantee ← a guarantee which promises to return your money if you are not satisfied with a product or service

一家自己動手的商店

a **do-it-yourself** store ← a store which allows you to make or repair things yourself instead of buying them

一套訂做的衣服

a **custom-made** suit ← a suit which is made for a particular person

雙贏的局面

a **win-win** situation ← a situation which will end well for everyone involved in it

一種複製、剪下、貼上的操作方法

a **copy-cut-and-paste** method ← a method by meams of which text is reproduced

---

第十五節　沒有主詞 = 必須確認並且提供主詞

中文句子常常可以省略主詞，例如，「活到老，學到老」；英文句子必須提供明確的主詞或利用虛主詞引導〔請參考 7.5.3〕。在祈使句中，中英文的主詞都可以省略。

如果我們只為自己而活，就不會真正地感到快樂。（96 學測）

If we only live for ourselves, **we** will not feel really happy.

比較：If we only live for ourselves, we will not really feel happy.

為了我們自身的健康，在購買食物前我們應仔細閱讀包裝上的說明。（101 指考）

For our own health, we should carefully read the instructions on the package before **we** buy any food.

第十六節　N + 介系詞 = 介系詞 + N

英文的介系詞是前置詞 (preposition)，是介系詞+名詞以形成介系詞片語；相反地，中文的介系詞是後置詞 (postposition)，是名詞+介系詞以形成介系詞片語。但是中文的介系詞片語與英文的介系詞片語當修飾語時，詞序不一樣，中文的介系詞片語是屬於前位修飾，要放在所修飾的名詞前面，而且有時候介系詞標記「在」未必顯示。英文的介系詞片語是屬於後位修飾，要放在所修飾的名詞後面，而且介系詞一定要顯示出來。

（在）都會區的高房價（102 學測） high house prices **in** city areas
許多（在）臺灣製作的影片（101 學測） many films produced **in** Taiwan
包裝上 **on** the package（101 指考）
在網路上 **on** the Internet（98 指考）
在這個小島上 **on** this small island（94 指考）
（在）我的心裡 **in** my heart

（在）河邊 **by** the river

（在）校園裡面 **on** the campus

報紙上面 **in** the newspaper

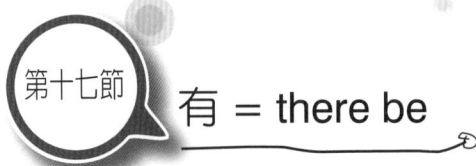

第十七節　有 = there be

　　中文用「有」、「發生」來表示「存在」；英文則利用介系詞片語 **with** ... 來表示「有」，利用虛詞 "there" 與 **be** 或 **exist/lie/remain/stand** 等動詞的句構，或用介系詞片語 **with** ... 來表示「存在」、「發生」。

有了高速鐵路（96 指考） **with** the high-speed rail; **with** the High-Speed Rail
一條有二個頭的蛇 a snake **with** two heads
一間有三個臥室的公寓 an apartment **with** three bedrooms
一本附有二片 CD 的詞典 a dictionary **with** two CDs
那裡以前有個夜市。 **There used to be** a night market there.
昨天臺北市發生了一場火警。 **There was** a fire in Taipei yesterday.
這個計畫有一些問題。 **There are** some problems in the project.
這個制度存在著一些問題。 **There remain** a number of problems in the system.

第十八節 V +（不）結果 =（否定）V + 質詞／介副詞

中文的結果動詞結構，例如吃完、吃不完，在英文中常以片語動詞（即動詞加質詞/介副詞），例如 eat up；或是動詞後面接上表示結果的形容詞，例如 pull open（拉開）來表達。英文的片語動詞常可以「類轉」成為名詞。〔請參考 10.8〕中文的結果動詞結構，只要在表結果的單詞或片語前面加上「不」即可形成否定，例如吃不完，打不開；英文常常必須在片語動詞前面加上「表否定」的（情態）助動詞例如 cannot eat up, cannot pull open 來形成否定。有時候，中英對譯會有語義上的差異，例如，吃不完 vs. 不吃完 vs. 無法吃完等。

吃完；脫掉；用盡；關閉 eat **up**; take **off**; run **out of**; shut **down**（動詞加質詞/介副詞） 比較：推開 push **open**；吹乾 blow **dry**；濕透 soak **wet**；脫光 strip **naked**
二十個伏地挺身 twenty **push-ups**（類轉）
幾十個得來速 dozens of **drive-throughs/drive-thrus**（類轉）
有才華的大學輟學生／退學生 talented college **dropouts**（類轉）
許多離家出走的青少年 a number of **teenage runaways**（類轉）
南臺灣第一個「露天汽車電影院」 the first "**drive-in**" (movie theater) in southern Taiwan（類轉）
舉行靜坐示威 to hold a **sit-in**（類轉）

第十九節　抽象形容詞或副詞 = 介系詞片語

中文的抽象形容詞或副詞，在英文中常用介系詞片語（介系詞，特別是 with，加上相關的抽象名詞）來表示。

今天我們在台灣驕傲和自信地告訴全世界......

Today, we in Taiwan tell the world, **with great pride and self-confidence**, that ...

(**very proudly and confidently**)

委員會謹慎地在選擇地點。

The committee is choosing the location **carefully/with care**.

那位參賽者充滿信心地走上講台。

The contestant went onto the podium **confidently/with confidence**.

遊客們匆匆忙忙走出遊覽車。

The visitors stepped out of the tour bus **quickly/in a hurry**.

他們的計畫一定會非常成功。

Their plan will **meet with great success/be very successful**.

第二十節　可能會用到的符號

1. 中文的句中省略用...... =英文的句中省略用 ...〔當代英語也有人用於句尾省略〕

...... 民有、民治、民享 ......（六個點）

... of the people, by the people, for the people ...（三個點）

2. 中文的句尾省略用......。 =英文的句尾省略用....〔請參考 5.2.6〕

民有、民治、民享的政府......。（六個點加句號）

Government of the people, by the people, for the people....（三個點加上句號成為四個點）

3. 中文短暫停頓或平行結構用「、」=英文短暫停頓或平行結構用「,」

   民有、民治、民享 = of the people, by the people, for the people

4. 中文書名號用《 》=英文書名號用底線＿＿＿＿＿或*斜體字*
   〔當代英語常用*斜體字*〕

   《傲慢與偏見》= Pride and Prejudice = *Pride and Prejudice*

5. 中文直接引述用「……」= 英文直接引述用 "..."

   她大聲喊著說：「走開！」= She shouted: "Go away!"

6. 中文引述中的引述用『……』= 英文引述中的引述用 '...'

   時機：在引述說話內容中又有直接的引述。中文：外單內雙；英文：外雙內單。（單=單引
   　　　號；雙=雙引號）

   那位記者堅持說：「主持人說：『錢可以買到真愛。』。」
   "The host said: 'Money can buy real love.'" insisted the reporter.

   　表示直接引述時，美式英語常用雙引號（" "），而英式英語常用單引號（' '）。如果引
   述內容中又有直接引述時，美式英語常用單引號，而英式英語常用雙引號。〔請參考 5.10〕

7. 與／或 = **and/or**

   現金與/或支票
   cash and/or check

   研究生與/或大學部學生
   graduate and/or undergraduate students

8. 對，訴＝versus/vs./v.〔常用於體育比賽或訴訟〕

休士頓火箭隊對紐約尼克隊

the Houston Rockets versus/vs. the New York Knicks

國民健康局訴臺北市一案

Bureau of Health Promotion v. Taipei City

（v. 常用於訴訟）

附錄 1

著名演說詞

蓋茨堡演說詞

背景資料

　　亞伯拉罕‧林肯 (Abraham Lincoln) 是美國第 16 任總統 (1861-1865)。當時正值美國內戰 (the American Civil War) 期間 (1861-1865)，1863 年 7 月支持聯邦政府各州的「聯邦軍」(the Union Army) 在蓋茨堡戰役 (the Battle of Gettysburg) 中戰勝了「南部邦聯軍」(the Confederate States Army)。這場舉世聞名的演說 (the Gettysburg Address) 是林肯總統於 1863 年 11 月 19 日在蓋茨堡所發表的，為了紀念在該戰役中犧牲的五萬多名士兵，而在賓州蓋茨堡 (Gettysburg, Pennsylvania) 建了國家軍人公墓 (Soldiers' National Cemetery)。這篇精雕細琢、語氣真誠堅定的演說詞，雖然只有 278 個單詞，10 個句子，全長二分多鐘，但是它卻是後人公認美國史上最有名的演說詞之一。

演說詞全文

Four score and seven years ago *our fathers brought forth on this continent, a new nation, conceived in Liberty*[1], and dedicated to the proposition that all men are created equal.

Now we are engaged in a great civil war, testing whether that nation[2], or any nation so conceived and so dedicated, can long endure. We are met on a great battlefield of that war. We have come to dedicate a portion of that field, as a final resting place for *those who here gave their lives that that nation might live*[3]. *It is altogether fitting and proper that we should do this*[4].

But, in a larger sense, *we cannot dedicate--we cannot consecrate-we cannot hallow this ground*[5]. The brave men, living and dead, who have struggled here, have consecrated it, far above our poor power to add or detract. *The world will little note, nor long remember what we say here, but it can never forget what they did here*[6]. It is for us the living, rather, to be dedicated here to the unfinished work which they who fought here have thus far so nobly advanced. *It is rather for us to be here dedicated to the great task remaining before us*[7]*--that* from these honored dead we take increased devotion to that cause for which they gave the last full measure of devotion--*that* we here highly resolve that these dead shall not have died in vain--*that* this nation, under God, shall have a new birth of freedom--and *that* government *of the people, by the people, for the people*[8], shall not perish from the earth.

精讀分析

1. ... our fathers brought forth on this continent, a new *nation*, *conceived* in Liberty....

　　將片語動詞 (brought forth) 的受詞 a new nation 往後移動，因此不會使得後位修飾語 conceived ... 造成「誤置修飾語」的問題，也就是說 conceived 清楚地修飾 nation (a new nation which was conceived in Liberty) 而不是修飾 continent。

　　比較*... our fathers brought forth a new nation on **this continent**, **conceived** in Liberty....（誤置修飾語）

2. Now we are engaged in a great civil war, *testing* whether that nation....

　　在完整句子的句尾加上逗號，然後接上一個分詞構句，清晰呈現彼此的邏輯關係。我們可以試著將句子還原為 Now we are engaged in a great civil war, because we are testing whether that nation....

3. ... those who here gave their lives *that that* nation might live.

　　形容詞子句 who here gave their lives 修飾先行詞 those；副詞子句 that that nation might live 呈現跟前句的「因果」關係。這個句子接連出現二個 that，第一個 that 是從屬連接詞（= so that），第二個 that 是限定詞，等於冠詞或指示詞的功能。

　　同系衍生詞：live-lives。

　　參考：*live* a happy *life*; *dream* an impossible *dream*; *sing* a beautiful *song*; *smile* a warm *smile*;
　　　　　die a natural *death*

4. *It* is altogether fitting and proper that we should do this.

　　用了一個由虛主詞 it 引導的句子，使得句型和句長有變化。在第三段，作者接連又用了二個由虛主詞 it 引導的句子，而且變化遣詞用字。

5. ... we cannot dedicate--we cannot consecrate--we cannot hallow--this ground.

這個句子同時用了二個修辭格，一個是加強語氣的重複，一個是三節格律法。〔請參考 10.3〕

6. The world *will little* note, nor *long* remember what we *say* here, but it *can* never forget what they *did* here.

有三組對照值得討論。第一是副詞 little vs. long 押頭韻，第二是名詞子句 what we say here vs. what they did here 時式的對照，第三是情態助動詞 will vs. can。另外，作者在文章中用了一個 will，三個 shall，很顯然地，這二種情態助動詞所呈現的語義或情態並不相同，shall 有強調「必然」的語義。這一點也可以在甘迺迪總統就職演說詞 ... we shall pay any price ...（第五段）得到佐證。

7. *It* is rather for us to be here dedicated to the great task remaining before us--that....

用了虛主詞 it 取代「冗長的」真主詞 for us to be here dedicated to the great task remaining before us。作者巧妙地利用高潮迭起的修辭格，連續用了四個由 that 引導的名詞子句，共六十九個單詞，占全文長度的四分之一，同時作 the great task 的同位語。

8. ... government *of the people, by the people, for the people, shall* not perish from the earth.

用了「三節格律法」，三個平行的介系詞片語 "of the people, by the people, for the people"（「民有、民治、民享」）的重要性和緊湊性逐漸增強。另外，就是前面提過的情態助動詞 shall (not) 表示強調「必然（不會）」的語義。

甘迺迪總統就職演說詞

背景資料

　　約翰・費茲傑羅・甘迺迪 (John Fitzgerald Kennedy) 是一位美國傳奇人物。他是經由選舉當選的最年輕的美國總統，當時年僅 43 歲。甘迺迪在 1960 年的美國總統選舉中，以些微的差距擊敗對手，時任副總統的共和黨候選人理查・尼克森 (Richard Nixon)。底下是甘迺迪於 1961 年 1 月 20 日宣誓就職美國第 35 任總統時所發表的演說詞。這篇就職演說詞 (inaugural address) 全文一千三百多個單詞，五十多個句子，文字簡潔平易鏗鏘有力，一直被公認是美國歷史上最好的總統就職演說之一。演說詞中有二句話常被後人引用："Let us never negotiate out of fear. But let us never fear to negotiate."「讓我們永遠不因畏懼而談判。但讓我們永遠不要畏懼談判。」"And so, my fellow Americans: ask not what your country can do for you--ask what you can do for your country."「所以，同胞們：不要問國家能為你們做什麼，而是要問你們能為國家做什麼。」

演說詞全文

Vice President Johnson, Mr. Speaker, Mr. Chief Justice, President Eisenhower, Vice President Nixon, President Truman, Reverend Clergy, fellow citizens:

We observe today *not a victory of party but a celebration of freedom, symbolizing an end as well as a beginning, signifying renewal as well as change*[1]. For I have sworn before you and Almighty God the same solemn oath our forebears prescribed nearly a century and three-quarters ago.

The world is very different now. For man holds in his mortal hands the power to abolish *all forms of human poverty and all forms of human life*[2]. And yet the same revolutionary beliefs for which our forebears fought are still at issue around the globe--the belief that the rights of man come not from the generosity of the state but from the hand of God.

We dare not forget today that we are the heirs of that first revolution. Let the word go forth from this time and place, to friend and foe alike, that the torch has been passed to a new generation of Americans, born in this century, tempered by war, disciplined by a hard and bitter peace, proud of our ancient heritage, and unwilling to witness or permit the slow undoing of *those human rights to which this nation has always been committed, and to which we are committed today*[3] at home and around the world.

Let every nation know, whether it wishes us well or ill, that *we shall pay any price, bear any burden, meet any hardship, support any friend, oppose any foe to assure the survival and the success of liberty*[4].

This much we pledge--and more.

To those old allies whose cultural and spiritual origins we share, we pledge the loyalty of faithful friends[5]. *United, there is little we cannot do in a host of cooperative ventures. Divided, there is little we can do*[6]; for we dare not meet a powerful challenge at odds and split asunder.

To those new states whom we welcome to the ranks of the free, we pledge[5] our word that one form of colonial control shall not have passed away merely to be replaced by a far more iron tyranny. We shall not always expect to find them supporting our view. But we shall always hope to find them strongly supporting their own freedom; and to remember that, in the past, those who foolishly sought power by riding the back of the tiger ended up inside.

To those people in the huts and villages of half the globe struggling to break the bonds of mass misery, we pledge[5] our best efforts to help them help themselves, for whatever period is required--not because the Communists may be doing it, not because we seek their votes, but because it is right. *If a free society cannot help the many who are poor, it cannot save the few who are rich*[7].

To our sister republics south of the border, we offer a special pledge: to convert our good words into good deeds in a new alliance for progress; to assist free men and free governments in casting off the chains of poverty. But this peaceful revolution of hope cannot become the prey of hostile powers. Let all our neighbors know that we shall join with them to oppose aggression or subversion anywhere in the Americas. And let every other power know that this Hemisphere intends to remain the master of its own house.

To that world assembly of sovereign states, the United Nations, our last best hope in an age where the instruments of war have far outpaced the instruments of peace, we renew our pledge of support, to prevent it from becoming merely a forum for invective, to strengthen its shield of the new and the weak, and to enlarge the area in which its writ may run.

Finally, to those nations who would make themselves our adversary, we offer not a pledge but a request: that both sides begin anew the quest for peace, before the dark powers of destruction unleashed by science engulf all humanity in planned or accidental self-destruction.

We dare not tempt them with weakness. For only when our arms are sufficient beyond doubt can we be certain beyond doubt that they will never be employed.

But neither can two great and powerful groups of nations take comfort from our present course[8]--both sides overburdened by the cost of modern weapons, both rightly alarmed by the steady spread of the deadly atom, yet both racing to alter that uncertain balance of terror that stays the hand of mankind's final war.

So let us begin anew remembering on both sides that civility is not a sign of weakness, and sincerity is always subject to proof. Let us never negotiate out of fear. But let us never fear to negotiate.

Let both sides explore what problems unite us instead of belaboring those problems which divide us.

Let both sides, for the first time, formulate serious and precise proposals for the inspection and control of arms--and bring the absolute power to destroy other nations under the absolute control of all nations.

Let both sides seek to invoke the wonders of science instead of its terrors. Together let us explore the stars, conquer the deserts, eradicate disease, tap the ocean depths, and encourage the arts and commerce.

Let both sides unite to heed, in all corners of the Earth the command of Isaiah to "undo the heavy burdens, and [to] let the oppressed go free."

And if a beachhead of cooperation may push back the jungle of suspicion, let both sides join in creating a new endeavor, not a new balance of power, but a new world of law, where the strong are just and the weak secure and the peace preserved.

All this will not be finished in the first one hundred days. Nor will it be finished in the first one thousand days, nor in the life of this administration, nor even perhaps in our lifetime on this planet[9]. But let us begin.

In your hands, my fellow citizens, more than mine, will rest the final success or failure of our course. Since this country was founded, each generation of Americans has been summoned to give testimony to its national loyalty. The graves of young Americans who answered the call to service surround the globe.

Now the trumpet summons us again; not as a call to bear arms, though arms we need; not as a call to battle, though embattled we are; but a call to bear the burden of a long twilight struggle, year in and year out, "rejoicing in hope, patient in tribulation"--a struggle against the common enemies of man: tyranny, poverty, disease, and war itself.

Can we forge against these enemies a grand and global alliance, North and South, East and West, that can assure a more fruitful life for all mankind? Will you join in that historic effort?

In the long history of the world, only a few generations have been granted the role of defending freedom in its hour of maximum danger. I do not shrink from this responsibility; I welcome it. I do not believe that any of us would exchange places with any other people or any other generation. The energy, the faith, the devotion which we bring to this endeavor will light our country and all who serve it. And the glow from that fire can truly light the world.

And so, my fellow Americans, *ask not what your country can do for you--ask what you can do for your country*[10].

My fellow citizens of the world, ask not what America will do for you, but what together we can do for the freedom of man.

Finally, whether you are citizens of America or citizens of the world, ask of us here the same high standards of strength and sacrifice which we ask of you. With a good conscience our only sure reward, with history the final judge of our deeds, let us go forth to lead the land we love, asking His blessing and His help, but knowing that here on Earth God's work must truly be our own.

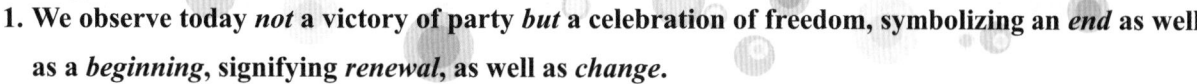

精讀分析

1. **We observe today *not* a victory of party *but* a celebration of freedom, symbolizing an *end* as well as a *beginning*, signifying *renewal*, as well as *change*.**

(1) 對照：not ...but; end vs. beginning; renewal vs. change

(2) 平行：not ... but; a victory of party, a celebration of freedom; symbolizing ..., signifying ...

(3) 押頭韻：symbolizing, signifying

　　參考：第三段的最後一句 not from the generosity of the state but from the hand of God 也有對照與平行的修辭格。

2. **For man holds in his mortal hands the power to abolish *all forms of human* poverty and *all forms of human* life.**

(1) 加強語氣的重複：all forms of human poverty, all forms of human life

(2) 將介系詞片語 in his mortal hands 前移。〔請參考蓋茨堡演說詞精讀分析 1〕

3. **... those human rights *to which* this nation has always been committed, and *to which* we *are committed* today....**

　　用了二個形容詞子句，後位修飾先行詞 those human rights，同時將在句尾落單的介系詞 to 移至 which 前面。另外，作者熟練地運用時式與時態來突顯動詞 commit 的從過去一直延續到現在。

　　比較：... those human rights which this nation has always been committed to, and which we are committed to today....

　　參考：本書第 233 頁 ... they were signing a promissory note *to which* every American was to fall heir.

4. **... we shall *pay* any *price, bear* any *burden*, meet any hardship, *support* any *friend, oppose* any *foe* to assure the *survival* and the *success* of liberty.**

(1) 對照：friend vs. foe; support vs. oppose。

(2) 押頭韻：pay-price; bear-burden; friend-foe; survival-success。

(3) 搭配：pay any price; bear any burden; support any friend; oppose any foe。

5. *To those* old allies whose *cultural* and *spiritual* origins we share, *we pledge* the loyalty of faithful friends. *To those ..., we pledge.... To those ..., we pledge....*

(1) 加強語氣的重複：To those ..., we pledge....。

　　參考：let both sides....。

(2) 押尾韻：cultural-spiritual。

(3) 押頭韻：faithful-friends。

6. *United*, there is *little* we *cannot* do in a host of cooperative ventures. *Divided*, there is little we can do....

(1) 分詞構句：United = If we are united; Divided = If we are divided。

(2) 「雙重否定」強於一個肯定：there is little we cannot do = there is a lot we can do。

7. If a free society cannot help the *many* who are *poor*, it cannot save the *few* who are *rich*.

(1) 對照：many vs. few; poor vs. rich。

(2) 變化：遣詞用字富於變化 help vs. save

8. But *neither can* two great and powerful groups of nations take comfort from our present course....

(1) 倒裝：... neither can two great and powerful groups of nations take comfort ...

　　比較：... two great and powerful groups of nations can neither take comfort ...

　　參考：In your hands, my fellow citizens, more than mine, will rest the final success or failure of our course.（第 228 頁）

　　比較：The final success or failure of our course will rest in your hands, my fellow citizens, more than mine.

(2) 詞序：great and powerful（一個音節 and 二個音節）

　　中譯：強大（的）（二聲-四聲）（註：英文的詞序是「大」and「強」。）

　　比較：powerful and great

9. All this will not be finished in the first one *hundred* days. Nor will it be finished in the first one *thousand* days, nor in the *life* of this *administration*, nor even perhaps in our *lifetime* on this *planet*.

(1)（層次）遞增：hundred-thousand; life-lifetime; administration-planet。

(2) 加強語氣的重複：... this will not be finished....; Nor will it be finished....。

(3) 倒裝：Nor will it be finished....。

10. ... *ask not* what your country can do for you--*ask* what you can do for your country.

(1) 平衡句：ask not ... ask....。

(2) ask not = do not ask。

《我有一個夢》

背景資料

　　《我有一個夢》"I Have a Dream" 是美國民權運動 (American Civil Rights Movement) 領袖馬丁 · 路德 · 金恩二世 (Martin Luther King, Jr.)，為了結束美國當時的種族主義 (racism in the United States) 於 1963 年 8 月 28 日在林肯紀念堂 (the Lincoln Memorial) 前，對串連到華盛頓參加為工作、為自由而遊行 (the March on Washington for Jobs and Freedom) 的支持者所發表的演講。演講的主要訴求是要終止種族隔離 (racial segregation) 與歧視 (discrimination) 政策。翌年，美國國會通過《1964 年民權法案》(Civil Rights Act of 1964)，這個法案被認為是美國民權立法的里程碑（landmark），明文規定對種族、民族、國籍、宗教的少數群體、女性的歧視是違法行為。金恩博士在演說詞中成功地運用了很多的修辭格，尤其是比喻修辭格。這篇演說詞被譽為二十世紀美國最好的演說詞。

演說詞全文

I am happy to join with you today in what will go down in history as the greatest demonstration for freedom in the history of our nation.

Five score years ago[1], a great American, in whose symbolic shadow we stand today, signed the Emancipation Proclamation. This momentous decree came as a great beacon light of hope to millions of Negro slaves who had been seared in the flames of withering injustice. It came as a joyous daybreak to end the long night of captivity.

But *one hundred years later*[2], we must face the tragic fact that the Negro still is not free. *One hundred years later*[2], the life of the Negro is still sadly crippled by the manacles of segregation and the chains of discrimination. *One hundred years later*[2], the Negro lives on *a lonely island of poverty in the midst of a vast ocean of material prosperity*[3]. *One hundred years later*[2], the Negro is still languished in the corners of American society and finds himself an exile in his own land.

And so we've come here today to dramatize an appalling condition. In a sense we've come to our nation's capital to cash a check. When the architects of our republic wrote the magnificent words of the Constitution and the Declaration of Independence, they were signing a promissory note to which every American was to fall heir. This note was a promise that all men, yes, black men as well as white men, would be guaranteed the inalienable rights of "Life, Liberty, and the pursuit of Happiness." It is obvious today that America has defaulted on this promissory note, insofar as her citizens of color are concerned. Instead of honoring this sacred obligation, America has given the Negro people a bad check which has come back marked "insufficient funds."

But we refuse to believe that the bank of justice is bankrupt. We refuse to believe that there are insufficient funds in the great vaults of opportunity of this nation. And so, *we've come to cash this check, a check*[4] that will give us upon demand the riches of freedom and the security of justice.

We have also come to this hallowed spot to remind America of the fierce urgency of Now. This is no time to engage in the luxury of cooling off or to take the tranquilizing drug of gradualism. *Now is the time*[2] to make real the promises of democracy. Now is the time to rise from the dark and desolate valley of segregation to the sunlit path of racial justice. *Now is the time*[2] to lift our nation *from the quicksands of racial injustice to the solid rock of brotherhood*[3]. *Now is the time*[2] to make justice a reality for all of God's children.

It would be fatal for the nation to overlook the urgency of the moment. This sweltering summer of the Negro's legitimate discontent will not pass until there is an invigorating autumn of freedom and equality. Nineteen sixty-three is not an end, but a beginning. And those who hope that the Negro needed to blow off steam and will now be content will have a rude awakening if the nation returns to business as usual. And there will be neither rest nor tranquility in America until the Negro is granted his citizenship rights. The whirlwinds of revolt will continue to shake the foundations of our nation until the bright day of justice emerges.

But there is something that I must say to my people, who stand on the warm threshold which leads into the palace of justice: In the process of gaining our rightful place, we must not be guilty of wrongful deeds. Let us not seek to satisfy our thirst for freedom by drinking from the cup of bitterness and hatred. We must forever conduct our struggle on the high plane of dignity and discipline. We must not allow our creative protest to degenerate into physical violence. Again and again, we must rise to the majestic heights of meeting physical force with soul force.

The marvelous new militancy which has engulfed the Negro community must not lead us to a distrust of all white people, for *many of our white brothers, as evidenced by their presence here today, have come to realize that their destiny is tied up with our destiny. And they have come to realize that their freedom is inextricably bound to our freedom*[5].

We cannot walk alone[6].

And as we walk, we must make the pledge that we shall always march ahead.

We cannot turn back[6].

There are those who are asking the devotees of civil rights, "When will you be satisfied?" We can never be satisfied as long as the Negro is the victim of the unspeakable horrors of police brutality. We can never be satisfied as long as our bodies, heavy with the fatigue of travel, cannot gain lodging in the motels of the highways and the hotels of the cities. We cannot be satisfied as long as the negro's basic mobility is from a smaller ghetto to a larger one. We can never be satisfied as long as our children are stripped of their self-hood and robbed of their dignity by signs stating: "For Whites Only." We cannot be satisfied as long as a Negro in Mississippi cannot vote and a Negro in New York believes he has nothing for which to vote. No, no, we are not satisfied, and we will not be satisfied until *"justice rolls down like waters, and righteousness like a mighty stream."*[7]

I am not unmindful that some of you have come here out of great trials and tribulations.[8] Some of you have come fresh from narrow jail cells. *And some of you have come from areas where your quest--quest*[4] for freedom left you battered by the storms of persecution and staggered by the winds of police brutality. You have been the veterans of creative suffering. Continue to work with the faith that unearned suffering is redemptive. Go back to Mississippi, go back to Alabama, go back to South Carolina, go back to Georgia, go back to Louisiana, go back to the slums and ghettos of our northern cities, knowing that somehow this situation can and will be changed.

Let us not wallow in the valley of despair, I say to you today, my friends.[6]

And so even though we face the difficulties of today and tomorrow, I still have a dream. *It is a dream deeply rooted in the American dream.* [6]

I have a dream that one day this nation will rise up and live out the true meaning of its creed: "We hold these truths to be self-evident, that all men are created equal."

I have a dream that one day on the red hills of Georgia, the sons of former slaves and the sons of former slave owners will be able to sit down together at the table of brotherhood.

I have a dream that one day even the state of Mississippi, a desert state, sweltering with the heat of injustice, sweltering with the heat of oppression, will be transformed into an oasis of freedom and justice.

I have a dream that my four little children will one day live in a nation where they will not be judged by the color of their skin but by the content of their character. [8]

I have a *dream* today!

I have a dream that one day, down in Alabama, with its vicious racists, with its governor having his lips dripping with the words of "interposition" and "nullification"--one day right there in Alabama *little black boys and black girls will be able to join hands with little white boys and white girls as sisters and brothers.* [9]

I have a *dream* today!

I have a dream that one day *every valley shall be exalted, and every hill and mountain shall be made low, the rough places will be made plain, and the crooked places will be made straight* [10]; "and the glory of the Lord shall be revealed and all flesh shall see it together."

This is our hope, and *this is the faith that I go back to the South with.*

With this faith [4], we will be able to hew out of the mountain of despair a stone of hope. *With this faith* [2], we will be able to transform the jangling discords of our nation into a beautiful symphony of brotherhood. *With this faith* [2], we will be able to work together, to pray together, to struggle together, to go to jail together, to stand up for freedom together, knowing that we will be free one day.

And this will be the day--this will be the day when all of God's children will be able to sing with new meaning:

"My country, 'tis of thee, sweet land of liberty, of thee I sing.

Land where my fathers died, land of the Pilgrim's pride,

From every mountainside, let freedom ring!"

And if America is to be a great nation, this must become true.

And so let freedom ring from the prodigious hilltops of New Hampshire.

Let freedom ring from the mighty mountains of New York.

Let freedom ring from the heightening Alleghenies of Pennsylvania.

Let freedom ring from the snow-capped Rockies of Colorado.

Let freedom ring from the curvaceous slopes of California.[10]

But not only that:

Let freedom ring from Stone Mountain of Georgia.

Let freedom ring from Lookout Mountain of Tennessee.

Let freedom ring from every hill and every molehill of Mississippi.

From every mountainside, let freedom ring.

And when this happens, when we allow freedom ring, when we let it ring from every village and every hamlet, from every state and every city, we will be able to speed up that day when all of God's children, black men and white men, Jews and Gentiles, Protestants and Catholics, will be able to join hands and sing in the words of the old Negro spiritual:

"Free at last! Free at last!

Thank God Almighty, we are free at last!"

精讀分析

1. Five *score* years ago....

變化：five score = one hundred

參考：林肯在蓋茨堡演說詞一開始用了 four score and seven years ago。

比較：作者在下一段改用 one hundred years later。

2. one hundred years later

加強語氣的重複：在同一段裡面，作者一連用了四次 "one hundred years later"。全文用了很多加強語氣的重複。

參考：Now is the time....

Will this faith....

3. a *lonely island* of *poverty* in the midst of a *vast ocean* of *material prosperity*

(1) 比喻：island, ocean

(2) 對照：lonely vs. vast; poverty vs. prosperity

(3) 押頭韻與押尾韻：poverty, prosperity

參考：from the quicksands of racial injustice to the solid rock of brotherhood

4. ...we've come to cash *this check, a check*....

(1) 聯珠：this check, a check

(2) 參考：And some of you have come from areas where your quest--quest....

... this is the faith that I go back to the south with. With this faith....

(3) 比喻：用「支票」(check)、「芭樂票」(bad check)、「退票」(a check which has come back)、「存款不足」(insufficient funds) 等引起共鳴。

5. ... many of our white brothers, as *evidenced* by their presence here today, *have come to realize* that their destiny is tied up with our destiny. And they *have come to realize* that their freedom is inextricably bound to our freedom.

(1) 類轉：evidence 作動詞用，等於 to prove。

(2) 加強語氣的重複：... have come to realize that....。

(3) 變化：遣詞用字富於變化 (is) tied up vs. (is inextricably) bound to。

6. We cannot walk alone.

　　變化：長短句交互使用

　　參考：We cannot turn back.

　　　　　Let us not wallow in the valley of despair, I say to you today, my friends.

　　　　　It is a dream deeply rooted in the American dream.

　　　　　I have a dream.

7. ... "justice rolls down *like waters*, and righteousness *like a mighty stream*."

(1) 引用：引用《聖經‧舊約》《阿摩司書》五章 24 節 (Amos 5:24) "justice rolls down like waters, and righteousness like a mighty stream."

(2) 參考：引用《聖經‧舊約》《以賽亞書》四十章 4~5 節 (Isaiah 40:4~5) "I have a dream that every valley shall be exalted...."。

(3) 比喻：like waters, like a mighty stream

(4) 省略：and righteousness (rolls down) like a mighty stream

(5) 詞序：justice（二個音節），righteousness（三個音節）

8. I have a dream that my four little children will one day live in a nation where they will *not* be judged by the *color* of their skin *but* by the *content* of their *character*.

(1) 平行：not ... but

(2) 對照：color vs. content

(3) 押頭韻：color, content, character

　　比較：will be judged not by the color of their skin but by the content of their character

9. ... little *black boys* and black *girls* will be able to join hands with *little white* boys and white girls as *sisters and brothers.*

(1) 對照：black vs. white; boys vs. girls
(2) 詞序：(little black) boys and (black) girls; (little white) boys and (white) girls; sisters and brothers
　　比較：ladies and gentlemen; young and old; friend and foe

10. ... every *valley shall* be exalted, and every *hill* and *mountain shall* be made low, the *rough places will* be made plain, and the *crooked places will* be made straight

(1) 變化：遣詞用字富於變化 valley, hill, mountain, rough places, crooked places
　　參考：prodigious (hilltops of New Hampshire); mighty (mountains of New York); heightening (Alleghenies of Pennsylvania); snow-capped (Rockies of Colorado); curvaceous (slopes of California)
(2) 搭配與邏輯：valley-exalt; hill and mountain-made low; rough-plain; crooked-straight
(3) 靈活選用情態助動詞：shall（五次）vs. will（27 次）（請參考林肯蓋茨堡演說詞精讀分析第六點）
　　參考：林肯總統蓋茨堡演說詞用了三次 shall，一次 will；甘迺迪總統就職演說詞用了五次 shall，七次 will；歐巴馬總統芝加哥勝選演說詞用了零次 shall，二次 will。

芝加哥勝選演說詞

背景資料

巴拉克‧海珊‧歐巴馬二世 (Barack Hussein Obama II)，現任（第 45 任）美國總統，美國第 44 任總統，為第一位非洲裔 (African American) 美國總統。他在 2008 年當選美國總統，並於 2012 年成功連任。歐巴馬 1961 年 8 月 4 日出生於美國夏威夷州檀香山市 (Honolulu, Hawaii)，是哥倫比亞大學 (Columbia University) 和哈佛大學 (Harvard University) 的校友。就讀哈佛法學院 (Harvard Law School) 期間，歐巴馬曾經擔任《哈佛法律評論》 (*Harvard Law Review*) 的會長。2008~2009 年期間，「歐巴馬」成為一種「現象」，全球興起一股「學習歐巴馬」的風潮。底下的演說詞是歐巴馬於 2008 年 11 月 4 日獲知總統選舉勝選後，在他的家鄉美國伊利諾州芝加哥市 (Chicago, Illinois) 葛蘭特公園 (Grant Park) 對二十多萬名擁護他的群眾所發表的演說。勝選演說詞 (election victory speech) 一開始就運用了「三節格律法」*，精彩激勵的表達方式，征服了全球億萬名「歐巴馬粉絲」。

*請參考第 10 章第 3 節有關「三節格律法」的討論。

演說詞全文

Obama's Victory Speech at Chicago's Grant Park

Hello, Chicago.

If there is anyone out there *who still doubts that America is a place where all things are possible, who still wonders if the dream of our founders is alive in our time, who still questions the power of our democracy*, tonight is your answer[1].

It's the answer[2] told by lines that stretched around schools and churches in numbers this nation has never seen, by people who waited three hours and four hours, many for the first time in their lives, because *they believed that this time must be different, that their voices could be that difference*[3].

It's the answer[2] *spoken by young and old, rich and poor, Democrat and Republican, black, white, Hispanic, Asian, Native American, gay, straight, disabled and not disabled*[4]--Americans who sent a message to the world that we have never been just a collection of individuals or a collection of red states and blue states; we are and always will be the United States of America.

It's the answer[2] that--that led those who've been told for so long by so many *to be cynical and fearful and doubtful about what we can achieve*[5] to put their hands on the arc of history and bend it once more toward the hope of a better day. It's been a long time coming, but tonight, because of what we did on this day, in this election, at this defining moment change has come to America.

A little bit earlier this evening, I received an extraordinarily gracious call from Senator McCain. *Senator McCain fought long and hard in this campaign*[6], *and he's fought even longer and harder for the country that he loves*[7]. He has endured sacrifices for America that most of us cannot begin to imagine. We are better off for the service rendered by this brave and selfless leader. I congratulate him, I congratulate Governor Palin for all that they've achieved, and I look forward to working with them to renew this nation's promise in the months ahead.

I want to thank my partner in this journey, a man who campaigned from his heart and spoke for the men and women he grew up with on the streets of Scranton, and rode with on the train home to Delaware, the vice president-elect of the United States, Joe Biden.

And I would not be standing here tonight without the unyielding support of my best friend for the last sixteen years, *the rock of our family, the love of my life, the nation's next First Lady*[1], Michelle Obama.

Sasha and Malia, I love you both more than you can imagine, and you have earned the new puppy that's coming with us to the White House.

And while she's no longer with us, I know my grandmother is watching, along with the family that made me who I am. *I miss them tonight*[6], and I know that my debt to them is beyond measure.

To my sister Maya, my sister Auma, all my other brothers and sisters, thank you so much for all the support that you've given me. *I am grateful to them*[6].

And to my campaign manager, David Plouffe--the unsung hero of this campaign, who built the best--the best political campaign I think in the history of the United States of America--to my chief strategist David Axelrod--who has been a partner with me every step of the way, to the best campaign team ever assembled in the history of politics--you made this happen, and I am forever grateful for what you've sacrificed to get it done.

But above all, I will never forget who this victory truly belongs to. *It belongs to you. It belongs to you*[8].

I was never the likeliest candidate for this office. We didn't start with much money or many endorsements. Our campaign was not hatched in the halls of Washington. *It began in the backyards of Des Moines and the living rooms of Concord and the front porches of Charleston*[9]. It was built by working men and women who dug into what little savings they had to give $5s and $10s and $20s to the cause. It grew strength from the young people who rejected the myth of their generation's apathy--who left their homes and their families for jobs that offered little pay and less sleep. *It drew strength from the not-so-young people who braved the bitter cold and scorching heat to knock on doors of perfect strangers*[10], and from the millions of Americans who volunteered and organized and proved that more than two centuries later a government of the people, by the people, and for the people has not perished from the Earth. This is your victory.

精讀分析

1. If there is anyone out there who still *doubts* that America is a place where all things are possible, who still *wonders* if the dream of our founders is alive in our time, who still *questions* the power of our democracy, tonight is your answer.

(1) 三節格律法：who still doubts ..., who still wonders ..., who still questions....
(2) 變化：遣詞用字富於變化 doubt, wonder, question，三個不同單詞表示相同語義。

　　參考：that America ...（名詞子句），if the dream ...（名詞子句），the power of our democracy（名詞片語）。

2. ... tonight is your *answer. It's the answer[2] told* by.... *It is the answer spoken* by.... *It is the answer that led*....

(1) 聯珠：... tonight is your answer. It's the answer
(2) 加強語氣的重複：it is the answer
(3) 變化：told, spoken, that led

3. ... they believed *that* this time must be *different, that* their voices could be *that difference*.

(1) 平行：二個名詞子句 that ..., that....
(2) 變化：句構、遣詞用字富於變化 must, could; different, difference。
(3) 同系衍生詞：different-difference。

　　參考：*that* their voices could be *that* difference: 第一個 that 是引導名詞子句的從屬連接詞，第二個 that 是限定詞。請參考林肯蓋茨堡演說詞精讀分析第三點。

4. ... young and old, rich and poor, Democrat and Republican, black, white, Hispanic, Asian, Native American, gay, straight, *disabled* and *not disabled*.

(1) 詞序：young and old（老少）；rich and poor（貧富）；disabled and not disabled（殘障與正常）
(2) 避免語言上的冒犯與歧視：Native American；disabled

比較：Indians（印第安人）；handicapped（殘疾人士）

參考：the physically challenged; the differently abled（身心障礙人士）

5. ... to be *cynical* and *fearful* and *doubtful* about what we can achieve

(1) 押尾韻：cynical, fearful, doubtful

(2) 省略：to be cynical (about) and (to be) fearful (about) and (to be) doubtful about

比較：to be cynical about and fearful for/of and doubtful about

6. Senator McCain fought long and hard in this campaign.

變化：句長富於變化，長短句交互使用。

參考：I miss them tonight.

I am grateful to them.

7. (Senator McCain fought *long and hard* in this campaign.) And he's fought even *longer and harder* for the country that he loves.

(1) 加強語氣的重複：... fought long and hard....; ... fought even longer and harder....。

(2) 層次遞增：long-longer; hard-harder。

8. It belongs to you. It belongs to you.

(1) 加強語氣的重複：It belongs to you.。

(2) 變化：句長富於變化，長短句交互使用。

9. It began in the *backyards* of *Des Moines* and the *living rooms* of *Concord* and the *front porches* of *Charleston*.

(1) 邏輯：由後面而中間再到前面，backyard（後院），living room（客廳），front porch（前廊）。從位於美國中西部 (Midwestern)，號稱美國地理中心 (the American Heartland) 的愛荷華州 (Iowa) 的 Des Moines 開始，接著是位於美國東北部 (northeastern) 的新罕布希州 (New Hampshire) 的 Concord，然後是位於美國東南部 (southeastern) 的南卡羅

萊納州 (South Carolina) 的 Charleston。

(2) 具體：利用大家熟悉的地名，引起讀者共鳴。請參考《我有一個夢》演說詞精讀分析第十
　　點。

10. It drew strength from the *not-so-young* people who *braved* the bitter cold and scorching heat to knock on doors of perfect strangers.

(1) 避免語言上的冒犯與歧視：用 not-so-young 代替 old。

(2) 類轉：brave 作動詞用，等於 to go out in bad weather

(3) 擬人化：bitter cold（嚴寒），用 bitter（痛苦）修飾 cold（寒冷）。scorching heat（酷
　　　　　熱），用 scorch（烤焦）修飾 heat（熱）。

(4) 對照：cold vs. heat。

(5) 押頭韻：strength-stranger。

附錄 2

轉承語

　　「轉承語」又稱為「轉折語」或「轉折詞」，它是文章中連接上下文的一個單詞或片語，最主要的功能就是「轉」和「承」。「轉」是轉換改變，「承」是承前接後。因此，一篇文章要利用轉承句，一個段落要利用轉承語，來做漂亮的前後連貫。

　　為了讓讀者很快瞭解，我們把轉承語比喻成騎機車或開汽車時候的換擋。換擋如果換的順，駕駛汽車的人，也就是作者，通行無阻揮灑順暢；坐在車上的人，也就是讀者，好比在愜意地喝著咖啡，不用擔心咖啡會灑在身上，而且可以和作者平行交流，用不著無助地在揣摩作者的心思。比方說，作者利用「第一、第二、第三、最後」給讀者很清楚的信號，用來說明系列的順序。利用「因為所以，雖然但是」告訴讀者相關的邏輯關係與步驟。利用「前後左右，東南西北」指示讀者相關的方位。我們在前面提過時間、空間、邏輯等概念，有一定的約定俗成，必須按部就班。除非是有自己的風格的作家，否則我們還是「乖乖地」按照順時鐘或是逆時鐘方向來描述空間，按照時間發生的先後順序來處理事件。先有因後有果，先同後異，後浪推前浪。先吃沙拉，再吃主菜，最後吃甜點。先酒駕，再被開罰單，然後不服上訴，最後無罪定讞，接著申請國賠。先考試，再送甄試書審資料，然後面試，最後通知錄取等一般大眾最熟悉認同的邏輯推理方式來使用轉承語。我們將「好使」常用的轉承語分類討論如下：

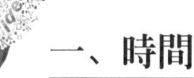

一、時間

1. 開始：	at first; in the beginning; before then The school was conducting an investigation; *at first*, she did not want to tell us anything about the school bullying.
2. 中間：	in the meantime; at the same time; simultaneously; meanwhile Kids will leave us eventually, but *in the meantime* they need our support.
3. 結束：	at last; in the end; finally; eventually; thereafter We had many days of negotiations, *and finally* my son decided not to become a monk.
4. 期間：	shortly after/before; day after day; for a long time; recently The bank turned down our loan application, *but shortly* my daughter found a job as an assistant.

二、對等

1. 相同:	similarly; likewise; moreover; furthermore; in the same way; in addition; equally important People today do not have time for exercise; ***moreover,*** they eat too much fast food.
2. 相異:	however; nevertheless; on the contrary; in contrast; instead; rather Honesty is a great virtue; ***however,*** today's politicians never hesitate to tell lies.
3. 重申:	in other words; that is (to say); to put it differently I don't want to work with or for you any more; ***in other words,*** I quit.

三、邏輯

1. 因果:	therefore; as a result; thus; hence; accordingly; consequently He usually drank and drove; ***as a result,*** he was fired by the company.
2. 讓步:	after all; of course; naturally; nevertheless; nonetheless; otherwise Rumors about her health are being spread; ***naturally,*** she felt frustrated.
3. 舉例:	for example; for instance; in particular; namely; ... to name just a few; specifically There are many ways to prevent unwanted pregnancies. ***For example***, you can use condoms during sexual intercourse.
4. 系列:	in the first place; in the second place; in addition; finally; first, second, third, last Many people in the tourist information center can speak English. ***In addition,*** they give tourists bilingual maps for free.
5. 結論:	all in all; in conclusion; to sum up; in short; in words; in brief Challenges are waiting for you; ***in conclusion,*** today you are proud of your school, and tomorrow your school will be proud of you.
6. 比較:	similarly; likewise A mother recognizes her baby's cry; ***similarly,*** a baby memorizes her mother's voice.
7. 對照:	by/in contrast; on the contrary, in spite of Boy students may be liberal and independent; ***in contrast,*** girl students may be conservative and dependent.

8. 限制：in terms of; speaking of; as far as ... be concerned; as long as ... be concerned
The program is designed to better your written English. ***As far as English writing is concerned/In terms of English writing***, many high school students are not good at it.

說明

(一)轉承語具有連接副詞的功能，可以用於一個句子的開始，也可以在一個句子的後面用分號，在轉承語的後面接上逗號，接著連上後面的句子，以完成承前接後的使命。例如，The cheerleaders practiced very hard**; however,** they failed to win the contest.

(二)學會了轉承語後，我們可以靈活運用甚至於內化創新，例如，「換句話說」我們可以用 "To put it differently,...." 或 "Putting it differently,...." 或 "Putting it in another way,...." 或 "Put differently...." 等；「同樣」我們可以用 "similarly" 或 "likewise" 或 "in a like manner" 或 "in a similar way" 等。

附錄 3

數字

（節錄自書林 (2013) 出版，蔣炳榮所著之《簡明當代英文法》第 383-398 頁。）

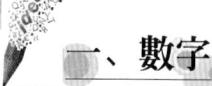

一、 數字

數字是表明金額、度量衡、溫度、成績、年份、時間、緯度、指數等觀念的一種「詞類」。使用數字應遵循三個原則：1. 約定俗成。2. 簡明精確。3. 尊重地區性的差異。正確使用數字能夠讓你的語言活動更明確更量化。

1. 一千可以用十個一百來表示，以此類推。

   1,000 = one thousand = ten hundred

   1,600 = one thousand and six hundred = sixteen hundred

2. 一萬用十個一千來表示，以此類推。

   20,000 = twenty thousand

   36,000 = thirty-six thousand

3. 十萬用一百個一千來表示，以此類推。

   100,000 = one hundred thousand

   785,000 = seven hundred (and) eighty-five thousand

   hundreds of thousands of examinees 好幾十萬名考生

4. 千萬用十個一百萬來表示，以此類推。

   10,000,000 = ten million

   50,000,000 = fifty million

5. 一億用一百個一百萬來表示，以此類推。

   100,000,000 = one hundred million

   365,200,000 = three hundred and sixty-five million, two hundred thousand

   hundreds of millions of copies 好幾億本

6. 長又複雜的數字，常直接用阿拉伯數字表示。

   1,234,567,891 = one billion, two hundred and thirty-four million, five hundred and sixty-seven thousand, eight hundred and ninety-one

7. 超過一千（含）以上的數字，常在百位數與千位數（第 3 位與第 4 位數），十萬位數與百萬位數（第 6 位與第 7 位數），億位數與十億位數（第 9 位與第 10 位數）之間，以逗號（，）隔開，以此類推。如此亦方便閱讀者唸出相關的位數：由右而左，第一個逗號是 thousand（千），第二個逗號是 million（百萬），第三個逗號是 billion（十億），第四個逗號是 trillion（兆），以此類推。

二、常見的序數表示

1. 表排列順序，常冠以定冠詞 the。

   the Second World War

   = World War Two 第二次世界大戰

   the third largest city in the US 美國第三大城市

2. 表第幾世紀。

   the seventies of the twentieth century

   = the 70s of the 20th century 二十世紀七〇年代

   at the beginning of the twenty-first century 二十一世紀之初

3. 表名次、成績等。

   take/win first place 贏得第一名

   get/win third prize 贏得第三獎

4. 當限定詞用時，序數排在基數前面。

   the *first two* weeks 最初的二個星期

   the *last three* months 最後的三個月

5. 表家族成員的排序。以羅馬數字書寫，讀音常維持序數的讀法。

   King Henry IV 英王亨利四世

   John D. Rockefeller II 約翰·洛克菲勒二世

6. 表分數的分母。

   one-*eighth* 八分之一

   two-*thirds* 三分之二

7. 表乘方。

    The third of three is 27.   3 的 3 次方是 27。

    參考：The cube of 3 is 3 x 3 x 3, which is 27.

             2 to the 5th power is 32.   2 的 5 次方等於 32。

三、分數 (vulgar fractions)

1. 形成分數時，分子用基數，分母用序數。分子大於 1 時，分母的序數用複數形。先讀寫分子，再讀寫分母。分子與分母之間也常以連字號（-）連接。

    1/3 = one third; one-third; a third

    2/3 = two thirds; two-thirds

    1/8 = one eighth; one-eighth

    3/8 = three eighths; three-eighths

2. 1/4 可以用 one-fourth 或 a quarter 或 one quarter 表示。

    參考：3/4 = three-fourths = three quarters

3. 1/2 可以用 a half 或 one half 表示。

    比較：a half hour = a half-hour = one half hour = half an hour 半小時

4. 超過 1 以上的分數，整數的部分用基數，再用 and 連接分數。

    $2\frac{1}{2}$ = two and a half = two and one half

    $3\frac{1}{4}$ = three and a quarter = three and one-fourth

    $7\frac{3}{4}$ = seven and three quarters = seven and three-fourths

5. 「複雜的」分數，例如分子、分母大於 10 時，則分子、分母均用基數，介以 over 來表示。

    18/61 = eighteen over sixty-one

    13/80 = thirteen over eighty

6. 百分之……數也可以用 percent (per cent) 或 % 表示。

    1/2 = a half = fifty percent = 50%

四、小數 (decimal fractions)

小數點讀成 point；小數點之前以基數讀出，小數點之後每一個數字（如十分位，百分位，千分位等）均單獨逐一讀出。小數點前面為「零」時，將零讀成 zero 或 nought，亦可省略不予讀出。

6.23	six point two three
18.417	eighteen point four one seven
0.69	(nought/zero) point six nine
0.45	(nought/zero) point four five
123.579	one hundred (and) twenty-three point five seven nine

五、使用數字的場合

1. 一般數字。

230 trucks	230 輛卡車
365 days	365 天
1,440 minutes	1440 分鐘
over 300 pages	超過 300 頁
60 lbs	60 磅（重）

2. 金額。

$320 = US$320	美元 320 元 ($ = dollar; US$ = US dollar)
NT$6,500	新台幣 6,500 元 (NT$ = New Taiwan dollar)
CN￥30,200	人民幣 30,200 元 (CN￥ = China Yuan)
	參考：RMB = renminbi 人民幣
￡75	75 英鎊 (￡ = pound)
€740	740 歐元 (€ = euro)
￥4,000	4,000 日元 (￥ = yen)

3. 日期。

May 21, 1979	1979 年 5 月 21 日（美式用法）

(5/21/79 =5/21/1979 = 5-21-79)

21 May 1979　　　　　　　　　　　　　　（歐式用法）

(21/5/79 = 21/5/1979 = 21.5.79)

June 22nd　　　　　　　　　　6 月 22 日

April 1 = April 1st = April first　　　　4 月 1 日

4. 時間。

8:05 a.m. = 8:05 A.M. = 8:05 AM 早上八點零五分

（a.m. = ante meridiem [before noon] 午前；上午）

4:20 p.m. = 4:20 P.M. = 4:20 PM 下午四點二十分

（p.m. = post meridiem [after noon] 午後；下午）

5. 年代。

1915　　nineteen fifteen

1998　　nineteen ninety-eight

2006　　two thousand (and) six

2010　　twenty ten/two thousand ten

A.D. 440 = AD 440 = 440 AD = 440 = 440 CE　　　　西元 440 年

18 B.C. = 18 BC = 18 BCE　　　　　　　　　　公元前 18 年

（AD = Anno Domini [in the year of the Lord]; [in the year since the birth of Christ] 西元）

（BC = before Christ 西元前）

（CE = Common Era 西元）

（BCE = before the Common Era 西元前）

6. 世紀。

the 18th century　　　　　第十八世紀

the 21st century　　　　　第二十一世紀

7. 溫度。

37°C (thirty-seven degrees Celsius/centigrade)　　　攝氏 37 度

(° = degree(s); C = Celsius)

65°F(sixty-five degrees Fahrenheit)　　　華氏 65 度

(F = Fahrenheit)

-2°C(minus two (degrees) Celsius)　　　攝氏零下二度

8. 體育運動。

(a height of) 1.95m = (a height of) one point nine five meters

一米九五的高度

(a height of) 6'2" = (a height of) six feet two inches	6 英尺 2 英寸的高度
1500m = 1500 meters = (the) fifteen hundred meters	1500 米（賽跑）
1600 meter relay	1600 米接力
4×100m relay = four by one hundred meters relay	400 米接力
200 meter breaststroke	200 米蛙式
the 800 meter freestyle champion	800 米自由式冠軍
95-88 ninety-five (points) to eighty-eight	95（分）比 88（分）
14:3 fourteen (points) to three	14（分）比 3（分）
15:0 fifteen love	15 比零（網球）
3:3 three all	3 比 3；3 平
3:0 three nothing = three zero	3 比零
49ers 27-Giants 20	49 人隊 27 比巨人隊 20

9. 度量衡。

34-25-36	34, 25, and 36 inches	三圍是 34-25-36（英寸）
86-65-89	86, 65, and 89 centimeters	三圍是 86-65-89（公分）
$8^{1/2}$"×11"	$8^{1/2}$ inches by 11 inches	$8^{1/2}$ 英寸 × 11 英寸
5'10"	five feet ten inches	5 英尺 10 英寸
12'×16"	twelve feet by sixteen inches	12 英尺 × 16 英寸
2'25"	two minutes twenty-five seconds	2 分 25 秒
38°26'25"N	at latitude 38 degrees 26 minutes 25 seconds north	
	北緯 38 度 26 分 25 秒	
500 miles	five hundred miles	500 英里

【註：表測量時，foot 可用以代替複數形式的 feet。】

10. 數學用語。

(1) 等於 (=): A is equal to B; A equals B

Three plus five is equal to eight.

= Three plus five equals eight.

3 加 5 等於 8。(3+5 = 8)

(2) 大於 (＞)：A is greater/more than B

Three-eighths is greater/more than one-fourth/a quarter.

八分之三大於四分之一。(3/8 > 1/4)

(3) 小於 (＜)：A is less than B

Twice three is less than three plus five.

= Two times three is less than three plus five.

3 乘以 2 小於 3 加 5。(3×2＜3+5)

(4) 加（上）(＋)：A plus B; A and B

What is nine plus four?

= What is nine and four?

9 加 4 等於幾？(9+4 = ?)

(5) 減（去）(－)：A minus B; take away A from B

Eighty minus twenty-five is equal to fifty-five.

80 減去 25 等於 55。

Take away two percent from fifteen percent and you get thirteen percent.

百分之十五減百分之二等於百分之十三。

(6) 乘（以）(×)：A multiplied by B; multiply A by B; A times B

參考：length by width (by height)（長×寬（×高））

Three multiplied by six is equal to 18.

6 乘以 3 等於 18。

If you multiply seven by twelve, you get eighty-four.

7 乘以 12 等於 84。

The library has 25 cubicles, 12 foot by 9 foot by 7 foot.

圖書館有 25 個小房間，長 12 英尺，寬 9 英尺，高 7 英尺。

(7) 除（以）(÷)：A divided by B; divide A by B

Twenty divided by five is equal to four.

20 除以 5 等於 4。（20 被 5 除等於 4。）

Divide thirty-six by four and you get nine.

36 除以 4 等於 9。（4 除 36 等於 9。）

(8) 比(：)：A：B；A is to B

Two is to five as four is to ten.

2 比 5 等於 4 比 10。(2:5 = 4:10)

11. 地址。

9500 Gilman Drive, Mail Code: 0108

University of California, San Diego

La Jolla, CA 92093-0108

USA

> 參考：美式英語在書寫地址時，第一行為街道名稱與號碼，第二行為城市名稱，然後為州或省的名稱（通常是縮寫），中間以逗號隔開，然後是郵遞區號，第三行為國家名稱，通常是縮寫，即頭字詞。

Macmillan Oxford

Between Towns Road

Oxford, OX4 3PP, UK

六、含有數字的一些實例

1. The temperature will fall to eight degrees Celsius tonight.
   今天晚上溫度將下降到攝氏八度。

2. The suspect is a 22-year-old male.
   嫌犯是一名男性，22 歲。

3. My husband weighs about 170 pounds.
   我丈夫體重大約 170 磅。

4. My grandmother is in her 70s.
   我奶奶今年 70 幾歲。

5. She thinks about her son 24/7.
   她時時刻刻惦記著她的兒子。
   〔24/7 讀做 twenty-four seven〕

6. The sergeant has a fashionable 4x4.
   那位中士有一輛時髦四輪驅動的車子。
   〔4x4 讀做 four by four〕

7. The flight takes off at five (minutes) to nine A.M.
   班機早上八點五十五分起飛。

8. The ceasefire will come into effect at 2400 hours/at 0000 hours/at midnight.
停火命令午夜生效。

9. The commencement is scheduled (on) Saturday, June 7, 2014.
畢業典禮訂於 2014 年 6 月 7 日星期六舉行。

10. Louis XV was the King of France from AD 1715 to AD 1774.
路易十五是法國國王，在位期間西元 1715 年至西元 1774 年。

11. The exhibition will be held on December 21st-23rd.
本次展覽期間為 12 月 21 日至 12 月 23 日。

12. The SUV does 0 to 60 miles per hour in only 6.5 seconds.
這款越野休旅車從靜止到每小時 60 英里只要 6.5 秒。

13. Please find enclosed a check of $50.50 and a money order of NT$200,000.
茲附上一張美元五十元五角的支票與一張新台幣二十萬元的匯票。

14. Coffee is 70 ¢. Lemonade is 25 ¢. Draft beer is $1.50. (¢ = cent)
咖啡七角。檸檬水二角五分。生啤酒一元五角。

15. My monthly income is £2,500. Her annual income is about €30,000.
我的月薪是二千五百英鎊。她的年收入是三萬歐元左右。

16. Her telephone number is +886-2-2345-6789. Our fax number is +886-7-551-7386.
她的電話號碼是 +886-2-2345-6789。我們的傳真號碼是 +886-7-551-7386。

17. His e-mail address is isky0875@yahoo.com.
他的電子郵件信箱是 isky0875@yahoo.com。〔@讀做 at；．讀做 dot〕

18. If you should have any complaints, please call our customer services department at (404) 555-1718 EXT 3216.
投訴請電客服專線 (404) 555-1718，分機 3216。

19. The groom is five feet and ten inches (5'10" (five foot ten)) tall. He takes a 15" collar and 42" sleeves.
新郎身高 5 英尺 10 英寸。他的領子周長是 15 英寸，袖長是 42 英寸。

20. The model, (aged) 21, was second runner-up in the 2010 Miss University Contest. Her measurements are 34-23-35.
這位模特兒芳齡 21，2010 年大學小姐選美第三名。三圍是 34-23-35。

21. A marathon is a running race of about 26 miles or 42.195 kilometers. It originated in 490 BC.

　　馬拉松是一種賽跑，大約 26 英里，亦即 42.195 公里。馬拉松起源於西元前 490 年。

22. The new warehouse is 400 foot/feet long, 200 foot/feet wide, and 12 foot/feet high. The rent is $1,400 per week.

　　新的貨倉佔地 400 英尺長，200 英尺寬，12 英尺高。租金每星期一千四百美元。

23. The speed limit on a US freeway is 60 MPH or about 96 KM.

　　美國高速公路的速限為每小時 60 英里，也就是大約 96 公里。

　　(MPH = miles per hour)

24. A4 paper is 210mm×297mm.

　　A4 紙張尺寸為 210×297 毫米。

25. He won third in the men's 400 meter hurdles.

　　他參加男子 400 米跨欄賽跑獲得第三名。

26. His daughter swam for her school in the women's hundred meter (100M) butterfly. She came in sixth place.

　　他女兒代表學校參加女子 100 米蝶泳比賽。獲得第六名。

27. The Chicago Bulls were leading by thirty-four to twenty-nine (34:29) at halftime, but the Orlando Magic won eighty-three to seventy-seven (83:77).

　　芝加哥公牛隊上半場以 34 比 29 領先，但是奧蘭多魔術隊終場以 83 比 77 獲勝。

28. Specialists have predicted that the San Francisco 49ers will defeat the New York Giants by 10 points. The odds are 2.3 to 1.

　　專家們預測舊金山 49 人隊會贏紐約巨人隊 10 分。賠率是 2.3 比 1。

29. We can give the first 10 customers a 20 to 25 percent discount.

　　我們可以給前十名訂購的顧客 20% 到 25% 的折扣。

30. The mobile disk has a memory of 512MB (512 megabytes).

　　這支隨身碟有 512MB。

31. How many megabytes equal one gigabyte?

　　多少個百萬位元組等於一個十億位元組?

　　參考：MB = Mb = megabyte 百萬位元組；GB = Gb = gigabyte 十億位元組；TB = Tb = terabyte 兆位元組

32. Our team won the men's doubles by three sets to two, six three, six four, two six, four six, six three.

我們的代表隊贏得男子網球雙打，三盤贏二盤輸，比數分別是六比三，六比四，二比六，四比六，六比三。

33. Homework for next week is pp. 119~35, Ch. VI.

下星期的家庭作業是預習第六章，第 119 頁至第 135 頁。

34. Senior citizens (over 65) and children under three will get a subsidy of NT$3,150 per month for no more than 18 months.

退休人員（65 歲以上）和三歲以下的幼童將可獲得每個月新台幣三千一百五十元的津貼。本項津貼最長補助 18 個月。

35. According to the article, the average American consumes the meat of seven 1,100-pound (500-kilogram) steers in a lifetime.

根據這篇報導，平均每個美國人一生當中會吃掉七隻每隻重達一千一百磅（五百公斤）的肉用公牛。

36. Today 130,000 farmers in 10 counties pay less than NT$400 a month per lamb on 50 million acres (20 million hectares) of public land.

今天十個縣市中的十三萬名酪農佔用五千萬英畝（二千萬公頃）的公有土地，卻只支付每隻羊每個月不到新台幣四百元的費用。

附錄 4

常用字首、字根、字尾
（按字母順序排列）

 **附錄 4.1　字尾**

 名詞

字尾綴詞	意義	英文例子與中文翻譯	
-al	狀態	refusal 拒絕	proposal 提議
-ance	行為	endurance 忍耐力	insurance 保險
-ancy	狀態	constancy 恒常不變	discrepancy 差異
-ant	行為者	assistant 助理	accountant 會計師
-ard	行為者	drunkard 酒鬼	dullard 笨人
-(a)(t)ion	行為	communication 溝通	education 教育
-cy	狀態	accuracy 精確	infancy 嬰兒期
-dom	狀態	freedom 自由	kingdom 王國
-ee	受行為者	employee 員工	interviewee 參加面試者
-eer	行為者	mountaineer 登山者	engineer 工程師
-ence	行為	dependence 依賴	insistence 堅持
-ency	狀態	currency 貨幣	fluency 流利
-er	行為者	cleaner 清潔劑	dancer 舞者
-ery	性質	bravery 勇氣	rivalry 競爭
-ery	聚集	poetry 詩	jewelry 珠寶
-ery/ary/ory	地方	bakery 麵包店 library 圖書館	eatery 餐館 crematory 火葬場
-ess	女性	actress 女演員	waitress 女侍者
-ette	小的；女性	kitchenette 小廚房	usherette 女引座員
-hood	狀態	childhood 童年	neighborhood 社區
-ian	行為者	physician 醫生	musician 音樂家
-ics	學科	linguistics 語言學	economics 經濟學
-ism	主義	capitalism 資本主義	feminism 女權主義

字尾綴詞	意義	英文例子與中文翻譯	
-ist	行為者	activist 積極分子	feminist 女權主義者
-ity	行為	purity 純潔	sincerity 誠摯
-ium	化學元素	sodium 鈉	ammonium 銨
-ium	地方	auditorium 禮堂	stadium 體育場
-let	小的；不重要	booklet 小冊子	starlet 小女明星
-ling	幼小	duckling 小鴨	gosling 小鵝
-ment	結果	movement 運動	government 政府
-ness	狀態	kindness 仁慈	softness 柔軟
-or	行為者	director 導演	advisor 顧問
-ship	狀態；身份	friendship 友誼	professorship 教授職位
-ship	技能；集體	musicianship 音樂技藝	membership 全體人員
-(s)ion	行為	decision 決定	collision 碰撞
-th	行為；序數	growth 成長	seventh 第七
-ty	十	sixty 六十	seventy 七十
-ty	狀態	cruelty 殘忍	popularity 流行
-ure	行為	failure 失敗	seizure 沒收
-y	行為	discovery 發現	inquiry 詢問
-y/ie	小的	kitty 小貓	piggy 小豬
-y/ie	暱稱	daddy 爹爹	Johnnie 強尼

動詞

字尾綴詞	意義	英文例子與中文翻譯	
-ate	使成為	associate 聯想	activate 使活動
-en	使成為	soften 軟化	strengthen 強化
-(i)fy	使成為	beautify 美化	purify 淨化
-ing	動名詞	finding 發現	teaching 教導
-ise（英式）	使成為	civilise 使文明	organise 籌備

字尾綴詞	意義	英文例子與中文翻譯	
-ize（美式）	使成為	modernize 現代化	computerize 電腦化
子音濁音化	使成為	strife-strive 衝突	safe-save 拯救

形容詞

字尾綴詞	意義	英文例子與中文翻譯	
-able	具有……特質	eatable 可食用的	workable 行得通的
-al	關於……的	emotional 情感的	magical 魔法的
-an	關於……的	urban 城市的	metropolitan 大都會的
-ant	進行……動作的	pleasant 愉快的	significant 重要的
-ar	具有……特質	polar（南、北）極的	triangular 三角形的
-ary/ory	關於……的	honorary 榮譽的 introductory 引導的	elementary 初級的 derogatory 貶低的
-ate	具有……特質	affectionate 愛心的	passionate 狂熱的
-ed	具有特徵；情緒	talented 有才能的	surprised 驚訝的
-en	具有……特質	golden 金的	wooden 木頭的
-ent	進行……動作的	different 不同的	dependent 依賴的
-ern	方向的	eastern 東方的	northern 北方的
-ful	充滿	helpful 有幫助的	useful 有用的
-ic(al)	關於……的	economic 經濟上的	economical 節約的
-ing	具有特徵；性質	amazing 令人驚喜的	boring 無聊的
-ish	像……似的	childish 幼稚的	foolish 愚笨的
-ive	具有……特質	expensive 昂貴的	active 主動的
-less	沒有	careless 不小心的	useless 沒用的
-like	像……似的	childlike 孩子般的	ladylike 淑女般的
-ly	像……似的	brotherly 兄弟般的	heavenly 天國的
-ous	充滿	dangerous 危險的	poisonous 有毒的
-some	有……傾向的	fearsome 觸目驚心的	lonesome 孤獨的

字尾綴詞	意義	英文例子與中文翻譯	
-ward	向著	forward 向前的	backward 向後的
-y	充滿	scary 恐怖的	rainy 多雨的

副詞

字尾綴詞	意義	英文例子與中文翻譯	
-ly	以......方式	carefully 小心地	confidently 自信地
-ward(s)	向著	eastwards 朝東地	backwards 向後
-ways	向著	lengthways 縱向地	sideways 斜向一邊地
-wise	以......方式／向	likewise 同樣地	clockwise 順時針方向地

附錄 4.2 字首與字根

字首／字根	意義	英文例字與中文翻譯	
a-	state 狀態	asleep 睡著	awake 醒著
ab-（a-, abs- 等）	away from 離開	abridge 刪節	abnormal 不正常的
ad-（ac-, af- 等）	to, toward 朝向	accumulate 累積	adhere 附著
ambi-	both 二者（都）	ambiguous 歧義的	ambidextrous 左右手都靈巧的
a (n)-	without 不；無	atheism 無神論	anonymous 匿名的
ante-	before 在前面	antecedent 先行詞	anteroom 前廳
anti-	against 反對	antisocial 反社會	antifreeze 防凍劑
aqua-	water 水	aqualung 水肺	aquarium 水族館
arch-	chief 主要的	archbishop 大主教	archenemy 主要敵人
audio-	sound 聲音的	audio-visual 視聽的	audiobook 有聲讀物
aut(o)-	self 自己的	autobiography 自傳	automatic 自動的
bene	good 好的	benefit 益處	benevolence 慈善

字首／字根	意義	英文例字與中文翻譯	
bi-	two 二	bicycle 自行車	bilingual 雙語的
bi(o)-	life 生命	biology 生物學	biography 傳記
capit	head 頭	capitalism 資本主義	capital 死刑的
cent(i)-	hundred 一百	century 世紀	centimeter 公分
chron(o)-	time 時間	chronic 慢性的	chronology 年代學
circum-	around 周圍	circumference 圓周	circumstance 狀況
co-	with 共同	cooperate 合作	coworker 同事
contra-	against 反對	contradict 反駁	contraception 避孕
de-	opposite 相反	decline 拒絕	decrease 減少
de-	remove 除去	defog 除霧	defrost 除霜
di-	two 二；雙	dichotomy 二分法	dioxide 二氧化物
dia-	throughout 始終	diachrony 歷時性	diachronic 歷時的
dia-	through 通過	diagnose 診斷	diameter 直徑
dis-	negate 相反	disagree 反對	dishonest 不誠實
dorm	sleep 睡眠	dormant 冬眠的	dormitory 宿舍
en-	cause 使成為	enlarge 變大	enrich 使富裕
ex-	out 外面	external 外部的	export 出口
ex-	former 以前的	ex-husband 前夫	ex-girlfriend 前任女友
extra-	additional 超出	extracurricular 課外的	extraordinary 非凡的
fore-	before 前面	foresee 預見	foreground 前景
hemi-	half 一半	hemisphere 半球	hemiplegia 半身不遂
hydr(o)-	water 水	hydrant 消防栓	hydrophobia 恐水病的
hyper-	over 過度	hyperactive 過動的	hyperlink 超鏈結
inter-	between 之間	interchange 交換	international 國際的
intra-	inside 之內	intradepartmental 系內的	intrapersonal 個人內在的
macro-	large 大的	macrocosm 整個宇宙	macroeconomics 宏觀經濟學
mania	madness 瘋狂；癖	kleptomania 偷竊狂	nymphomania 女色情狂
meter	measure 計；儀	odometer 里程表	thermometer 溫度計

字首／字根	意義	英文例字與中文翻譯	
micro-	small 微小的	micro-computer 微電腦	micro-organism 微生物
mono-	one 單一	monopoly 獨佔	monotone 單調
multi-	many 很多	multilingual 多語言的	multifunctional 多功能的
neo-	new 新的	neoclassicism 新古典主義	neolithic 新石器時代的
nym	name 名字；詞義	synonym 同義詞	antonym 反義詞
oct(o)-	eight 八	octogenarian 八旬老人	octagon 八角形
pan-	all 全部	pan-Asia 泛亞	panchromatic 全色的
para-	beside 旁；近	paramedic 護理人員	paramenstrual 經期前的
path(o)-	disease 疾病	pathography 病史	pathology 病理學
path(y)	feel 感覺	sympathy 同情	telepathy 心靈感應
p(a)ed(o)-	children 兒童	pediatrician 兒科醫師	paedophilia 戀童癖
pedi-	feet 足	pedicure 足部治療	pedestrian 行人
penta-	five 五	pentagon 五角形	pentathlon 五項運動
per-	through 通過	perceive 意識到	perennial 長久的
phil(o)-	liking 喜愛	philanthropist 慈善家	philosophy 哲學
phobia	extreme fear 極端恐懼	claustrophobia 幽閉恐懼症	hydrophobia 恐水症
phone	sound 聲音	phonograph 留聲機	phonetics 語音學
phone	sound 聲音	telephone 電話	microphone 麥克風
photo-	light 光線	photography 攝影	photocopy 影印本
poly-	many 多	polygamy 一夫多妻	polytheism 多神論
post-	after 後	postwar 戰後	postscript 信末附筆
pre-	before 先於	preview 預習	precaution 預防
pseudo-	false 假；擬	pseudonym 假名	pseudo-science 假科學
psych(o)-	mind 精神；靈魂	psychology 心理學	psychiatry 精神病學
retro-	backwards 向後	retrogress 退步	retrospect 回顧
se-	apart 分離	seduce 誘騙	segregate 隔離
sect	cut 切開	bisect 二等分	dissect 解剖
semi-	half 一半	semifinal 半決賽	semicircular 半圓形的
soph (ia)	wisdom 智慧	philosophy 哲學	sophist 詭辯者

字首／字根	意義	英文例字與中文翻譯	
sub-	under 下面；次	subway 地鐵	subtitle 副標題
super-	above 上面；超	supermarket 超市	superpower 超級強國
therm-	heat 熱	thermonuclear 熱核的	thermometer 溫度計
trans-	across 橫穿；改變	transaction 交易	transplant 移植
uni	one 單；獨	unisex 男女皆宜的	uniform 制服

附錄 5

易混淆單詞

英語有許多拼寫相似、讀音雷同、語義近似的單詞，例如 *liter* **vs.** *litter*; *premiere* **vs.** *premier*; *fair* **vs.** *fare; stationary* **vs.** *stationery; president* **vs.** *precedent; economic* **vs.** *economical; endangered* **vs.** *dangerous; lose* **vs.** *loose; basis* **vs.** *bases* **vs.** *base*。有些是拼寫一模一樣的「同形詞」（minute 分鐘；微小的）；讀音一模一樣的「同音詞」（bear 熊；忍受；生出）；有些是語義十分接近的「同義詞」（beautiful 美麗的；pretty 漂亮的）。這些「同形詞」、「同音詞」、「同義詞」在用法上常常是截然不同，我們稱之為「易混淆單詞」。辨識、征服這類容易混淆的單詞，可以幫助我們遣詞用字「精確得宜」。

請比較底下這二組例句：

* The new cabinet is devoted to social, political, and *economical* reforms.
（economical 經濟的；省錢的 vs. economic 經濟上的）

改寫：The new cabinet is devoted to social, political, and *economic* reforms.
新內閣致力於社會、政治與經濟的改革。

*The *contents* of the video game are not suitable for young children.
（contents；文章內容〔常用複數〕；目錄 vs. content 節目內容〔常用單數〕）

改寫：The *content* of the video game is not suitable for young children.
這個電玩的內容不適合兒童。

問題是如何征服所謂的「易混淆單詞」呢？我們的建議是儘量吸取「正確的」語言輸入，也就是不要接觸「錯誤的」語言輸入。哪裡有「正確的」輸入呢？答案是聽「好的、可靠的」英語，例如，英美人士推崇的廣播、電視與網路節目與/或剪輯等；讀「好的、可靠的」英文，例如，研究英語的專家學者所公認的、推薦的報章雜誌書籍等。初學階段不妨遵循一個原則：英美人士怎麼用，我們就怎麼用。平常在聽讀英語的時候，要督促自己提高語言的敏感度，遇到有疑問的單詞、片語、句子，可以從可靠嚴謹的詞典或提供同義字與反義字的類語辭典 (thesaurus) 以及專門討論比較用法 (usage) 的詞典，作整理、作辨識、作分析、作比較，進而增進自己英語遣詞選字的功力，使自己用錯字詞的情形降到最低，使寫出來的文章字字真切，句句有效。

附錄練習 5.1

說明：請選出正確的選項。必要時，請參考詞典。

舉例：North of the Himalayas, in the eastern part of Asia, (A. lies   B. lays) China.

答案：A

1. The committee allowed two student representatives to (A. set B. sit C. seat) in on their meetings.
2. Please (A. set B. sit) the plates and silverware at this end of the table.
3. Please be (A. sat B. seated). The valedictorian is about to deliver her commencement address.
4. The elderly couple had (A. laid B. lain) there unattended for hours before the ambulance arrived.
5. Many historians have agreed that President Theodore Roosevelt (A. laid B. lied C. lay) the foundation for a government-guided free market.
6. Having (A. laid B. lain) back in the couch, the patient felt relieved and comfortable.
7. The widow devoted her life to (A. rising B. raising) her children.
8. Skyscrapers (A. rise B. raise C. arise) from the sidewalks into the sky.
9. I was (A. arose B. aroused) by the traffic noise at about two in the morning.
10. Trouble will (A. arise B. arouse) when people have no food or shelter.
11. Believe it or not, my boss has (A. risen B. raised C. aroused) my salary by 10%.
12. I was so tired that I (A. felt B. fell C. felled) asleep during the meeting.
13. (A. Feeling B. Falling C. Felling) embarrassed, I turned away silently.
14. Should they (A. fall B. fell) and burn the trees that are badly infected?
15. The organization is privately (A. funded B. found) by a successful entrepreneur.
16. According to the documents, the party was (A. funded B. founded C. found) in 1912.
17. My grandson has (A. funded B. founded C. found) some interesting books in his university library.
18. Julia's parents decided to (A. grind B. ground) her for two weeks.
19. Because of the bird flu, all the passengers were (A. grounded B. ground).
20. I can't believe that this dish is made from (A. ground B. grounded) beef. It's delicious.
21. Who is going to take the (A. minute B. minutes) of our meeting?
22. The (A. custom B. customs) officers were checking our luggage.
23. Let's toss a coin to decide. (A. Heads or tails? B. Head or tail?)
24. In a sense, (A. economic B. economical) and political reforms are two sides of the same coin.
25. (A. Congratulation B. Congratulations)! You have passed the exam.
26. My uncle has coached me how to invest my money on government (A. security B. securities).
27. We greatly enjoyed our dinner. Please give my (A. compliments B. compliment) to the

chef.

28. In the press conference, the two players exchanged (A. greetings B. greeting).

29. The hotel manager gave us a lecture about international table (A. manner　B. manners).

30. The research has focused on the rich cultural heritage of the native (A. people　B. peoples) of South America.

附錄練習 5.2

說明：請選出正確的選項。必要時，請參考詞典。

舉例：Dr. Lin is a professor of (A. economy　B. economics) at National Taiwan University.

答案：B

1. My sister applied for (A. admittance　B. admission) to Harvard Law School.

2. Grammar does not seem to play an important role in (A. every day　B. everyday) conversation.

3. The child was abused; he has developed (A. imaginative　B. imaginary) fears.

4. It is (A. uneasy　B. not easy) for an adult to master a foreign language.

5. My ex-husband had seven marriages and eleven (A. unlawful　B. illegitimate) children.

6. Will the new film have its (A. premiere　B. premier) at the 2014 Taipei Golden Horse Film Festival?

7. It is not (A. economical　B. economic) to own a car which burns too much gasoline.

8. The association is devoted to helping (A. alone　B. lonely) people.

9. Only two of the candidates went to the interview; Patrick and (A. others　B. the others) did not show up.

10. I was born and (A. bred　B. brought up) in a small village in Hualian, Taiwan.

11. What languages do you speak (A. beside　B. besides) Chinese and English?

12. Please (A. take　B. bring) your dictionary to every class for English Writing.

13. Can I come and see you (A. sometime　B. sometimes) next week?

14. Our boat was nearly (A. stationary　B. stationery) on the lake.

15. The United States is always faced with a problem: illegal (A. emigrants　B. immigrants).

16. The witness (A. verified　B. testified) that she saw the police officers hit the black singer in the face.

17. More and more people (A. observe　B. notice) Christmas as a holiday.

18. My advisee is a very ambitious and (A. conscious　B. conscientious) graduate student.

19. Sometimes it is challenging for students in the United States to move from (A. elementary B. primary) school to middle school.

20. In her story, Hello Kitty will bring forth a (A. liter　B. litter) of kittens.

21. Mrs. Robinson took a shower and (A. wore　B. dressed) up in a beautiful, sexy silk gown.

22. May I be (A. forgiven　B. excused) form the table?

23. The retired professor's most (A. noticeable　B. notable) achievement was to have his experiment published.

24. Thanks for the (A. loan　B. borrow) of your digital camera.

25. The new auditorium has an 800-seat (A. capability　B. capacity).

26. Let's take a little time and (A. say　B. tell) a prayer for the tsunami victims.

27. The Miami Heat beat the San Antonio Spurs and (A. won　B. accomplished) the 2013 NBA Championship.

28. The flight attendant seems to have plenty of (A. female　B. feminine) charm.

29. The per (A. capital　B. capita) consumption of sugar has increased over the last decade.

30. The new conductor of the symphony orchestra is (A. a gay　B. a homosexual).

附錄 6

英語語音系統簡介

一般來說，英語有 24 個子音，有 17 個母音。

子音 / 輔音 (consonant)

[p] pie	[b] buy	塞音 (stop)
[t] tie	[d] die	塞音
[k] kite	[g] guy	塞音

[tʃ] choose	[dʒ] juice	塞擦音 (affricate)

[f] fine	[v] vine	擦音 (fricative)
[θ] thigh	[ð] thy	擦音
[s] sip	[z] zip	擦音
[ʃ] ship	[ʒ] pleasure	擦音
[h] high		擦音

[m] sum	[n] sun	[ŋ] sung	鼻音 (nasal)

[l] late	[r] rate	流音 (liquid)

[w] wet	[j] yet	滑音 (glide)

濁音，又稱帶聲音，（發音時，聲帶振動）(voiced)：

[b d g dʒ v ð z ʒ m n ŋ l r w j]

清音，又稱不帶聲音，（發音時，聲帶不振動）(voiceless)：

[p t k tʃ f θ s ʃ h]

母音 / 元音 (vowel)

[i]	feet	前—高母音
[ɪ]	fit	前—中高母音
[e]	fate	前—中母音
[ɛ]	mess	前—中低母音
[æ]	mass	前—低母音

[ʌ]	luck	中—低母音（強）
[ə]	sofa	中—低母音（弱）
[ɚ]	locker	捲舌中—低母音（弱）
[ɝ]	nurse	捲舌中—央母音（強）

[u]	pool	後—高母音
[ʊ]	pull	後—中高母音
[o]	poll	後—中母音
[ɔ]	call	後—中低母音
[ɑ]	lot	後—低母音

[aɪ]	mice	雙母音 / 雙元音
[ɔɪ]	voice	雙母音 / 雙元音
[aʊ]	mouse	雙母音 / 雙元音

響度等級表

高響度 --> 低響度								
ɑ ɔ o ʊ u	æ ɛ e ɪ i	w j	r l	m n ŋ	v ð z ʒ f θ s ʃ	ʤ ʧ	b d g p t k	h
後母音	前母音	滑音	流音	鼻音	擦音	塞擦音	塞音	擦音

說明：其他條件相同情況下，判斷響度的高低的原則如下。

　　　　（> 表示響度高於後者）

1. 母　音 > 子音
2. 後母音 > 前母音
3. 低母音 > 高母音
4. 濁　音 > 清音
5. 捲舌音 > 非捲舌音

附錄 7

評分說明與等級標準

附錄 7.1　102 學測英文作文評分說明（資料來源：大學入學考試中心）

1. 評分標準與歷年相同。
2. 採分項式評分，分項得分加總之後，給予一個總體分數（0-20 分）。
3. 依考生在內容（5 分）、組織（5 分）、文法句構（4 分）、字彙拼字（4分）及體例（2 分）之表現評分。
4. 分為下述五等級：特優（19-20 分）、優（15-18 分）、可（10-14 分）、差（5-9 分）、劣（0-4 分）。
5. 內容是否切題、組織是否具連貫性、句子結構與用字是否能妥適表達文意，以及拼字與標點符號是否使用正確等要項進行評分。
6. 字數明顯不足，扣總分 1 分。
7. 每份試卷皆由二位閱卷委員分別評分，最後成績以二位委員給分之平均為準。第一閱與第二閱分數超過差分標準時（差距大於 5 分），再由第三位委員評閱。
8. 比較：101 學年度：「字數嚴重不足，扣總分 1 分；多寫，不扣分。」
      100 學年度：「字數明顯不足，扣 1 分；未分段，扣 1 分；寫多段，不扣分。」

附錄 7.2　102 指考英文作文評分說明（資料來源：大學入學考試中心）

1. 評分標準與歷年相同。
2. 考生是否能運用詞彙、語法、修辭知識，寫出切合主題、具統一性、連貫性之短文。
3. 分為五等級：特優（19-20 分）、優（15-18 分）、可（10-14 分）、差（5-9 分）、劣（0-4 分）。
4. 字數明顯不足，扣總分 1 分。
5. 每份試卷皆由二位閱卷委員分別評分，最後成績以二位委員給分之平均為準。第一閱與第二閱分數超過差分標準時（差距大於 5 分），再由第三位委員評閱。

附錄 7.3　102 學測中譯英評分說明節錄（資料來源：大學入學考試中心）

1. 評分標準與歷年相同。
2. 考生能否運用熟悉的詞彙，與基本句型，將中文句子翻譯成正確、通順、達意的英文句子之能力。
3. 所測驗之標的詞彙都控制在大考中心參考詞彙表四級內之詞彙。
4. 參考：100 學年度中譯英差分標準為大於 2 分。

附錄 7.4 102 指考中譯英評分說明節錄（資料來源：大學入學考試中心）

1. 評分標準與歷年相同。

2. 評量考生使用高中詞彙及基本句型，將中文翻譯成正確、通順且達意的英文句子的能力。

3. 所測驗之標的詞彙都控制在大考中心參考詞彙表四級內之詞彙。

附錄 7.5

 **英文作文分項式評分指標**

項目＼等級	優	可	差	劣
內容	主題（句）清楚切題，並有具體、完整的相關細節支持。（5~4分）	主題不夠清楚或突顯，部分相關敘述發展不全。（3分）	主題不明，大部分相關敘述發展不全或與主題無關。（2~1分）	文不對題或沒寫（凡文不對題或沒寫者，其他各項均以零分計算）。（0分）
組織	重點分明，有開頭、發展、結尾，前後連貫，轉承語使用得當。（5~4分）	重點安排不妥，前後發展比例與轉承語使用欠妥。（3分）	重點不明、前後不連貫。（2~1分）	全文毫無組織或未按提示寫作。（0分）
文法、句構	全文幾無文法錯誤，文句結構富變化。（4分）	文法錯誤少，且未影響文意之表達。（3分）	文法錯誤多，且明顯影響文意之表達。（2~1分）	全文文法錯誤嚴重，導致文意不明。（0分）
字彙、拼字	用字精確、得宜，且幾無拼字錯誤。（4分）	字詞單調、重複，用字偶有不當，少許拼字錯誤，但不影響文意之表達。（3分）	用字、拼字錯誤多，明顯影響文意之表達。（2~1分）	只寫出或抄襲與題意有關的零碎字詞。（0分）
體例	格式、標點、大小寫幾無錯誤。（2分）		格式、標點、大小寫等有錯誤，但不影響文意之表達。（1分）	違背基本的寫作體例或格式，標點、大小寫等錯誤甚多。（0分）

資料來源：大學入學考試中心

附錄 8

準備 50 個片語，
10 種句型

　　我們在第 4 章第 2 節二，建議同學在考試前，要自行準備 150 個單詞，50 個片語，10 種句型。這三個數字僅供參考而已。每個人的背景、訓練、需求不同，因此必須作自我期許與調整。底下的 50 個片語，10 種句型是為了拋磚引玉，希望同學能夠舉一反三，因應自己的實際需求來做完善的準備。有一點要提醒同學的是，依據大學入學考試中心所公佈之 102 學測中譯英評分說明，「詞彙亦控制在大考中心詞彙表四級內之詞彙」，因此掌握高中 7000 單詞，就考試而言，綽綽有餘。

附錄 8.1　50 個片語

1.	**abandon oneself to** grief/sorrow/despair	陷入憂傷 / 悲傷 / 絕望
2.	**a controversial issue** on euthanasia/mercy killing	有關安樂死的爭議性議題
3.	**put an advertisement** in newspaper/on TV	在報紙 / 電視上登廣告
4.	student/car/home **loan**	就學 / 汽車 / 房屋貸款
5.	**the Nobel Prize in Physics** for 2013	2013年諾貝爾物理獎
6.	the 2013 **Taipei Golden Horse Film Festival**	2013臺北金馬影展
7.	**on Saturday, June 9, 2013**, at 3:00 p.m.	102年六月九日星期六下午三點
8.	nuclear/financial/economic **crisis**	核災 / 金融 / 經濟危機
9.	body/official/sign/**native language**	肢體 / 官方語言 / 手語 / 母語
10.	food/alcohol **poisoning**	食物 / 酒精中毒
11.	**poison the minds** of young students	毒害年輕學子的思想
12.	**conservative** bureaucracy/estimate/attitude	保守的官僚 / 估計 / 態度
13.	be charged with **bribery and corruption**	被控貪汙與賄賂罪
14.	**hold a (campus) carnival**/election/meeting	舉辦園遊會 / 選舉 / 會議
15.	an opening/closing/**graduation ceremony**	開幕 / 閉幕 / 畢業典禮
16.	**deliver an** (inaugural) **address/speech**	發表（就職）演說
17.	women's /civil/**human rights movement**	女 / 民 / 人權運動
18.	boycott fakes/forgeries/bad products	抵制贗品 / 偽造品 / 無良貨品
19.	sugar/alcohol/**caffeine consumption**	糖 / 酒精 / 咖啡因的食用
20.	**drunk driving**/(DUI) driving under the influence	酒駕
21.	**abnormal behavior**/weather conditions	變態行為 / 反常的天氣
22.	**be popular with** students/young people/voters	受學生 / 年輕人 / 選民歡迎
23.	**brush up on** my English/Japanese/the chess rules	複習英語 / 日語 / 象棋規則

24.	medical /political/literary/**fashionable circles**	醫學 / 政治 / 文學 / 時尚界
25.	**good**/bad (academic) **performance at school**	學業成績優秀 / 欠佳
26.	devote/**dedicate oneself to** helping the poor	致力於幫助窮人
27.	**racial**/sexual harassment/**discrimination**	種族 / 性騷擾 / 歧視
28.	**problems of bullying**/drug trafficking **on campuses**	校園霸凌 / 販毒問題
29.	dangerous/**run-down crammers**/bushibans	危險 / 破舊的補習班
30.	morning/**evening rush hour**	早上 / 傍晚的交通高峰期
31.	**protest against high tuition fees**/injustice	抗議昂貴的學費 / 不公平
32.	**domestic**/racial/ethnic **violence**	家庭 / 種族 / 族群暴力
33.	**capital**/physical/severe **punishment**	死刑 / 體罰 / 嚴懲
34.	lose/**gain weight**	減肥 / 變胖
35.	**energy conservation** and **emission reduction**	節能減碳
36.	**try/do one's best** to save the earth	盡全力救地球
37.	**environmental pollution**/risks/damage	環境污染 / 威脅 / 危害
38.	**natural**/human/financial **resources**	自然 / 人力 / 財力資源
39.	the public/**the majority of**/a minority of **people**	大眾 / 大多數 / 少數人
40.	nothing but a **copy-cut-and-paste** process	只是複製剪下貼上的處理
41.	**send**/receive **text messages**	發 / 接簡訊
42.	**in detail**/in sequence/in all	詳細 / 按順序 / 總共
43.	**in** public/person/private/**secret**	公開 / 親自 / 私下 / 秘密地
44.	**launch a campaign**/an investigation	發起運動 / 進行調查
45.	**look up the new word** in the dictionary	查字典（翻閱詞典查單詞）
46.	**go on (a) vacation**/a picnic/50	度假 / 去野餐 / 快50歲
47.	**in the early/mid-90s**/in her late 60s	90年代初 / 中期 / 快70歲了
48.	**I look forward to hearing from** you.	我期待收到你的來信。
49.	**You win some, you lose some.**	你不可能事事都成功。
50.	put/call/turn/take/rip/**go**/cut/break/carry **off**	推遲 / 取消 / 關閉 / 脫；起飛 / 敲竹槓 / 爆炸；發出響聲 / 切掉；中斷 / 斷絕 / 勝任

附錄 8.2　10 種句型

　　靈活應用底下介紹的句型，加上第 7 章 5 節、第 9 章第 7 節、第 10 章所討論的句型和句構，當然可以讓你的文章達到「文句結構富變化」的要求。別忘了「熟能生巧」哦！

---

1. *It is scientifically proven that* too much sugar-sweetened beverages will cause health problems.
   科學證明吃太多加糖的飲料會導致健康問題。

   (scientifically = 副詞; proven = 過去分詞或形容詞) (= 可以換成其他的)

   說明：用虛主詞 "it" 作先行主詞，代替 that 引導的名詞子句。

   參考：It is never too late to give up bad habits such as smoking.

---

2. *Never* in all her life *has she felt* so depressed and confused.
   她這一生從來沒有如此地沮喪和困惑。

   (never = 否定副詞或地方副詞或冗長的修飾語; have = 一般/情態助動詞)

   說明：將動詞移到主詞前面的倒裝句。

   參考：Behind the tennis court are apartment complexes and a swimming pool.

---

3. The speaker, *an expert on bird flu*, will deliver an address on virus infections.
   講者是一位禽流感專家，他要作一場有關病毒感染的演講。

   (an expert = a world-known psychologist = my new roommate)

   說明：同位語 an expert... 是形容詞子句 who is an expert... 的縮減。

   參考：Our principal, a kind-hearted man in his early 50s, is an alumnus of our school.

---

4. *Not that* I love Chinese *less, but that* I love English *more*.
   我愛中文，我更愛英文。

   (Chinese/English = classical music/popular music; swimming/shopping)

   說明：not love ... A less, but love ... B more 不是愛 A 愛的少，而是愛 B 愛的多。

   參考："The world will little note, nor long remember what we say here, but it can never forget what we did here."

---

5. Last week I came across several foreign backpackers, *one of whom* gave me this souvenir--a one-dollar coin.
   上星期我碰見幾名外國背包客，其中有一位送給我這個紀念品，它是一枚美元一元的硬幣。

   (one = two/both/many; whom = which)

   說明：one of whom ... 形成形容詞子句，後位修飾先行詞 backpackers。

   參考：The paintings at the auction were by several China's 20th-century masters, one of whom was Zhang Daqian, who was famous for his ink paintings.

6. *Engrossed* in his new experiments, the scientist neither ate nor slept.
　那位科學家全神貫注在做新的實驗，既不吃飯也不睡覺。
　(Engrossed =（從屬連接詞）V-ing/（從屬連接詞）V-en
　　　　　　 = Having V-en/On V-ing/After V-ing
　　　　　　 = NP V-ing/V-en（獨立分詞構句）)
說明：利用分詞構句可以使句型富於變化。分詞構句可以在主要子句的前面與／或後面。
參考：The little boy began to sing the song, remembering his mother, thinking how much he missed her.
　　　After taking a shower, I would play my guitar and hummed some of my favorite songs.
　　　The rain having stopped, the cyclists continued their tour around the island.（獨立分詞構句）
　　　Other things being equal, I prefer cycling to driving.（獨立分詞構句）

---

7. There are kids playing in the park: *Some* are flying kites, *some* are in-line skating, *and still some* are skateboarding.
　公園裡有小孩在玩耍。有的在放風箏，有的在溜直排輪，還有的在玩滑板。
　（第二個和之後的 some = others）
說明：利用 there are 引導一群人物，再用不定代名詞 some 逐一描述。
參考：There are kids playing in the park: Some are flying kites, others are in-line skating, and still others are skateboarding.
　　　There are kids playing in the park: Some are flying kites; some are in-line skating; still some are skateboarding.（用分號；連接）

---

8. Students in big cities tend to have a *good* command of spoken English, *while* those in the south have relatively *poor* proficiency in spoken English.
　大城市裡的學生大多口語英語的能力很好，但是相對而言，南部的學生口語英語的能力就比較差。
　(while = whereas)
說明：利用從屬連接詞 while 連接二個獨立子句，用以表示「對比」，強調二種情況的區別。
參考：My son is conservative and easy-going whereas my daughter is liberal and ambitious.

---

9. *The more* we have, *the more* we want.
　我們有的愈多，我們想要的就愈多。
　(more = less = more knowledge = less sugar)
說明：利用二個比較級結構，來對照二個不同的情況。
參考：The less people earn, the less they spend.
　　　The fewer/less the tourists, the less the commission.

10. *Given that* the students have some learning disability, we the teachers still have to do our best to mainstream them. *Put differently*, we can never abandon any student.

鑒於學生們有一些學習障礙的問題，我們當老師的還是要盡全力幫助他們融入主流教育。換句話說，我們絕不能放棄任何一位學生。

(given = taking into account the fact = considering (the fact))

說明：given 當介系詞用，可以後接一個名詞子句或名詞片語，放在句首，引導所考慮的原因。分詞構句 put differently 放在句首，強調作者的觀點。

參考：Given his interest in cooking, we can send him to France for advanced culinary skills.

考慮到他喜歡做菜，我們可以送他到法國學習高階的烹飪技術。

附錄 9
主要參考書目

The American Heritage Dictionary of the English Language. Ed. William Morris. Boston: Houghton Mifflin, 1976.

Butler, Eugenia, et al. *Correct Writing*. 6th Edition. Lexington, Mass.: Heath and Co., 1995.

Collins COBUILD Advanced Learner's Dictionary. 5th Edition. Ed. John Sinclair. London: HarperCollins, 2006.

Collins COBUILD English Usage. Ed. John Sinclair. London: HarperCollins, 1992.

Crystal, David. A *Dictionary of Linguistics and Phonetics*. 4th Edition. Oxford: Basil Blackwell, 1997.

Fowler, Henry W. *A Dictionary of Modern English Usage*. Ed. Ernest Gowers. 2nd Edition. New York: Oxford UP, 1965.

Gibaldi, Joseph. *MLA Handbook for Writers of Research Papers*. 6th Edition. New York: The Modern Language Association of America, 2003.

Kramer, Melinda G., Glenn Leggett, and C. David Mead. *Prentice Hall Handbook for Writers*. 12th Edition. Englewood Cliffs: Prentice-Hall, 1995.

Langan, John. *College Writing Skills with Readings*. 8th Edition. New York: McGraw-Hill, 2011.

Macmillan English Dictionary for Advanced Learners of American English. Ed. Michael Rundell. Oxford: Macmillan, 2002.

Merriam-Webster's Dictionary of English Usage. Ed. E. Ward Gilman. Springfield, Mass.: Merriam-Webster, 1994.

Morris, Williams, and Mary Morris. *Harper Dictionary of Contemporary Usage*. 2nd Edition. New York: Harper & Row, 1985.

Ladefoged, Peter, and Keith Johnson. *A Course in Phonetics*. 6th Edition. Singapore: Cengage Learning, 2011

The Oxford English Dictionary. 2nd Edition. 20 vols. London: Oxford UP, 1989.

Quirk, Randolph, et al. *A Comprehensive Grammar of the English Language*. London: Longman, 1985.

The Random House Dictionary of the English Language. Ed. Jess Stein. New York: Random House, 1974.

The Random House Thesaurus. College Edition. Eds. Stein, Jess, and Stuart Berg Flexner. New York: Random House, 1984.

Ruszkiewicz, John, et al. *The Scott, Foresman Handbook for Writers*. 9th Edition. New York: Pearson Education, 2011.

Strunk, William Jr., and E. B. White. *The Elements of Style*. 4th Edition. New York: Longman, 2000.

Sullivan, Kathleen E. *Paragraph Practice: Writing the Paragraph and the Short Composition*. 6th Edition. New York: Macmillan, 1989.

Webster's Third New International Dictionary of the English Language. Ed. Philip Babcock Gove. Springfield, Mass.: Merriam-Webster, 1993.

思果《翻譯研究》，第 14 版，臺北：大地出版社，2003。
胡曙中《現代英語修辭學》，上海：上海外語教育出版社，2006。
覃先美、李陽《英語修辭學概論》，長沙：湖南師範大學出版社，2008。
蔣炳榮《英文文法與修辭 增訂版（下）》，臺北：中華電視公司，1999。

（以下為有關「詞序排列」的參考論文。）

Chiang, P. J. (2007). "The word order of Modern English coordinating parallels: A principle of relative sonority." *The Proceedings of the Fifth Annual Hawaii International Conference on Arts and Humanities* (pp. 937~949). Honolulu: Hawaii International Conference on Arts and Humanities.

〔應用「相對響度原則」分析英語二項式結構之詞序排列〕(2007)

Chiang, P. J. and Zhong, R. M. "The Word Order of Disyllabic Chinese Antonym Phrases in CFL Learning: An Application of "the Principle of Relative Tones," *Journal of Leader University*, vol. 7.1 (Dec. 2010).

〔漢語為外語的學習者應用「相對聲調原則」決定漢語雙音節反義並列詞組詞序〕(2010)

蔣炳榮、鍾瑞明 (2008)。應用「相對響度原則」與「相對聲調原則」探討英語反義二項式結構與漢語反義複詞對譯時之詞序排列。載於國立高雄第一科技大學舉辦之「21 世紀外語教學與應用」。2008 應用外語國際研討會論文集（頁 199~211），高雄市。

[Translating English Antonym Binomials into Disyllabic Chinese Antonym Phrases: An Application of the Principle of Relative Sonority and the Principle of Relative Tones] (2008)

蔣炳榮、鍾瑞明 (2007)。應用「相對響度原則」將漢語平行並列詞組翻譯成英語二項式結構。載於國立高雄第一科技大學舉辦之「超越『視』界—語言學習與應用新探索」。2007 應用外語國際研討會論文集（頁 552~566），高雄市。

[The Application of the Principle of Relative Sonority to the Translation from Chinese Parallel Phrases into English Binomials] (2007)

附錄 10

參考答案

練習 1

1. 答：

「講英語」時，

(1) 說、聽者雙方不會去查詞典。

(2) 言談之間的話語稍縱即逝。

(3) 我們看不到聲音也留不住聲音。

「寫英文」時，

(1) 落筆後，字裡行間用詞選字可不斷重複回溯。

(2) 寫作上必須鋪陳結構琢磨遣詞用字。

(3) 經常需要查一本以上的詞典以確定選用單詞、片語以及文法句構和修辭格式的正確使用方法。

2. 答：

(1) 確認拼寫正確。

(2) 確認美式英語與英式英語拼寫、語法和語義上的差異。

(3) 確認挑選精確的動詞以及字詞間的搭配。

(4) 參考例句的用法。

3. 答：

「學測」與「指考」的英文考科均有兩部分：選擇題（占 72 分）與非選擇題（占 28 分）。非選擇題又分為中譯英（占 8 分）與英文作文（占 20 分）。

中譯英有二個子題，每題四分。考生必須能夠將二個分別長達 20 至 30 個單詞的中文句子翻譯成「正確、通順、達意」的英文。

102 學測英文作文：

說明：1.依提示在「答案卷」上寫一篇英文作文。

2.文長至少 120 個單詞 (words)。

提示：請仔細觀察以下三幅連環圖片的內容，並想像第四幅圖片可能的發展，寫出一個涵蓋連環圖片內容並有完整結局的故事。

101 指考英文作文：

　　說明：1.依提示在「答案卷」上寫一篇英文作文。

　　　　　2.文長至少 120 個單詞 (words)。

　　提示：請以運動為主題，寫一篇至少 120 個單詞的文章，說明你最常從事的運動是什麼。文分兩段，第一段描述這項運動如何進行（如地點、活動方式、及可能需要的相關用品等），第二段說明你從事這項運動的原因及這項運動對你生活的影響。

4. 答：

我個人認為英文作文比較簡單。

寫英文作文有很明確的提示，文分兩段，不會或沒有把握的單詞、片語、句構等可以避開，換成自己事先準備、演練多時的單詞、片語、句構等。基本上，只要按部就班把平常的操練，從容有信心地再做一次就可以了。

練習 2

1. 答：(1)；(4)

2. 答：(1) 2; (2) 4; (3) 4; (4) 4; (5) 5。

3. 答：(1) 3 (break, fast, -s); (2) 3 (butter, fly, -s); (3) 3 (multi-, function, -al); (4) 4 (un- fortune, -ate, -ly); (5) 4 (globe, -al, -ize, -tion); (6) 4 (dis-, cover, -y, -s); (7) 3 (ex-, port, -s); (8) 4 (mis-, carry, -age, -s); (9) 3 (inter-, nation, -al); (10) 3 (fore-, word, -s)。

4. 答：(1) uploading (2) receivers (3) disestablisments (4) beancounters

　　　(5) unlawfully (6) antisocial (7) extraordinarily (8) globalization

　　　(9) microeconomically (10) dishonesty

練習 3

1. 答：A 組的每個成員的組成元素都是可以獨立存在的自由詞素，如 rain, bow 等；B 組的每個成員的組成元素其中至少有一個是不能夠獨立存在的附著詞素，如 re-, -er 等。

2. 答：

　　(1) a beautiful model; a model who is from South America; a model dancing on the catwalk

　　(2) to live a happy life; a life full of rises and falls; a poor but peaceful life

　　(3) the bright lights of the city; to look on the bright side; as bright as a button

　　(4) a flock of foreign reporters; reporters killed in the explosion; reporters who are free and independent

(5) homework given by English teachers; no homework to do; doing homework with my father's help

3. 答：

(1) I saw beautiful models from South America who are dancing happily on the catwalk.

(2) I am not rich and powerful but I am living a happy life.

(3) (What a beautiful view!) We can see the bright lights of the city below us.

(4) My answer is that I certainly do not want to be a fashion victim.

(5) According to the report, packaged food is becoming more and more popular with career women.

練習 4

1. 答：一致、連貫、支撐、遣詞用字和體例、有效變化與掌控時間。

2. 答：變化就是同中求異，必要時異中求同。寫英文作文可以營造四種變化：遣詞用字要變化，句長要變化，句型要變化，標點符號要變化。

3. 答：(1A) I was given a guitar by my sister for my birthday.

(1B) A guitar was given to me by my sister for my birthday.

(2A) It is important that we should use English-English dictionaries.

(2B) It is important for us to use English-English dictionaries.

(3A) Although the cheerleaders worked very hard, our team lost the game.

(3B) The cheerleaders worked very hard; however, our team lost the game

(4A) We are devoted to social reforms; we are devoted to judicial reforms.

(4B) We are devoted to social and judicial reforms.

(5A) Wanting to participate in the singing contest, my parents practiced day and night.

(5B) My parents practiced day and night so as to participate in the singing contest.

練習 5

1. 答：依照大考中心所公佈的學測指考英文作文分項式評分指標，體例占 2 分 (10%)，包括有格式、標點與大小寫。

2. 答：

(1) We completed our project ahead of schedule; we felt very proud.

(2) Hurry up. We are supposed to pick up the manager at 3:30 p.m.

(3) The patient screamed and shouted at the nurse, "Leave me alone!"

(4) The committee promised to give us an answer by October 18, 2013.

(5) The men's restrooms are on the 1st floor, the ladies' restrooms are on the 2nd floor, and we also have children's restrooms on the 3rd floor.

(6) <u>The old man and the sea</u> is a novel written by Hemingway in 1951.

(7) The picnic basket was filled with sandwiches, apples, drinks, and candy bars.

(8) When did the Internet come into being? The early 80s or the mid-90s?

(9) According to my dictionary, WHO is an abbreviation for World Health Organization.

(10) "... government of the people ... shall never perish...."

3. 答：

(1) The Art of Listening to Classical Music

(2) Elementary English Composition for High School Students: An Introduction

(3) Taiwan Stands Up! 或 Taiwan, Stand Up!

(4) Can Money Buy Everything for Us?

(5) The Future of Teaching English as a Second Language

練習 6

1. 答：(1) lift (2) tram (cart) (3) sweet (4) waistcoat (5) underground (6) soccer (7) line (8) French fries (9) movie theater (10) primary school

2. 答：(1) African American (2) Native Americans (3) chairperson; chair (4) fire fighter (5) the physically challenged (6) women writers; woman writers (7) senior citizens (8) (so) unbelievable (9) Chinese (10) young women; ladies

練習 7

1. 答：

(1) I want to go home.

(2) I want to go home. 正確

(3) The security guard forced my roommate to leave.

(4) The security guard forced my roommate to leave. 正確

(5) The security guard forced my roommate to leave.

(6) Enough! Stop calling her names in front of her peers.

(7) I double-checked the schedule to avoid making any mistakes.

(8) Students spend too many hours surfing the Internet.

(9) Slow and steady wins the race.

(10) The fact that the homeroom teacher is late for class is surprising.

(11) Those who are interested in the program can sign up before Friday.

(12) I am sure that the San Antonio Spurs will win the championship.

(13) There is a night club at the corner of the street.

(14) The answer keys to the exercises are included in the handbook.

(15) Many a boy and many a girl is at the party.

2. 答：(1) 單句 (2) 合句 (3) 單句 (4) 複句 (5) 合句 (6) 單句 (7) 複合句 (8) 複句 (9) 合句 (10) 複合句

3. 答：(1) SVC (2) SVOA (3) SVA (4) SVOO (5) SVC (6) SV (7) SVO (8) SVO prep O (9) SVOA (10) SVO

4. 答：(1) needy (2) gentlemen (3) never (4) relatives/family (5) spicy (6) bustle (7) drive (8) beautiful (9) order (10) balances (11) field (12) error (13) wane (14) fall (15) run (16) steady (17) economic (18) shoulders (19) explorer (20) conquered。

5. 答：(1) or (2) and (3) neither, nor 或 both, and 或 X, and (4) and (5) or (6) (Either,) or (7) but (8) Not, but (9) and (10) Not, but。

6. 答：(1) since (2) If, if (3) although 或 though 或 even though (4) so (that) (5) lest (6) whereas 或 while (7) When (8) as far as 或 as long as 或 so long as (9) as (10) Where。

7. 答：(1) however 或 nevertheless 或 nonetheless (2) therefore 或 consequently 或 as a result 或 accordingly (3) otherwise (4) therefore 或 consequently 或 as a result 或 accordingly (5) therefore 或 consequently 或 as a result 或 accordingly (6) moreover 或 in addition (7) likewise 或 similarly (8) instead 或 on the contrary (9) therefore 或 consequently 或 as a result 或 accordingly (10) therefore 或 consequently 或 as a result 或 accordingly。

8. 答：

(1) I know the woman who is the CEO of my company.

(2) I know the woman whom every man in my office loves.

(3) I know the woman of whom everyone in my office is proud.

(4) I know the woman whose son is the CEO of my company.

(5) The retired professor published a book which is about migratory birds.

(6) The retired professor published a book in which she discussed migratory birds.

(7) On my sixteenth birthday, my father gave me a guitar which he bought in Spain.

(8) On the campus they are shooting a film which the Parent-Teacher Association protests.
或 The Parent-Teacher Association protests the film which they are shooting on the campus.

(9) On my sixteenth birthday, my father gave me a guitar the strings of which are made of

precious black nylon.

　或 On my sixteenth birthday, my father gave me a guitar whose strings are made of precious black nylon.

(10) In the carnival I came across a beautiful Indian woman who was wearing a purple and gold silk sari.

　或 In the carnival I came across a beautiful woman from India who was wearing a purple and gold sari which is made of silk.

9. 答：

(1) if/whether your son can fly a jet plane

(2) if/whether you have taken drugs before

(3) when you will return the books to the library

(4) if/whether your husband works for the CIA

(5) that social networking plays an important role in our future success

10. 答：

(1) When I was swimming in the pool, the tile cut my right ankle.

(2) Bound in leather, an old dictionary was given to me by my grandfather.

　或 My grandfather gave me an old dictionary bound in leather.

(3) To get a refund, you must enclose both the receipt and the proof of purchase.

(4) To become a professional football player, you need constant practice.

(5) Before climbing the mountain, we must double-check our food supply.

11. 答：

(1) When I was three, my grandfather took me to Hong Kong Disneyland.

　或 At the age of three, I was taken to Hong Kong Disneyland by my grandfather.

(2) We walked nearly ten miles to buy some water to drink.

(3) The little boy who walked onto the podium bowed to the audience confidently.

　或 The little boy who confidently walked onto the podium bowed to the audience.

(4) The new LED TV which was bought last night was put in the living room.

(5) My husband took my car that needed to be repaired to the body shop.

12. 答：(1) humble (2) dangerous (3) generous (4) confident (5) explorer (6) romantic (7) comprehensive (8) diligent (9) wonderful (10) security。

13. 答：(1) prejudice (2) never (3) clear (4) furious (5) breakfast (6) family (7) foe (8) wane (9) prosperous (10) roll。

14. 答：

(1) My suitcase is larger than yours.

或 My suitcase is larger than your suitcase.

(2) This year's corn harvest is not as good as last year's.

　　或 This year's corn harvest is not as good as that of last year.

(3) The number of run-aways is larger than that of drop-outs.

(4) They are enthusiastic about and supportive of the new plan.

(5) We are told not to dispose of the used batteries.

(6) Your daughter is as diligent as if not more diligent than mine.

　　或 Your daughter is as diligent as if not more diligent than my daughter.

(7) "My dog barks a lot." "Mine too."

　　或 "My dog barks a lot." "My dog too."

　　或 "My dog barks a lot." "So does my dog."

(8) My wife always has remembered and will remember to pay the bills on time.

(9) My daughter is taller than any other girl on her team.

(10) I love you more than Jennifer loves you.

　　或 I love you more than I love Jennifer.

　　或 I love you more than Jennifer does.

15. 答：

(1) When a writer has finished her essay, she needs to edit it carefully.

　　或 When writers have finished their essays, they need to edit them carefully.

(2) My son said to his father, "I need to buy a new cell phone."

　　或 My son said to his father, "You need to buy a new cell phone."

　　或 My son told his father that my son needed to buy a new cell phone.

(3) My roommate is a famous photographer and he enjoys showing photographs to me.

　　或 My roommate is a famous photographer and she enjoys showing photographs to me.

(4) My new friend talked endlessly about his trip to Paris, and his story was boring.

(5) If a foreign student wants to participate in the field trip, he or she can sign up for it by next Tuesday.

　　或 If a foreign student wants to participate in the field trip, s/he can sign up for it by next Tuesday.

　　或 If foreign students want to participate in the field trip, they can sign up for it by next Tuesday.

練習 8

1. 答：二個段落。

2. 答：議論文、記敘文、描述文。

3. 答：如果我準備寫一篇由十個句子組成的二段式的文章，一般而言，我會以四句加六句的比例分配這十個句子。我第一段會寫四個句子，第二段會寫六個句子。如果是十二個句子。我第一段會寫五個句子，第二段會寫七個句子，以此類推。

4. 答：如果我準備寫一篇由 150 個單詞左右組成的二段式的文章，一般而言，我第一段會寫 60 個單詞左右，第二段會寫 90 個單詞左右。如果是 120 個單詞，我第一段會寫 50 個單詞左右，第二段會寫 70 個單詞左右，以此類推。

5. 答：議論文文體第一段的四個句子可以做如下的安排：第一句寫「主題句」；第二句寫「定義句」；第三句寫「數據句」；第四句寫「如下句」。

記述文文體第一段的四個句子可以做如下的安排：第一句寫「主題句」；第二句寫「實例鋪陳句」；第三句寫「背景資料句」；第四句寫「時空串連句」。

描述文文體第一段的四個句子可以做如下的安排：第一句寫「介紹人物句」；第二句寫「時空典故句」；第三句寫「特徵句」；第四句寫「原因句」。

6. 答：

議論文文體的第二段的六個句子可以做如下的安排：

「方法句 1」-「方法句 2」-「方法句 3」-「效果句 1」-「效果句 2」-「結論句」

記述文文體的第二段的六個句子可以做如下的安排：

「鋪陳句」－「時空句 1」－「時空句 2」－「時空句 3」－「效果句」－「結論句」

描述文文體的第二段的六個句子可以做如下的安排：

「時空特徵句 1」－「時空特徵句 2」－「時空特徵句 3」－「時空特徵句 4」－「收尾句 1」－「收尾句 2」

7. 答：

First, turn off all electronic devices when you are not using them. Remember to unplug them when you are leaving the room. Second, replace old light bulbs with fluorescent ones. By doing so, you will pay less for your electricity bills. Third, if possible and convenient, do your best to walk, to cycle, and/or to take public transportation because not only do cars take more time in rush hours but also they use a large amount of gasoline.

8. 答：

One week before our visit, we called our friend's family and the hospital for the timing, length and guidance. The hospice is located in the rural area, about 30 miles from our school; therefore, we have decided to go by bus. We have planned to visit the hospice for 20 minutes: Three minutes for giving flowers and cards; ten minutes for casual conversation; five minutes for a guitar performance; two minutes for praying for our friend and promising our next visit.

9. 答：

My most cherished card is a Christmas card given to me by my mother, who was then suffering from liver cancer and who braved the critical condition to accompany me to study as an exchange student between August 2011 and June 2012 in the United States. I have pinned this card on the board attached to the wall next to my desk. This card always reminds me of my good times and memory back then in Austin, Texas. I am now looking at the card. On the top half of the card are three gold fish swimming happily in the river, and on the bottom half are words from the bottom of my mom's heart: "My dearest Princess, You are my treasure forever. I have been so proud of you. I love you. Always have. Always will. Mom 12-25-2011." I will cherish the card forever.

練習 9

1. 答：

(1A) Information is power and power is everything.

(1B) The 21st century is a century of information, with which we can change the world.

(2A) The key elements to be a successful entrepreneur are creativity, partnership, and management.

(2B) The key elements to excel in English are curiosity, diligence, and perseverance.

(3A) There are four factors that will guarartee a successful graduation party: location, food and beverages, and activities.

(3B) The best way to guarantee an unforgettable graduation party is to contract a professional catering company to do it for the graduating class.

2. 答：

(1) A volunteer, by definition, is a person who willingly offers to help without being paid.

(2) Expertise refers to special kills or knowledge that someone has acquired by study, training, and/or experience.

(3) Bullying is a situation in which someone uses their strength or power to hurt and/or frighten other people who are weaker.

3. 答：

(1) According to a study by XYZ, more than 80% of people in Taiwan spend an average time of 30 hours a year visiting night markets in their neighborhood.

(2) A recent study by XYZ (June 2012) indicated that on average more than five million boxed

meals were sold per day from Mondays through Fridays in September 2011.

4. 答：

(1) What can we do to effectively improve our English listening comprehension? Some of the suggestions are as follows:

(2) As far as I am concerned, the top ways for you to lose weight and to get in shape are listed below:

5. 答：

(1) Successful time management can lead to on-schedule or ahead-of-schedule achievements with pride and enjoyment.

(2) Facing challenges is nothing but succeeding through our own efforts, or failing; you are left to sink or swim.

6. 答：

(1) Generally speaking, extracurricular activities are a laboratory for college students, for example, a ballroom dancing club can familiarize them with the waltz.

(2) I am interested in a number of hobbies. They include reading, cooking, and playing Chinese chess (Xiangqi).

7. 答：

(1) There are three major kinds of dictionaries essential for English learners: (1) dictionaries for advanced learners, (2) pronunciation dictionaries, (3) thesauruses.

(2) Based on different styles and forms, music can be divided into the following three categories: classical music, folk music, and popular music.

8. 答：

(1) My swimming coach, a graduate student in a university of sports, is a lady with a strong body and a tender heart.

(2) During our hospice trip last week, I met a veteran volunteer in the hospital who is an 80-year-old lady with big, sunny smiles.

9. 答：

(1) Our class won the 2013 High School Cheerleading Championship. To celebrate our victory, we voted to hold a class outing on the weekend after the mid-term exam.

(2) To the east side of the gate of our school is the auditorium, which is a domed building made of red brick, 300 feet long and 160 feet wide.

10. 答：

(1) Unhealthy eating habits, too many sugar-sweetened beverages, too much sedentary time, and lack of exercise will result in overweight problems.

(2) For many high school students, poor academic performance may be due to lack of sleep, bad family life, bullying (and dyslexia, which is a disorder involving difficulty with learning to read fluently).

11. 答：

(1) If students, staff, and faculty can respect each other, if we can provide students with a positive and supportive campus, if we can promise students a safe and secure campus, then we can minimize bullying on campus.

(2) If we can minimize carbon emission, if we can save energy, and if we can love the earth as a mother loves her baby, then we can have an Earth which is forever green.

12. 答：

(1) In summary, a friend who never hesitates to laugh and cry with you is a lifelong friend.

(2) In conclusion, living a simple life, slowing down the pace in your life, and sticking to the three Rs--rest, relax, recreate--can eliminate stress from your life.

14. 答：

（請參考本章節的範文。）

練習 10

1. 答：

(1) We shall fight against drunk driving, we shall fight against campus bullying, we shall fight against child abuse, and shall fight against bribery and corruption.

(2) If people believe that our civil servants are integral, if people believe that our civil servants are intelligent, and if people believe that our civil servants are independent....

2. 答：

(1) A computer is used to store a huge amount of information, to play video games, to write, send, and receive e-mails, and to prepare tables and illustrations in research papers.

(2) I have been jogging for five years because I want to lose weight, because I want to get in shape, because I want to have a strong heart, and most important of all, because I want to live a long life.

3. 答：

(1) prosperous (2) humid (3) confident (4) bustle (5) wealthy (6) blue

(7) management (8) cut; color; certification (9) security (10) purpose

4. 答：

(1) apple (2) bee (3) whistle (4) poor (5) fish (6) beet/rose (7) sheet/snow

(7) shoulders (9) sky (10) spoon (11) mountain (12) book (13) ears (14) cream

(15) tower

5. 答：

(1) nose/nosing (2) headed (3) eyed (4) handed (5) elbowed (6) mouthed

(7) shoulder (8) watered (9) starred (10) fingered

附錄練習 5.1

1~15　　BABBA　BBABA　BBABA

16~30　　BCBAA　BBAAB　BAABB

附錄練習 5.2

1~15　　BBBBB　AABBB　BBAAB

16~30　　BABAB　BBBAB　AABBB

國家圖書館出版品預行編目資料

學測指考英文作文的第一本書／蔣炳榮作.
--初版--.--臺北市：書泉，2014.03
　　面；　公分.
　　ISBN 978-986-121-899-1（平裝）

1.英語教學　2.作文　3.寫作法　4.中等教
育

524.38　　　　　　　　　　103001526

3AN9

學測指考 英文作文的第一本書
Elementary Enghish Composition for Chinese EFL Learners

作　　者 — 蔣炳榮

發 行 人 — 楊榮川

總 編 輯 — 王翠華

主　　編 — 朱曉蘋

封面設計 — 董子瑈

出 版 者 — 書泉出版社

地　　址：106台北市大安區和平東路二段339號4樓

電　　話：(02)2705-5066　傳　　真：(02)2706-6100

網　　址：http://www.wunan.com.tw

電子郵件：shuchuan@shuchuan.com.tw

劃撥帳號：01303853

戶　　名：書泉出版社

總 經 銷：朝日文化

進退貨地址：235新北市中和區橋安街15巷1號7樓

TEL：(02)2249-7714　　FAX：(02)2249-8715

法律顧問　林勝安律師事務所　林勝安律師

出版日期　2014年3月初版一刷

定　　價　新臺幣450元